Southern Living

# RECIPE REVIVAL

## Southern Classics Reinvented for Modern Cooks

Southern Living

# RECIPE
# REVIVAL

Southern Classics Reinvented
for Modern Cooks

Writer: Mary Allen Perry
Senior Editor: Katherine Cobbs
Project Editor: Melissa Brown
Senior Designer: Maribeth Jones
Compositor: Amy Bickell
Photographers: Iain Bagwell, Jennifer Causey, Greg Dupree, Alison Miksch,
    Hector Sanchez
Prop Stylists: Cindy Barr, Jessica Baude, Heather Chadduck, Kay E. Clarke,
    Mindi Shapiro Levine, Claire Spollen,
Food Stylists: Margaret Monroe Dickey, Kellie Gerber Kelley, Catherine Crowell Steele
Assistant Production Director: Sue Chodakiewicz
Senior Production Manager: Greg A. Amason
Copy Editors: Donna Baldone, Julie Gillis
Proofreader: Rebecca Brennan
Indexer: Mary Ann Laurens
Fellows: Audrey Davis, Rishon Hanners, Olivia Pierce, Natalie Schumann, Mallory Short
Models: Kylie Dazzo, Chris Melton

ISBN-13: 978-0-8487-5189-0
ISBN-10: 0-8487-5189-2
Library of Congress Control Number: 2016940261

First Edition 2016
Printed in China
10 9 8 7 6 5 4 3 2 1

Time Inc. Books products may be purchased for business or promotional use.
For information on bulk purchases, please contact Christi Crowley in the Special Sales
Department at (845) 895-9858.

We welcome your comments and suggestions about Time Inc. Books.
Please write to us at:
Time Inc. Books
Attention: Book Editors
P.O. Box 62310
Tampa, Florida 33662-2310

# Introduction

————◇————

IN THE PREFACE TO THE ORIGINAL 1951 EDITION OF MARION BROWN'S HALLMARK *THE SOUTHERN COOK BOOK*, SHE WRITES: "the Southern recipe cannot be rigidly defined. It may be a cherished old formula handed down for generations, or it may be relatively new—an adaptation, a combination, or an original idea, for Southerners have always wanted the best of the new along with the old, and the art of cooking in the South has never stood still." For 50 years, the *Southern Living* food pages have celebrated the best of the old and the new. We've featured nostalgic favorites from inside spiral-bound community cookbooks and showcased signature dishes from landmark restaurants and award-winning chefs. But it has always been the close relationship with our readers and the evolution of the extraordinary recipes they share that has set us apart from other publications.

Much is written today about the "new" global South, but flip through back issues of *Southern Living* and you'll find a culinary history of richly diverse recipes with centuries-old roots that continue to inspire and to tell the story of a multiethnic South—from the bayous of Cajun country and the tiny mountain towns of Appalachia to the coastal Lowcountry of South Carolina. In 1970, four years after the premier issue of *Southern Living* appeared on newsstands, we published our first collection of recipes, curated by founding Food Editor Lena Sturges. As the magazine's popularity soared, so did the submission of recipes from our readers—often thousands a month. Our editorial halls were soon lined with rows of mile-high metal filing cabinets filled with handwritten recipes for company-worthy pot roasts, fiery pickled chowchows, and foolproof squash soufflés. Treasured recipes for a great-grandmother's rose geranium pound cake or spiced holiday eye-of-round were carefully penned on monogrammed notecards. Secrets to homemade boudin, chocolate-colored roux, and perfectly set fig preserves were scrawled on tattered notebook paper. Those of us lucky enough to be a part of the *Southern Living* food staff at that time had the supreme joy of testing many of those wonderful recipes by gathering daily around the tasting table and breaking bread with the readers whose generous offerings are now woven into the larger culinary history of *Southern Living*.

In this, our latest collection of favorites, you'll find that the notion of "recipe revival" is about more than just turning up the flavor of an iconic dish by substituting a novel ingredient. A new generation of Southern cooks is far more inventive. With a thrifty wink to tradition, the rich coastal flavors of Maryland crab cakes reappear as indulgent crab-filled hush puppies at a Deep South fish fry. The cool sweet-and-sour brightness of a vintage tomato aspic translates into a colorful high-summer pairing of heirloom tomatoes and field pea-nectarine salsa. Spiked with fresh citrus and thyme, a featherlight buttermilk cornbread batter makes the continental leap from cast-iron cornstick pans to shell-shaped French madeleine pans. Classic lemon bars are elevated to new and elegant dinner-party heights as a swoon-worthy cheesecake wrapped in a rustic shortbread crust. The list goes on—deliciously, we might add.

We continue to document how the South cooks and eats, inviting readers to join us at our table and to share with us the bounty that is theirs. It's a tradition we hope continues for another 50 years.

— Mary Allen Perry

*Food has been featured on the cover of* Southern Living *more times than we can count over the past 50 years, but it took almost two years to get there. This December 1967 cover of a bountiful holiday spread was our first food cover.*

# 1
# BREAKFAST & BRUNCH

Break out your best linen napkins (yes, the ones with the monogram) and polish up the silver. What's on the menu? Oh-so-Southern morning favorites that *Southern Living* has celebrated right from the very start.

# THE WAY WE DINE

## 1960s Leisurely Brunch

Raise a glass to the relaxed midmorning meal that's an enduring Southern ritual. Classic quiche paired with roasted asparagus spears and a colorful melon salad make you wish morning would last forever.

Kane's Peppery Bloody Marys (page 54)
Caramelized Onion Quiche (page 38)
Simple Roasted Asparagus (page 284)
Minted Melon Balls (page 34)
Cajun Benne Seed Shortbread (page 137)

# Sweet Potato Biscuits with Pork Chops and Pear Preserves

Sweet potato biscuits are divine straight from the oven, but pair that earthy sweetness with the salty punch of a pan-fried pork chop and pear preserves and you've just built a near-perfect breakfast sandwich. Of course, today you might take it one step further and tuck in some baby arugula. Taste of the South Trivia: Cooks originally added sweet potatoes to baked goods as a way to extend costly refined wheat flour.

Serves 6   Hands-on 20 minutes   Total 35 minutes, including pork

## Biscuits:
¾ cup mashed cooked sweet potato (about 1 potato)
¾ cup buttermilk
½ cup melted butter
2 tablespoons brown sugar
2 cups all-purpose flour
2 teaspoons baking powder
½ teaspoon table salt
½ teaspoon baking soda
Parchment paper

## Pork Chops:
⅓ cup all-purpose flour
1 teaspoon table salt
1 teaspoon seasoned pepper
6 thin boneless pork chops (about 1 pound)
¼ cup vegetable oil
Pear preserves

1. Make the Biscuits: Preheat the oven to 450°F. Whisk together the first 4 ingredients. Combine the flour, baking powder, salt, and baking soda; add to the sweet potato mixture, stirring just until moistened. Turn the dough out onto a floured surface, and knead lightly 6 to 8 times.

2. Pat the dough to ¾-inch thickness; cut into 6 rounds using a 3-inch round cutter, gathering and patting scraps once. Place on a parchment paper-lined baking sheet.

3. Bake at 450°F for 15 to 17 minutes or until lightly browned.

4. Meanwhile, make the Pork Chops: Combine the flour, salt, and seasoned pepper in a shallow dish; dredge the pork in the flour mixture, shaking off excess.

5. Cook the pork, in 3 batches, in hot oil in a large skillet over medium-high 1 minute on each side or until browned. Drain on paper towels.

6. Serve the pork with biscuits and preserves.

1980s

# FRIED CHICKEN- THIGHS BISCUITS

Tender, high-rise buttermilk biscuits and insanely crunchy fried chicken thighs are a match made in breakfast heaven. This is an Ashley Christensen inspiration from Beasley's Chicken + Honey in Raleigh, North Carolina, where local honey and pickled green tomatoes offer a sweet-sharp counterpoint to the rich dark-meat flavor.

Serves 8   Hands-on 30 minutes   Total 1 hour 5 minutes

## FRIED CHICKEN THIGHS:

8 skinned and boned chicken thighs (about 2¼ pounds)
1 teaspoon table salt
½ teaspoon ground black pepper
⅛ teaspoon onion powder
1 cup buttermilk
1 large egg
Vegetable oil
2 cups all-purpose flour

## BISCUITS:

2 cups bread flour
2 cups all-purpose flour
2 tablespoons baking powder
2 tablespoons sugar
1 teaspoon table salt
1 cup butter, cut into cubes
1½ cups buttermilk
1 large egg
Parchment paper
Chopped pickled green tomatoes, local honey

1. Make the Chicken: Sprinkle the chicken thighs with the salt and next 2 ingredients. Whisk together 1 cup buttermilk and 1 egg in a large bowl; add chicken, tossing to coat.

2. Pour 1 inch of oil into a large cast-iron skillet; heat to 325°F. Place the flour in a shallow dish. Dredge the chicken, shaking off excess. Fry the chicken, in 2 batches, 5 to 6 minutes on each side or until golden and done. Drain on a rack over paper towels; keep warm.

3. Make the Biscuits: Combine the bread flour and next 4 ingredients in a large bowl. Place the cubed butter in a zip-top plastic freezer bag. Freeze the flour mixture and butter separately 10 minutes or until well chilled. Whisk together 1½ cups buttermilk and 1 egg in a bowl.

4. Cut the chilled butter into the flour mixture with a pastry blender or fork until crumbly. Add the buttermilk mixture; stir just until dry ingredients are moistened.

5. Preheat the oven to 450°F. Turn the dough out onto a lightly floured surface, and knead lightly 3 to 4 times. Pat or roll the dough to 1-inch thickness; cut into 8 squares, and place on a parchment paper-lined baking sheet.

6. Bake at 450°F for 15 to 16 minutes or until golden brown. Split biscuits; fill each with 1 cooked chicken thigh and desired toppings.

# Orange Rolls

Is there a better way to start the day than with sunny Florida citrus? We don't think so either. Homemade orange rolls are a charter member of the Southern bread basket hall of fame. Every recipe has its own special twist, and this one just happens to turn out tender, buttery spirals with a hint of cinnamon and a perfectly gooey sweet orange marmalade center.

Makes 15 rolls   Hands-on 25 minutes   Total 2 hours, including glaze

1 cup warm milk (105° to 115°F)
1 (¼-ounce) package active dry yeast
1 cup sugar
4 cups all-purpose flour
¼ cup plus ⅓ cup butter, melted
1 teaspoon table salt

1 teaspoon orange zest
2 large eggs, lightly beaten
Vegetable cooking spray
⅔ cup orange marmalade
¾ teaspoon ground cinnamon
Glaze

1. Combine the milk, yeast, and 1 teaspoon of the sugar in a 1-cup glass measuring cup, stirring to dissolve yeast; let stand 5 minutes.

2. Combine the flour, ¼ cup of the butter, salt, orange zest, eggs, and 3 tablespoons plus 2 teaspoons sugar in bowl of a heavy-duty electric stand mixer. Add the milk mixture; beat at low speed 1 to 2 minutes or until blended, using the dough hook attachment. Increase speed to medium-low, and beat 5 minutes or until the dough is smooth (dough will be soft and slightly sticky). Place the dough in a greased bowl; lightly grease top of dough with cooking spray. Cover and let rise in a warm place (80° to 85°F), free from drafts, 45 minutes to 1 hour or until doubled in bulk.

3. Combine the marmalade, remaining ⅓ cup butter, cinnamon, and remaining ¾ cup sugar in a small bowl.

4. Punch the dough down. Turn out onto a lightly floured surface; roll into a 15- x 12-inch rectangle (about ¼ inch thick). Spread the marmalade mixture over the dough, leaving a ½-inch border. Roll up, jelly-roll fashion, starting at 1 long side. Cut the dough into 15 (1-inch-thick) slices, and place in a well-greased 13- x 9-inch pan with sides touching. Cover and let rise 45 minutes or until almost doubled in bulk.

5. Preheat the oven to 350°F. Uncover the rolls, and bake 20 to 25 minutes or until light golden brown. Remove from the oven, and cool slightly. Drizzle the glaze over the warm rolls.

Glaze: Whisk together until blended 1 cup powdered sugar, 2 tablespoons melted butter, 1½ tablespoons milk, and ¼ teaspoon orange extract. Makes ⅔ cup

1970s

# CITRUS PULL-APART BREAD

It's all about the layered look. A few quick cuts and a fresh citrus zest filling was all it took for Test Kitchen Pro Pam Lolley to transform her famous orange roll recipe into the latest fashion: sweet, buttery loaves of pull-apart bread.

Makes 2 loaves   Hands-on 1 hour
Total 4 hours 55 minutes, including glaze

¼ cup warm water (100° to 110°F)
1 (¼-ounce) envelope active dry yeast
1 teaspoon granulated sugar
1 cup butter, softened
½ cup plus 1 cup granulated sugar
1 teaspoon table salt
2 large eggs, lightly beaten
1 cup milk
1 tablespoon fresh lemon juice
4½ cups bread flour
¼ teaspoon ground nutmeg
Vegetable cooking spray
4 tablespoons orange zest
2 tablespoons lemon zest
⅔ cup powdered sugar
¼ cup butter, melted
2 tablespoons honey
1 large egg white
Fresh Citrus Glaze (at right)

1. Combine the first 3 ingredients in a 1-cup glass measuring cup, and let stand 5 minutes.

2. Beat ½ cup of the softened butter at medium speed with a heavy-duty electric stand mixer until creamy. Gradually add ½ cup of the granulated sugar and 1 teaspoon salt; beat 3 minutes or until light and fluffy. Beat in the eggs and next 2 ingredients. Stir in the yeast mixture.

3. Combine the bread flour and nutmeg. Gradually add to butter mixture, and beat at low speed 2 minutes or until well blended.

4. Sprinkle a flat surface generously with bread flour. Turn out the dough; knead until smooth and elastic (about 5 minutes), sprinkling surface with the bread flour as needed. Coat a large bowl with the cooking spray. Place the dough in the bowl, turning to grease top. Cover with plastic wrap; let rise in a warm place (80° to 85°F) 1½ to 2 hours or until doubled in bulk.

5. Stir together the remaining 1 cup sugar, orange zest, and lemon zest until just combined.

6. Punch the dough down; turn out onto a lightly floured surface. Divide the dough in half. Roll 1 dough portion into a 20- x 12-inch rectangle. Spread with ¼ cup softened butter, and cut into 5 (12- x 4-inch) strips. Sprinkle 2 tablespoons of the zest mixture over 1 strip, and top with a second strip. Repeat with remaining strips and zest mixture, stacking strips as you go. Cut stack into 6 (4- x 2-inch) rectangles.

7. Lightly grease 2 (9- x 5-inch) loaf pans with the cooking spray. Place the stacked rectangles, cut sides up, into 1 prepared pan. Repeat with remaining dough, ¼ cup softened butter, zest mixture, and second pan. Sprinkle any remaining zest mixture over loaves.

8. Whisk together the powdered sugar, melted butter, honey, and egg white until blended. Spoon over loaves. Cover loosely with plastic wrap; let rise in a warm place (80° to 85°F) 1 hour or until doubled in bulk.

9. Preheat the oven to 350°F. Bake at 350°F for 30 to 35 minutes or until golden brown, shielding with aluminum foil after 25 minutes to prevent excessive browning, if necessary. Cool in pans on a wire rack 10 minutes. Remove from pans to a wire rack; brush with Fresh Citrus Glaze. Cool 5 minutes.

## FRESH CITRUS GLAZE

2 cups powdered sugar
2 tablespoons butter, softened
2 teaspoons orange zest

2 to 3 tablespoons fresh orange juice
1 tablespoon fresh lemon juice

Beat the powdered sugar and butter at medium speed with an electric mixer until blended. Add the orange zest, orange juice, and lemon juice; beat until smooth. (Stir in an additional 1 tablespoon orange juice, 1 teaspoon at a time, if desired.) Makes ¾ cup

# Apple Coffee Cake

It's fresh, uncomplicated, and perfect for serving a crowd. Reminiscent of the Mountain South, sweet-tart chunks of apple are folded into a rich sour cream batter and topped with a scattering of black walnuts. Feel free to substitute pecans, but you'll miss out on the distinctive smoky flavor that black walnuts deliver.

Serves 12   Hands-on 20 minutes   Total 50 minutes

½ cup butter, softened
1 cup granulated sugar
1 teaspoon vanilla extract
½ teaspoon table salt
2 large eggs
2½ cups all-purpose flour
1 teaspoon baking powder

1 teaspoon baking soda
1 cup sour cream
2 cups peeled, chopped apples
¾ cup chopped walnuts
½ cup firmly packed brown sugar
1 teaspoon ground cinnamon

1. Preheat the oven to 350°F. Beat first 4 ingredients at medium speed with an electric mixer until light and fluffy. Add the eggs, 1 at a time, beating until blended after each addition. Whisk together the flour, baking powder, and baking soda; add to the butter mixture alternately with the sour cream, beginning and ending with the flour mixture. Beat at low speed just until blended after each addition. Fold in the apples.

2. Spread the batter in a greased 13- x 9-inch pan. Sprinkle with the walnuts. Combine the brown sugar and cinnamon; sprinkle over the nuts.

3. Bake at 350°F for 30 minutes or until a wooden pick inserted in center comes out clean.

1960s

# CARAMEL APPLE COFFEE CAKE

You know what they say about apples and temptation. Well, just imagine the sweet snap of crisp fall apples baked between layers of moist butter cake and crisp pecan streusel. Then top all that with a wickedly delicious caramel sauce. Who could resist? Not us, that's for sure. Bonus: It's deceptively easy. A springform pan (not a culinary degree) is all it takes to get today's crafty artisan look.

Serves 8 to 10    Hands-on 35 minutes
Total 4 hours 50 minutes, including topping and sauce

| | |
|---|---|
| 2 tablespoons butter | 1 cup sugar |
| 3 cups peeled and sliced Granny Smith apples (about 3 large) | 2 large eggs |
| | 2 cups all-purpose flour |
| | 2 teaspoons baking powder |
| Streusel Topping (at right) | ½ teaspoon table salt |
| Caramel Sauce (at right) | ⅔ cup milk |
| ½ cup butter, softened | 2 teaspoons vanilla extract |

1. Preheat the oven to 350°F. Melt 2 tablespoons butter in a large skillet over medium-high; add the apples, and sauté 5 minutes or until softened. Remove from heat; cool completely (about 30 minutes).

2. Meanwhile, make the Streusel Topping and Caramel Sauce. Reserve ½ cup Caramel Sauce for another use.

3. Beat ½ cup butter at medium speed with an electric mixer until creamy; gradually add the sugar, beating well. Add the eggs, 1 at a time, beating until blended after each addition.

4. Combine the flour, baking powder, and salt; add to the butter mixture alternately with the milk, beginning and ending with the flour mixture. Beat at low speed until blended after each addition. Stir in the vanilla. Pour batter into a greased and floured shiny 9-inch springform pan; top with apples. Drizzle with ½ cup Caramel Sauce; sprinkle with Streusel Topping.

5. Bake at 350°F for 45 minutes. Cover loosely with aluminum foil to prevent excessive browning; bake at 350°F for 25 to 30 more minutes or until center is set. (A wooden pick will not come out clean.) Cool in the pan on a wire rack 30 minutes; remove sides of the pan. Cool completely on the wire rack (about 1½ hours). Drizzle with ½ cup Caramel Sauce.

## FLASHBACK

### September Apple Days

That irresistible pull of fall baking always starts just about the time our September issue comes out. Around the Test Kitchen and editorial offices, it's known as the apple issue because years ago we began featuring insanely delicious apple desserts on the cover—all of which led to a fresh crop of new recipes in the magazine. We always include a few savory offerings for good measure (and to keep the doctor away), but it's those irresistible caramel apple coffee cakes and cream cheese Bundt cakes that everyone really craves. So we continue the tradition. And each year, when the apple harvest comes in at the local farmers' market, we start dreaming up another September cover. Did someone say double-crust toffee apple pie?

## STREUSEL TOPPING

1½ cups all-purpose flour
1 cup chopped pecans
½ cup butter, melted
½ cup firmly packed light
    brown sugar

¼ cup granulated sugar
1½ teaspoons ground
    cinnamon
¼ teaspoon table salt

Stir together the flour, pecans, melted butter, brown sugar, granulated sugar, cinnamon, and salt until blended. Let stand 30 minutes or until firm enough to crumble into small pieces. Makes about 2 cups

## CARAMEL SAUCE

1 cup firmly packed light
    brown sugar
½ cup butter

¼ cup whipping cream
¼ cup honey

Bring the brown sugar, butter, whipping cream, and honey to a boil in a medium saucepan over medium-high, stirring constantly; boil, stirring constantly, 2 minutes. Remove from heat, and cool 15 minutes before serving. Store in an airtight container in the refrigerator up to 1 week. To reheat, microwave at HIGH 10 to 15 seconds or just until warm; stir until smooth. Makes about 1½ cups

# Cheesy Grits with Bacon

The secret to these ultra-creamy cheese grits? Supreme meltability. And it can be found only in a golden loaf of Velveeta. Yes, we know it's considered lowbrow these days, but it still tempers the graininess of aged sharp Cheddar brilliantly. Together, they create the perfect balance of creaminess and flavor.

Serves 10 to 12   Hands-on 25 minutes   Total 1 hour 5 minutes

5 cups water
1½ cups uncooked regular grits
1 teaspoon table salt
¾ cup butter
1 (8-ounce) package pasteurized prepared
  cheese product, cubed

1 cup milk
5 large eggs, beaten
8 to 10 bacon slices, cooked and crumbled
1 cup (4 ounces) shredded Cheddar cheese

1. Preheat the oven to 375°F. Bring 5 cups water to a boil in a saucepan, and whisk in the grits; reduce heat, and stir in salt. Cover and cook, stirring occasionally, 10 minutes or until grits are creamy and tender. Stir in the butter and prepared cheese product until melted.

2. Combine the milk and eggs; stir in a small amount of hot grits. Stir the milk mixture into the remaining grits, stirring constantly until well blended. Stir in the bacon. Spoon the mixture into a greased 13- x 9-inch baking dish. Sprinkle with the Cheddar cheese.

3. Bake at 375°F for 40 minutes.

Note: We tested with Velveeta for pasteurized prepared cheese product.

1970s

# BAKED GRITS AND GREENS

What's not to love about buttery garlic croutons and piles of freshly shredded Parm? Granted, the Caesar salad spin is not the classic take on cheese grits, but trust us, it's definitely brunch worthy.

Serves 8 to 10   Hands-on 35 minutes   Total 1 hour 10 minutes

1 teaspoon garlic salt
4 cups water
1 cup uncooked quick-cooking grits
⅓ cup finely chopped red onion
5 tablespoons butter
2 large eggs
1 (10-ounce) package frozen chopped spinach, thawed and drained

1½ cups (6 ounces) shredded Parmesan cheese
½ cup bottled creamy Caesar dressing
½ teaspoon freshly ground black pepper
1¼ cups coarsely crushed garlic-flavored croutons

1. Preheat the oven to 350°F. Bring the garlic salt and 4 cups water to a boil in a large saucepan over medium-high; gradually stir in the grits. Reduce heat to medium, and cook, stirring often, 5 minutes or until thickened. Remove from heat, and stir in the onion and 3 tablespoons of the butter.

2. Whisk together the eggs and next 4 ingredients in a large bowl. Stir about one-fourth of grits mixture gradually into egg mixture; add remaining grits mixture, stirring constantly. Pour into a lightly greased 13- x 9-inch baking dish.

3. Melt remaining 2 tablespoons butter, and toss with coarsely crushed croutons; sprinkle over the grits mixture.

4. Bake at 350°F for 30 to 35 minutes or until mixture is set and croutons are golden brown.

NOTE: We tested with Oscar Mayer Real Bacon Bits.

# Brother Boniface's Pumpkin Bread

Pumpkin bread was trending way before the spiced latte craze. We already had a long list of favorites dating back to the 60s, when Brother Boniface, from Mepkin Abbey near Charleston, shared his recipe. Twenty-five years later, his is still a versatile standout. Our latest spin? Pumpkin bread bruschetta: thinly sliced, toasted, and topped with goat cheese and apricot preserves.

Makes 2 loaves   Hands-on 10 minutes   Total 3 hours 5 minutes

4 cups all-purpose flour
3 cups sugar
1 (15-ounce) can pumpkin
1 cup vegetable oil
²⁄₃ cup milk
2 teaspoons baking soda
1½ teaspoons table salt
1 teaspoon baking powder

1 teaspoon ground cinnamon
½ teaspoon ground ginger
½ teaspoon freshly grated nutmeg
½ teaspoon ground allspice
½ teaspoon ground cloves
4 large eggs
1 cup chopped toasted pecans

1. Preheat the oven to 350°F. Beat first 14 ingredients at medium speed with an electric mixer just until blended. Fold in the pecans. Spoon into 2 greased and floured 9- x 5-inch loaf pans.

2. Bake at 350°F for 1 hour and 15 minutes or until a wooden pick inserted in the center comes out clean. Cool in the pans on wire racks 10 minutes; remove from the pans to wire racks, and cool completely (about 1½ hours).

1990s

# STICKY BUN PUMPKIN MUFFINS

When you fuse the buttery brown sugar goodness of a pecan sticky bun with super-moist pumpkin bread, you get the most outrageously delicious muffin ever. In fact, it's so good it just might reignite 80s muffin mania. Bonus: Topped with a beehive of glazed pecans, they tumble from the pan perfectly coiffed and party ready.

*Makes about 2 dozen   Hands-on 25 minutes   Total 1 hour*

½ cup butter, melted
½ cup firmly packed light brown sugar
2 tablespoons light corn syrup
2 cups toasted pecan halves and pieces
3½ cups all-purpose flour
3 cups granulated sugar
1 tablespoon pumpkin pie spice
1 teaspoon baking soda
1 teaspoon table salt
1 (15-ounce) can pumpkin
1 cup canola oil
4 large eggs
⅔ cup water

1. Preheat the oven to 350°F.

2. Stir together the melted butter and next 2 ingredients. Spoon 1 rounded teaspoonful butter mixture into each cup of 2 lightly greased 12-cup muffin pans, and top each with 1 rounded tablespoonful pecans.

3. Stir together the flour and next 4 ingredients in a large bowl, and make a well in the center of the mixture. Whisk together the pumpkin, next 2 ingredients, and ⅔ cup water; add to the dry ingredients, stirring just until moistened.

4. Spoon the batter into the prepared muffin pans, filling three-fourths full. Place an aluminum foil-lined jelly-roll pan on the lower oven rack to catch any overflow.

5. Bake at 350°F on the middle oven rack for 25 to 30 minutes or until a wooden pick inserted in center comes out clean. Invert the pan immediately to remove the muffins, and arrange the muffins on a wire rack. Spoon any topping remaining in muffin cups over the muffins. Cool 5 minutes.

## FLASHBACK
### Morning Exchange

Most quick bread recipes in our archives can also be baked in muffin pans. You don't need to adjust the recipe or change the oven temperature when making the switch, but you do need to change the bake time. There are no hard and fast rules, but muffins usually bake in a little less than half the time it takes for the original loaf. Sticky Bun Pumpkin Muffins (using the same batter) bake in 25 to 30 minutes. The secret to making both muffins and quick breads is all in the mixing technique. Those with a delicate fine-crumbed texture use the same technique as cakes, beating butter and sugar together until light and fluffy. Others use oil, stirring liquid and dry ingredients together separately so they can be quickly combined without overmixing.

# Cheese-Stuffed French Toast

◆

An over-the-top 90s take on New Orleans-style pain perdu. Cornflake-crusted and pan-fried golden brown before a fast oven finish, this French toast has a crunchy coating that stays crisp even when topped with syrup.

Serves 8   Hands-on 50 minutes   Total 1 hour 15 minutes, plus chill time

8 (2-inch-thick) slices French bread
¾ cup (3 ounces) shredded mozzarella cheese
½ (8-ounce) package cream cheese, softened
1 tablespoon ricotta cheese
3 tablespoons apricot jam
2 large eggs, lightly beaten
½ cup milk
1 cup cornflake crumbs
2 tablespoons plus ¼ cup butter
1 (12-ounce) bottle apricot syrup
2 tablespoons sugar
2 teaspoons ground ginger
16 peach slices
Sifted powdered sugar

1. Starting from 1 side, split each bread slice, leaving the opposite side attached (so that when open, the bread looks like butterfly wings). Using a fork, hollow out a shallow pocket on the inside of each slice, discarding crumbs; set aside. Combine the cheeses; stir in the apricot jam. Spoon about 2 tablespoons of the cheese mixture into each bread slice, and place the slices in a 13- x 9-inch baking dish. Cover and chill 8 hours.

2. Preheat the oven to 400°F. Combine the eggs and milk; dip the bread in the mixture, and dredge in the cornflake crumbs. Melt 2 tablespoons of the butter in a large skillet over medium; cook the bread 2 minutes on each side or until golden brown. Place in a lightly greased 13- x 9-inch baking dish. Bake at 400°F for 15 minutes.

3. Cook the syrup in a saucepan over low until thoroughly heated; remove from heat, and keep warm.

4. Combine remaining ¼ cup butter, sugar, and ginger in a large skillet over medium; add the peach slices, and cook 3 minutes, stirring gently. Arrange the French toast on individual plates; top each serving with the peaches, and sprinkle with the powdered sugar. Serve with the syrup.

1990s

# PRALINE-PECAN FRENCH TOAST

If French toast somehow morphed into a wildly delicious, custardy, upside-down cake, this would be it. And yet, simplicity rules. A golden trifecta of brown sugar, butter, and maple syrup caramelizes in the bottom of the dish, coating the bread as it bakes. It's make-ahead, and totally hands-off. Just add a scattering of berries for a fresh finish.

Serves 8 to 10    Hands-on 15 minutes    Total 55 minutes, plus chilling time

1 (16-ounce) French bread loaf
1 cup firmly packed light brown sugar
⅓ cup butter, melted
2 tablespoons maple syrup
¾ cup chopped pecans

4 large eggs, lightly beaten
1 cup 2% reduced-fat milk
2 tablespoons granulated sugar
1 teaspoon ground cinnamon
1 teaspoon vanilla extract

1. Cut 10 (1-inch-thick) slices of bread. Reserve remaining bread for another use.

2. Stir together the brown sugar and next 2 ingredients; pour into a lightly greased 13- x 9-inch baking dish. Sprinkle with the chopped pecans.

3. Whisk together the eggs and next 4 ingredients. Arrange the bread slices over the pecans; pour the egg mixture over the bread. Cover and chill 8 hours.

4. Preheat the oven to 350°F. Bake at 350°F for 35 to 37 minutes or until golden brown. Serve immediately.

# Minted Melon Balls

Thirty years ago, melon ballers were an essential tool in the kitchen drawer of every progressive hostess. Anyone could master a simple fruit salad, but there was definitely an art to turning out perfect spheres of melon for beautifully carved cantaloupe shells. And we must say, infused with mint-flavored simple syrup, they still make a standout offering on the brunch buffet.

Makes 4 cups   Hands-on 10 minutes   Total 2 hours 10 minutes

½ cup sugar
⅓ cup water
½ cup loosely packed fresh mint leaves

4 cups mixed melon balls
Garnish: fresh mint leaves

1. Bring the sugar and ⅓ cup water to a boil in a small saucepan, stirring occasionally. Remove from heat.

2. Process the sugar mixture and mint in a blender until mint is finely chopped.

3. Toss the melon with mint mixture, and chill at least 2 hours before serving. Serve with a slotted spoon.

1980s

# MELON-PLUM SALAD

Honeydew melon balls enter the 21st century riding on the high-fashion heels of the watermelon-mint-feta trend. Tender watercress leaves and pepper-jelly vinaigrette add a fresh, spicy bite to the salty-sweet mix.

Serves 6   Hands-on 30 minutes   Total 30 minutes

4 cups seeded and cubed watermelon

4 cups honeydew melon balls

3 red plums, sliced

2 cups torn watercress

1 cup crumbled feta cheese

¼ cup rice wine vinegar

¼ cup hot jalapeño pepper jelly

1 tablespoon chopped fresh mint

1 tablespoon grated onion

1 tablespoon fresh lime juice

¼ cup canola oil

1. Gently toss together first 5 ingredients. Arrange on a platter.

2. Whisk together the vinegar, pepper jelly, mint, onion, and lime juice. Gradually add the oil in a slow, steady stream, whisking until smooth. Drizzle the salad with the vinaigrette, and season to taste.

# Perfect Quiche Lorraine

———— ◇ ————

This 70s cream-rich quiche Lorraine set the standard for the decade of the quiche that followed. In the 80s, we published more than 50 recipes for quiche, treating readers to a culinary world tour of our favorites. The highlights? Greek Spinach and Feta Quiche, Swiss Alpine Quiche, and Scandinavian Salmon Quiche inlaid with feathery sprigs of fresh dill. Not to be forgotten: 1987's cocktail brunch quichelets.

Serves 6   Hands-on 20 minutes   Total 1 hour 15 minutes

½ (14.1-ounce) package refrigerated piecrusts
1 (16-ounce) package bacon slices
1½ cups (6 ounces) diced Swiss cheese
4 large eggs, beaten
1 cup whipping cream

1 cup half-and-half
1 tablespoon all-purpose flour
¾ teaspoon table salt
Dash of ground black pepper
Dash of ground nutmeg

1. Preheat the oven to 375°F. Fit a piecrust into a 10-inch quiche dish or pie plate according to package directions; fold the edges under, and crimp.

2. Bake at 375°F for 5 minutes. Cool on a wire rack.

3. Meanwhile, cook the bacon in a large skillet over medium-low until crisp; drain on paper towels.

4. Crumble the bacon, and place in the crust; sprinkle with cheese.

5. Stir together the eggs and next 6 ingredients; pour over cheese.

6. Bake at 375°F for 50 minutes or until set, shielding the crust after 30 minutes to prevent excessive browning.

1970s

# CARAMELIZED ONION QUICHE

We still love quiche and we're not ashamed to say it (those who are call it a tart). Our latest favorite updates the classic quiche Lorraine with a Deep-South Georgia twist, layering hickory-smoked bacon and Gruyère with caramelized Vidalia onions. The perfect foil for all that richness? A fresh herb salad scattered over the top just before serving: Toss flat-leaf parsley, basil, and mint with a tiny splash of fresh lemon juice and olive oil.

Serves 6 to 8   Hands-on 45 minutes   Total 2 hours

1 (14.1-ounce) package refrigerated piecrusts
3 large sweet onions, sliced (about 1½ pounds)
2 tablespoons olive oil
½ cup chopped fresh flat-leaf parsley
6 cooked bacon slices, crumbled
2 cups (8 ounces) shredded Gruyère cheese
1½ cups half-and-half
4 large eggs
½ teaspoon table salt
¼ teaspoon freshly ground black pepper
¼ teaspoon ground nutmeg
Garnish: fresh herbs

1. Preheat the oven to 425°F. Unroll the piecrusts; stack on a lightly greased surface. Roll the stacked piecrusts into a 12-inch circle. Fit the piecrust into a 10-inch deep-dish tart pan with removable bottom; press into the fluted edges. Trim off the excess piecrust along the edges. Line the piecrust with aluminum foil or parchment paper, and fill with pie weights or dried beans. Place the pan on a foil-lined baking sheet. Bake at 425°F for 12 minutes. Remove weights and foil, and bake 8 more minutes. Cool completely on a baking sheet on a wire rack (about 15 minutes). Reduce the oven temperature to 350°F.

2. Meanwhile, cook the onions in hot oil in a large skillet over medium-high, stirring often, 15 to 20 minutes or until the onions are caramel-colored. Remove from heat, and stir in the parsley and bacon. Place half of the onion mixture in the tart shell, and top with half of the cheese; repeat with the remaining onion mixture and cheese.

3. Whisk the half-and-half with the next 4 ingredients; pour over the cheese.

4. Bake at 350°F for 40 to 45 minutes or until set. Cool on a baking sheet on a wire rack 15 minutes before serving.

## SOUTHERN HOSPITALITY

### Garnish the Morning in Style

Clever presentation was paramount for the Southern hostess, even at an early morning hour, and we were happy to share our 1982 expertise: "Whether the entrée you've chosen for your brunch is simple or elaborate, an attractive garnish will add a great deal of eye appeal." Readers learned the fine art of twirling paper-thin tomato peelings into roses, fluting lemon slices with a citrus stripper, and sculpting mushroom caps with the tip of a paring knife. Need to dress up a spiral-cut ham for a buffet? Frothy egg whites and a pastry brush create a winter wonderland of sweet sugar-frosted grapes. And, for the hostess who liked to plan ahead and freeze, plastic candy molds popped out decorative butter pats by the dozens.

# Eggs Hussarde

◆

The original Eggs Benedict dates back to late 19th-century New York, but it's the city of New Orleans that later made it a Southern classic with indulgent twists like Brennan's Eggs Hussarde. Crisp Holland rusks replaced the traditional English muffin, and the bright acidity of Marchand de Vin Sauce, made with a red wine reduction, perfectly balanced the richness of the hollandaise.

Serves 4   Hands-on 15 minutes   Total 55 minutes, including sauces

4 large, thin ham slices
4 tomato slices
½ teaspoon white vinegar
4 large eggs

4 Holland rusks
1⅓ cups Marchand de Vin Sauce
⅓ cup Hollandaise Sauce
Garnish: paprika

1. Cook the ham and tomatoes, in batches, in a large grill pan or nonstick skillet 1 to 2 minutes or until lightly browned and grill marks appear.

2. Pour water to a depth of 3 inches in a large saucepan. Bring to a boil; reduce heat, and maintain at a light simmer. Add the vinegar. Break the eggs, and slip them into water, 1 at a time, as close as possible to surface. Simmer 3 to 5 minutes or to desired degree of doneness. Remove with a slotted spoon. Trim edges, if desired.

3. Place 1 ham slice on each rusk on individual serving plates, and top with Marchand de Vin Sauce. Top with tomatoes, eggs, and Hollandaise Sauce.

## Marchand de Vin Sauce

3 tablespoons butter
½ cup minced cooked ham
½ cup finely chopped onion
⅓ cup finely chopped mushrooms
⅓ cup finely chopped shallots
1 garlic clove, minced
2 tablespoons all-purpose flour

½ teaspoon table salt
⅛ teaspoon freshly ground black pepper
Dash of ground red pepper
¾ cup beef broth
½ cup dry red wine

Melt the butter in a 10-inch skillet over medium. Add the ham and next 4 ingredients; sauté 7 minutes or until onion is very tender. Stir in the flour, salt, black pepper, and red pepper; cook 5 minutes or until lightly browned, stirring often. Stir in broth and wine; bring to a simmer. Cook, stirring often, 5 minutes or until thickened. Makes 1½ cups

# Hollandaise Sauce

4 large egg yolks
2 tablespoons fresh lemon
  juice

1 cup butter, melted
¼ teaspoon table salt

1. Pour water to a depth of 1 inch in the bottom of a double boiler over medium heat; bring to a simmer (do not boil).

2. Whisk together the egg yolks and lemon juice in top of double boiler over barely simmering water. Cook over low 2 to 3 minutes. Gradually whisk in the butter, whisking constantly until warm to the touch. Whisk in the salt. Cook 2 minutes until thickened. Makes 1½ cups

1970s

# BLT BENEDICT WITH AVOCADO-TOMATO RELISH

It's a summer-fresh, 20-minute take on the classic Benedict. Keep in mind that such divine simplicity calls for primo ingredients. Every component counts. So put away the Texas toast and spring for a loaf of brioche or a rustic artisan bread that you can carve into thick slices and toast. If you're seriously missing the hollandaise, we wouldn't say no to gilding the lily. Make it the traditional way (page 41) or use the blender method at left.

Serves 6   Hands-on 15 minutes   Total 25 minutes

1 cup halved grape tomatoes
1 avocado, diced
1 tablespoon chopped fresh basil
1 garlic clove, minced
2 tablespoons olive oil
1 tablespoon red wine vinegar

6 large eggs
1/4 cup mayonnaise
6 (3/4-inch-thick) bakery bread slices, toasted
3 cups firmly packed arugula
12 thick bacon slices, cooked

1. Combine the tomatoes, next 4 ingredients, 2 1/2 teaspoons of the red wine vinegar, and salt and pepper to taste in a small bowl.

2. Add water to a depth of 3 inches in a large saucepan. Bring to a boil; reduce heat, and maintain at a light simmer. Add remaining 1/2 teaspoon red wine vinegar. Break the eggs, and slip them into the water, 1 at a time, as close as possible to the surface. Simmer 3 to 5 minutes or to desired degree of doneness. Remove with a slotted spoon. Trim edges, if desired.

3. Spread the mayonnaise on 1 side of each bread slice. Layer each with 1/2 cup arugula, 2 bacon slices, and 1 egg, and top with the tomato mixture.

## FRESH TAKE

### Hollandaise

Hollandaise can be tricky to make, especially for the novice cook. In a pinch, you could brighten a packaged mix by adding some fresh lemon zest or create a totally faux hollandaise with mayo and sour cream, but it's nowhere near as good as the real thing. This foolproof twist delivers all the silky-rich flavor of the classic.

**Blender Hollandaise:**
Melt 1/2 cup butter in a small saucepan over medium; reduce heat to low, and keep warm. Process 4 large egg yolks, 2 Tbsp. fresh lemon juice, 1/2 tsp. kosher salt, 1/8 tsp. ground white pepper, and 1 Tbsp. water in a blender 2 to 3 minutes or until pale and fluffy. With blender running, add melted butter in a slow stream, processing until smooth. Makes 2/3 cup

# Buttermilk Breakfast Scones

Tender, flaky, and filled with buttery biscuit goodness, the scone was the Cronut of the 80s. Crisp, sugar-crusted tops and currants plumped in buttermilk just made them all the more party-perfect. Plus, they had a certain chameleon quality that let them transition easily from a formal seated brunch to a casual afternoon coffee with friends. That's why, aside from being crazy good, they're a trend that's never lost traction.

Serves 8   Hands-on 10 minutes   Total 30 minutes

1/3 cup dried currants
3/4 cup plus 2 tablespoons buttermilk
2 cups all-purpose flour
2 teaspoons baking powder
1 1/2 teaspoons orange zest
1/4 teaspoon baking soda

1/8 teaspoon table salt
3 1/2 tablespoons sugar
1/3 cup cold butter, cut into pieces
Parchment paper
1 tablespoon milk

1. Preheat the oven to 425°F. Soak the currants in buttermilk 5 minutes.

2. Whisk together the flour, next 4 ingredients, and 2 tablespoons of the sugar. Cut in the butter with a pastry blender until the mixture is crumbly. Gradually add the currants and buttermilk, stirring just until dry ingredients are moistened. Turn the dough out onto a lightly floured surface, and knead lightly 2 or 3 times.

3. Pat the dough into an 8-inch round (3/4 inch thick); cut into 8 wedges with a floured knife. Separate the wedges, and place on a parchment paper-lined baking sheet. Brush the scones with milk, and sprinkle with the remaining 1 1/2 tablespoons sugar.

4. Bake at 425°F for 16 to 18 minutes or until lightly browned.

1980s

# BEST-EVER SCONES

When reader Betty Joyce Mills from Birmingham, Alabama, shared her cranberry scone recipe with us, we thought it was the best we had ever tasted. No tricky techniques were involved—just perfectly balanced ratios and the added richness of heavy cream. The real genius of the recipe? You can make dozens of sweet and savory variations from one master dough.

Serves 8   Hands-on 15 minutes   Total 35 minutes

2 cups all-purpose flour
1/3 cup sugar
1 tablespoon baking powder
1/2 teaspoon table salt

1/2 cup cold butter, cut into
   1/2-inch cubes
1 cup whipping cream

1. Preheat the oven to 450°F. Stir together first 4 ingredients in a large bowl. Cut the butter into the flour mixture with a pastry blender until crumbly. Freeze 5 minutes. Add 3/4 cup plus 2 tablespoons of the cream, stirring just until dry ingredients are moistened.

2. Turn the dough out onto wax paper; gently press or pat dough into a 7-inch round (mixture will be crumbly). Cut the round into 8 wedges. Place the wedges 2 inches apart on a lightly greased baking sheet. Brush the tops of the wedges with the remaining 2 tablespoons cream just until moistened.

3. Bake at 450°F for 13 to 15 minutes or until golden.

## FRESH TAKE

### Downsizing

Once we'd exhausted the sweet and savory possibilities of these Best-Ever Scones, we decided it might be a good idea to make them tiny (you know, for teas and such) and add a glaze. Never fearing too much of a good thing, we went for it.

**Bite-Size Scones:** Pat the dough into 2 (4-inch) rounds. Cut each round into 8 wedges. Bake as directed in the original recipe but decrease the time to 12 or 13 minutes. If, post baking and cooling, you want to add a glaze, start with 1 cup powdered sugar and whisk in 1 Tbsp. cream and 1/2 tsp. vanilla extract; or 1 Tbsp. fresh lemon juice and 1 tsp. zest; or 1 Tbsp. almond, coffee, or praline liqueur. Drizzle over scones. Makes 16 scones

## SWEET VARIATIONS

**Chocolate-Cherry Scones:** Stir in ¼ cup dried cherries, coarsely chopped, and 2 oz. coarsely chopped semisweet chocolate with the cream.

**Apricot-Ginger Scones:** Stir in ½ cup finely chopped dried apricots and 2 Tbsp. finely chopped crystallized ginger with the cream. Drizzle with Cream Cheese Anglaise (page 50), if desired.

## SAVORY VARIATIONS

**Bacon, Cheddar, and Chive Scones:** Omit the sugar. Stir in ¾ cup (3-oz.) shredded sharp Cheddar cheese, ¼ cup finely chopped cooked bacon, 2 Tbsp. chopped fresh chives, and ½ tsp. freshly ground black pepper with the cream.

**Pimiento Cheese Scones:** Omit the sugar. Stir in ¾ cup (3-oz.) shredded sharp Cheddar cheese and 3 Tbsp. finely chopped pimiento with the cream.

# Cream Cheese Pancakes

❖

It happens all the time. Someone in the Test Kitchen says, "You know what would be great with this?" And just like that, a forgotten favorite is resurrected from the archives. Former Editor-in-Chief John Floyd and his wife, Pam, always paired their Bananas Foster Sauce with a buttered-rum pound cake that first ran in 1983. It's just as extraordinary with Cream Cheese Pancakes—and the perfect excuse to have dessert for breakfast.

Serves 6   Hands-on 15 minutes   Total 25 minutes, including sauce

2 cups self-rising flour
2 tablespoons sugar
1 large egg, lightly beaten
1¼ cups milk
1 (3-ounce) package cream cheese, softened

1 tablespoon butter, melted
½ teaspoon vanilla extract
Bananas Foster Sauce (see below)

1. Combine the flour and sugar in a large bowl; make a well in center of mixture. Whisk together the egg and next 4 ingredients in a small bowl; add to the dry ingredients, stirring just until the dry ingredients are moistened.

2. Pour about ¼ cup batter for each pancake onto a hot, lightly greased griddle. Cook the pancakes until tops are covered with bubbles and edges look cooked; turn and cook other side. Serve with Bananas Foster Sauce.

## Bananas Foster Sauce

¼ cup butter
½ cup firmly packed brown sugar
¼ teaspoon ground cinnamon

4 bananas, peeled and sliced
⅓ cup dark rum

1. Melt the butter in a large skillet over medium. Stir in the brown sugar and cinnamon; cook 1 minute or until bubbly. Stir in the bananas; cook 1 minute.

2. Remove from heat; stir in the rum. Ignite with a long match; let flames die down. Return to medium, and cook, stirring constantly, 1 minute or until smooth. Makes 2¾ cups

1990s

# HUMMINGBIRD PANCAKES

After we published Mrs. L.H. Wiggins' triple-layer Hummingbird Cake in 1978, it became the most requested recipe in *Southern Living* history. So we wondered: Could all that blissfully moist sweetness be captured in a stack of pancakes? Indeed. We included a delicious riff on the cream cheese frosting too.

Makes about 18 pancakes   Hands-on 1 hour
Total 1 hour, including sauce

1 1/2 cups all-purpose flour
2 teaspoons baking powder
3/4 teaspoon table salt
1/2 teaspoon ground cinnamon
1 1/2 cups buttermilk
1 cup mashed very ripe bananas
1/2 cup drained, canned crushed pineapple in juice
1/3 cup sugar

1 large egg, lightly beaten
3 tablespoons canola oil
1/2 cup chopped toasted pecans
Cream Cheese Anglaise (see below)
Garnishes: sliced bananas, chopped fresh pineapple

Stir together first 4 ingredients in a large bowl. Whisk together the buttermilk and next 5 ingredients in another bowl. Gradually stir the buttermilk mixture into the flour mixture just until the dry ingredients are moistened. Fold in the toasted pecans. Pour about 1/4 cup batter for each pancake onto a hot buttered griddle or large nonstick skillet. Cook 3 to 4 minutes or until tops are covered with bubbles and edges look dry and cooked. Turn and cook 3 to 4 minutes or until done. Place in a single layer on a baking sheet, and keep warm in a 200°F oven up to 30 minutes. Serve with Cream Cheese Anglaise.

## CREAM CHEESE ANGLAISE

1 1/2 cups half-and-half
1/2 (8-ounce) package cream cheese, softened
1/3 cup sugar
3 large egg yolks

1 tablespoon cornstarch
1/8 teaspoon table salt
2 tablespoons butter
1 teaspoon vanilla extract

Process the half-and-half, cream cheese, sugar, egg yolks, cornstarch, and salt in a blender until smooth. Bring mixture to a boil in a medium saucepan over medium heat, whisking constantly. Boil, whisking constantly, 1 minute. Remove from heat, and whisk in the butter and vanilla. Serve immediately. Makes 1 3/4 cups

# Breakfast Casserole

———◇———

Countless versions of this classic casserole exist, many dating back to
our first issues in the 60s. Ham sometimes stands in for sausage, more
sophisticated cheeses may upstage the Cheddar. All well and good, but
when it comes to replacing the pillowy-soft cushions of white bread with
brioche or croissants, be forewarned: You will be serving only a mere
strata, not an authentic Southern breakfast soufflé.

Serves 8   Hands-on 20 minutes
Total 1 hour 5 minutes, plus 8 hours for chilling

1 pound mild ground pork sausage*
10 white sandwich bread slices, cubed
   (6 cups)
1 (8-ounce) block sharp Cheddar
   cheese, shredded
6 large eggs

2 cups milk
1 teaspoon table salt
1 teaspoon dry mustard
¼ teaspoon Worcestershire sauce
Garnish: chopped fresh parsley

1. Cook the sausage in a skillet over medium, stirring often, 8 minutes or until meat
crumbles and is no longer pink; drain well.

2. Place the bread in a lightly greased 13- x 9-inch baking dish; sprinkle with the cheese,
and top with the sausage crumbles.

3. Whisk together the eggs and next 4 ingredients; pour over the sausage. Cover and
chill 8 hours.

4. Preheat the oven to 350°F. Bake at 350°F for 45 minutes or until set.

*2 cups cubed cooked ham may be substituted.

1990s

# BREAKFAST ENCHILADAS

This bold Tex-Mex twist on the vintage morning casserole gets a cowboy kick with hot sausage and jalapeño Jack. Folding still-warm cheese sauce into the eggs keeps this make-ahead marvel über-moist.

*Serves 6 to 8  Hands-on 45 minutes*
*Total 1 hour 15 minutes, including sauce*

1 (1-pound) package hot ground
   pork sausage
2 tablespoons butter
4 green onions, thinly sliced
2 tablespoons chopped cilantro
14 large eggs, beaten
¾ teaspoon table salt
½ teaspoon ground black
   pepper

Cheese Sauce (see below)
8 (8-inch) flour tortillas
1 cup (4 ounces) shredded
   pepper Jack cheese
Toppings: grape tomatoes,
   sliced green onions,
   fresh cilantro

1. Preheat the oven to 350°F. Cook the sausage in a large nonstick skillet over medium-high, stirring until sausage crumbles and is no longer pink. Remove from pan; drain well on paper towels.

2. Melt the butter in a large nonstick skillet over medium. Add the green onions and cilantro, and sauté 1 minute. Add the eggs, salt, and pepper, and cook, without stirring, until eggs begin to set on bottom. Draw a spatula across bottom of pan to form large curds. Cook until eggs are thickened but still moist; do not stir constantly. Remove from heat; fold in 1½ cups Cheese Sauce and sausage.

3. Spoon about ⅓ cup egg mixture down the center of each flour tortilla; roll up. Place, seam side down, in a lightly greased 13- x 9-inch baking dish. Pour remaining Cheese Sauce evenly over tortillas; sprinkle evenly with pepper Jack cheese.

4. Bake at 350°F for 30 minutes or until bubbly. Serve warm.

# CHEESE SAUCE

⅓ cup butter
⅓ cup all-purpose flour
3 cups milk
2 cups (8 ounces) shredded
   Cheddar cheese

1 (4.5-ounce) can chopped
   green chiles, undrained
¾ teaspoon table salt

Melt the butter in a saucepan over medium-low; whisk in the flour. Cook, whisking constantly, 1 minute. Gradually whisk in the milk over medium heat, whisking constantly, 5 minutes or until thickened. Remove from heat; whisk in remaining ingredients. Makes 4 cups

# Sunrise Omelet

◆

The 80s may have been the decade of the quiche, but omelets were also trending, and we were their biggest cheerleader. We encouraged readers to "Start the Day With an Omelet," "Turn Out the Perfect Omelet," and (noting that timing is everything when manning an omelet station) "Turn Omelets Into a Party." No such suspense here. Just a delicious diner breakfast for two.

Serves 2   Hands-on 30 minutes   Total 30 minutes

2 bacon slices
1 cup peeled, chopped baking potatoes
4 large eggs
1 tablespoon chopped fresh flat-leaf parsley
¼ teaspoon seasoned salt
Dash of onion powder

Dash of ground black pepper
1 tablespoon butter
½ cup (2 ounces) shredded extra-sharp Cheddar cheese
Garnishes: cherry tomato slices, fresh parsley sprigs

1. Cook the bacon in a 10-inch omelet pan or heavy skillet 6 minutes or until crisp; remove bacon, reserving drippings in the skillet. Crumble bacon.

2. Cook the potatoes in hot drippings in a skillet over medium, stirring often, 8 minutes or until golden brown. Remove from the skillet.

3. Whisk together the eggs, parsley, seasoned salt, onion powder, and pepper.

4. Melt the butter in a skillet over medium; rotate pan to coat bottom. Pour egg mixture into the skillet. As the mixture starts to cook, gently lift edges of omelet with a spatula, and tilt pan so uncooked portion flows underneath, cooking until almost set (about 2 minutes).

5. Sprinkle the center of the omelet with bacon, cheese, and potatoes; continue to cook until egg mixture is set. Fold right and left sides of omelet over filling. Gently slide omelet onto a serving plate. Serve immediately.

1980s

# CORNBREAD OMELETS

Totally smitten with the cornbread omelets we sampled at the National Cornbread Festival in South Pittsburg, Tennessee, we returned home, omelet pans in hand, to put our own spicy chorizo spin on the festival favorite.

Serves 5  Hands-on 50 minutes  Total 50 minutes

¾ pound chorizo sausage, casings removed (about 3 links)
6 tablespoons butter
3 green onions, chopped
1 small red bell pepper, chopped
2 jalapeño peppers, minced
1 cup self-rising white cornmeal mix
½ cup buttermilk
½ cup milk
¼ cup all-purpose flour
1 large egg, lightly beaten
Vegetable cooking spray
1 cup (4 ounces) shredded Mexican cheese blend
Garnish: sliced green onions

1. Sauté the chorizo in an 8-inch nonstick omelet pan or skillet with sloped sides 7 to 10 minutes or until browned. Remove from the skillet, and drain on paper towels. Wipe the skillet clean.

2. Melt 1 tablespoon of the butter in skillet, and sauté the green onions, bell pepper, and jalapeño peppers over medium-high 3 to 5 minutes or until tender. Transfer to a bowl; stir in the chorizo. Wipe the skillet clean.

3. Whisk together the cornmeal mix, buttermilk, milk, flour, and egg.

4. Coat the skillet with cooking spray; melt 1 tablespoon of the butter in skillet over medium-high, rotating pan to coat bottom evenly. Pour about ⅓ cup cornmeal mixture into skillet. Tilt pan so uncooked portion flows around to coat bottom of pan, cooking until almost set, bubbles form, and edges are dry (about 1½ minutes). Gently flip with a spatula.

5. Sprinkle 1 side of the omelet with about ½ cup onion mixture and about 3 tablespoons cheese. Fold the omelet in half; cook 30 seconds or until cheese is melted. Transfer to a serving plate; keep warm. Repeat procedure 4 times with remaining butter, cornmeal mixture, onion mixture, and cheese. Serve immediately.

# Classic Charleston Breakfast Shrimp

Before shrimp and grits made it inland to upscale restaurants, it was a simple but hearty breakfast for coastal fishermen.

Serves 2  Hands-on 30 minutes  Total 35 minutes, including grits

¾ pound peeled and deveined medium-size raw shrimp
2 tablespoons lemon juice
¼ teaspoon table salt
⅛ teaspoon ground red pepper
⅛ teaspoon freshly ground black pepper
4 bacon slices

½ cup finely chopped onion
⅓ cup finely chopped green bell pepper
2 teaspoons minced garlic
2 tablespoons all-purpose flour
1 cup bottled clam juice
Creamy Grits (see below)

1. Combine the shrimp and the next 4 ingredients in a bowl.

2. Cook the bacon in a large skillet over medium-low 8 to 10 minutes or until crisp; drain on paper towels, reserving 3 tablespoons drippings in skillet. Crumble bacon.

3. Cook the onion, bell pepper, and garlic in hot drippings over medium-high, stirring constantly, 5 minutes. Sprinkle the flour over vegetables; cook, stirring constantly, 2 minutes or until flour begins to brown. Add the shrimp and ¾ cup of the clam juice; cook, stirring constantly, 2 to 3 minutes or until shrimp turn pink and gravy is smooth. Stir in remaining ¼ cup clam juice. (Add water or additional clam juice to reach desired consistency, if desired.)

4. Serve immediately over Creamy Grits. Sprinkle with bacon.

## Creamy Grits

2 cups water
½ cup uncooked regular grits
1 teaspoon table salt

1 cup whipping cream
4 tablespoons butter, cut into pieces

1. Bring 2 cups water to a boil in a heavy saucepan. Stir in the grits and salt; return to a boil over medium. Reduce heat, and cook, stirring occasionally, 10 minutes or until thickened. Stir in the whipping cream; simmer 10 minutes, stirring occasionally.

2. Remove from heat, and gradually add the butter, stirring until melted after each addition. Serve immediately. Serves 2

1990s

# GRILLED SHRIMP AND SMOKY-GRILLED CORN GRITS

Summery notes of grilled shrimp (flash-marinated with lemon, garlic, and olive oil) and charred-corn grits tinged with the smoky heat of chipotles redefine the traditional breakfast notion of shrimp and grits. A purist might be skeptical, but we say try it anyway. No doubt you'll be convinced to round out your brunch repertoire on sunny weekends.

Serves 4 to 6   Hands-on 55 minutes   Total 1 hour 15 minutes

16 (6-inch) wooden skewers
2 ears fresh corn
1 teaspoon table salt
4 cups water
1 cup uncooked quick-cooking grits
1 cup (4 ounces) shredded Cheddar cheese
2 teaspoons minced canned chipotle pepper in adobo sauce
½ cup olive oil

¼ cup fresh lemon juice
1 garlic clove, pressed
½ teaspoon freshly ground black pepper
1 pound peeled, jumbo raw shrimp with tails, deveined
1 pint grape tomatoes
½ (8-ounce) package fresh mushrooms, quartered
1 small green bell pepper, cut into 1-inch pieces
⅓ cup fresh cilantro

1. Preheat the grill to 350° to 400°F (medium-high). Soak wooden skewers in water 30 minutes. Grill the corn, covered with grill lid, 10 minutes or until done, turning once. Cut kernels from cobs. Discard cobs.

2. Bring the salt and 4 cups water to a boil in a medium saucepan over medium-high. Gradually whisk in the grits. Cook, stirring occasionally, 8 minutes or until thickened. Stir in the corn kernels, cheese, and chipotle pepper. Cover and keep warm.

3. Stir together the olive oil and next 3 ingredients in a large bowl. Toss the shrimp with the olive oil mixture; let stand at room temperature 3 minutes.

4. Remove the shrimp from marinade, discarding marinade. Thread the shrimp onto skewers alternately with the tomatoes, mushrooms, and bell pepper.

5. Grill the kabobs, covered with a grill lid, 4 to 5 minutes on each side or just until shrimp turn pink. Serve the kabobs with the grits, and sprinkle with the cilantro just before serving.

## FLASHBACK

### Canned Shrimp... So Convenient

In 1979, long before landlocked grocers stocked flash-frozen shrimp, we offered the time-pressed reader a tasty alternative: "Have you ever discovered at the last moment that you need shrimp to make that perfect dish? Then next time, reach for a can." We featured recipes for Polynesian Seafood Salad, twice-baked-potato Shrimp Boats, a Shrimp-Crab Puff (yes, that would be singular, as in one Southern-style soufflé), and Shrimp Mousse. Not just any Shrimp Mousse, but THE luxe, coral-colored classic made with cream cheese, mayo, and canned tomato soup. Sculpted in a fish-shaped aspic mold, it was, for decades, the culinary centerpiece of swank cocktail parties and receptions.

# 2

# LUNCHTIME

Hosting the garden club? Longing for an authentic muffuletta or seafood gumbo? Look no further. These are some of our favorite recipes to add to your repertoire.

# ◆ THE WAY WE DINE ◆

## 1970s Ladies Luncheon

Inspired by the white-gloved halcyon days of feminine dining, we set the table for a classic lunch with the girls. Pass the bread basket, please!

# Tomato Pie

According to Texas songwriting legend Guy Clark, there are only two things that money can't buy: true love and homegrown tomatoes. We'd like to amend that list to include tomato pie—not just any tomato pie, but one with perfectly ripe tomatoes, sliced and layered in a crisp biscuit crust while they're still warm from the sun. You can't buy that kind of summer garden bliss, but you sure can make it at home.

Serves 6   Hands-on 30 minutes   Total 2 hours

## Pastry:
1¼ cups all-purpose flour
2 teaspoons baking powder
½ teaspoon table salt
½ teaspoon dried basil
½ cup shortening
½ cup sour cream

## Filling:
3 medium tomatoes, peeled and sliced
1 tablespoon butter
1 cup sliced fresh mushrooms
½ cup chopped onion
½ cup chopped green bell pepper
½ teaspoon table salt
¼ teaspoon ground black pepper
1½ cups (6 ounces) shredded Cheddar cheese
½ cup mayonnaise
Garnish: fresh parsley

1. Make the Pastry: Combine first 4 ingredients in a bowl; cut in the shortening with a pastry blender until mixture is crumbly. Add the sour cream; stir with a fork just until dry ingredients are moistened. Shape into a ball. Wrap in plastic wrap, and chill 1 hour.

2. Roll the dough to ⅛-inch thickness on a lightly floured surface. Fit in a 9-inch pie plate; fold edges under, and crimp.

3. Make the Filling: Preheat the oven to 375°F. Arrange half of the tomatoes in the piecrust.

4. Melt the butter in a large skillet over medium-high; add the mushrooms and next 4 ingredients. Sauté 6 minutes or until the mushrooms are lightly browned and the vegetables tender. Cool slightly.

5. Stir together the cheese, mayonnaise, and mushroom mixture. Spread half of the mixture over the tomatoes in the piecrust. Top with the remaining tomatoes and mushroom mixture.

6. Bake at 375°F for 30 to 35 minutes.

1980s

# TOMATO, CHEDDAR, AND BACON PIE

We turned up the volume on the classic tomato pie with the salty sharpness of freshly grated Parmigiano-Reggiano and summer herbs. A buttery homemade crust, peppered with smoky bits of crumbled bacon, fits neatly into a deep-dish fluted tart pan. For best results, seed the tomatoes and drain the slices before baking.

Serves 6   Hands-on 1 hour 35 minutes   Total 3 hours, plus stand time

CRUST:

2¼ cups self-rising soft-wheat flour (such as White Lily)
1 cup cold butter, cut up
8 cooked bacon slices, chopped
¾ cup sour cream

FILLING:

2¾ pounds assorted large tomatoes
2 teaspoons kosher salt
1½ cups (6 ounces) freshly shredded extra-sharp Cheddar cheese
½ cup (4 ounces) freshly shredded Parmigiano-Reggiano cheese

½ cup mayonnaise
1 large egg, lightly beaten
2 tablespoons fresh dill sprigs
1 tablespoon chopped fresh chives
1 tablespoon chopped fresh flat-leaf parsley
1 tablespoon apple cider vinegar
1 green onion, thinly sliced
2 teaspoons sugar
¼ teaspoon freshly ground black pepper
1½ tablespoons plain yellow cornmeal
Garnishes: fresh dill, parsley, chives

1. Make the Crust: Place the flour in the bowl of a heavy-duty electric stand mixer; cut in the cold butter with a pastry blender or fork until mixture is crumbly. Chill 10 minutes.

2. Add the bacon to the flour mixture; beat at low speed just until combined. Gradually add the sour cream, ¼ cup at a time, beating just until blended after each addition.

3. Spoon the mixture onto a heavily floured surface; sprinkle lightly with flour, and knead 3 or 4 times, adding more flour as needed. Roll into a 13-inch round. Gently place dough in a 9-inch fluted tart pan with 2-inch sides and a removable bottom. Press dough into pan; trim off excess dough along edges. Chill 30 minutes.

4. Meanwhile, make the Filling: Cut 2 pounds of the tomatoes into ¼-inch-thick slices, and remove seeds. Place tomatoes in a single layer on paper towels; sprinkle evenly with 1 teaspoon of the salt. Let stand 30 minutes.

5. Preheat the oven to 425°F. Stir together the Cheddar cheese, next 10 ingredients, and remaining 1 teaspoon salt in a large bowl until combined.

6. Pat the tomato slices dry with a paper towel. Sprinkle the cornmeal over the bottom of the crust. Lightly spread ½ cup of the cheese mixture onto the crust; layer with half of the tomato slices in slightly overlapping rows. Spread with ½ cup of the cheese mixture. Repeat layers, using remaining tomato slices and cheese mixture. Cut remaining ¾ pound tomatoes into ¼-inch-thick slices, and arrange on top of pie.

7. Bake at 425°F for 40 to 45 minutes, shielding edges with foil during the last 20 minutes to prevent excessive browning. Let stand 1 to 2 hours before serving.

# Pimiento Cheese Spread

Purists prefer their pimiento cheese with few embellishments. A whisper
of finely grated onion? No problem. A splash of Worcestershire sauce?
Sure. But toss in candied jalapeños or pecans and you've gone too far. More
daring cooks defy tradition and stir in the unexpected with stellar results.

Makes 3½ cups   Hands-on 15 minutes   Total 15 minutes

4 cups (16 ounces) shredded extra-sharp
   Cheddar cheese
1 (4-ounce) jar diced pimiento, drained
¾ cup chopped pecans
¾ cup mayonnaise
¼ cup chopped pimiento-stuffed Spanish
   olives

2 tablespoons dry sherry
1 tablespoon olive juice from pimiento-
   stuffed Spanish olives
1 teaspoon sugar
½ teaspoon freshly ground black pepper
½ teaspoon hot sauce

Stir together all ingredients until well blended. Cover and chill until ready to serve.

1970s

# FOOD SHARK'S PIMIENTO CHEESE

We'll admit it. We were skeptical when we first read the ingredient list for this pimiento cheese: pepperoncini, horseradish, Havarti, and fresh dill? That's one big intersection of street-food flavor going on in Marfa, Texas. We stirred up a big batch anyway. Turns out, it's every bit as amazing as we'd heard.

Makes 6 cups   Hands-on 15 minutes   Total 15 minutes

1 (12-ounce) jar roasted red bell peppers, drained and finely chopped
1 cup mayonnaise
¼ cup finely chopped red onion
¼ cup chopped fresh parsley
1 tablespoon chopped fresh dill
2 tablespoons Dijon mustard
2 tablespoons chopped jarred pepperoncini salad peppers

1 tablespoon liquid from pepperoncini salad peppers
1 teaspoon grated fresh horseradish
4 cups (16 ounces) shredded sharp Cheddar cheese
3 cups (12 ounces) shredded Havarti cheese
Garnish: fresh flat-leaf parsley

Stir together the roasted red bell peppers, mayonnaise, red onion, chopped parsley, chopped fresh dill, Dijon mustard, pepperoncini salad peppers, liquid from pepperoncini salad peppers, and horseradish. Gently stir in the Cheddar cheese and Havarti cheese until blended. Cover and chill until ready to serve.

## FLASHBACK
### Taste of the South

This wildly popular column was dedicated to sharing iconic Southern recipes like this vintage pimiento cheese recipe (see below), inherited from a staff member's great-grandmother who ran a boarding house in Tuscaloosa. It won out as the all-time favorite in our search for the definitive blend.

**Pimiento Cheese:**
Stir together 1½ cups mayonnaise; 1 (4-oz.) jar diced pimiento, drained; 1 tsp. Worcestershire sauce; 1 tsp. finely grated sweet onion; and ¼ tsp. ground red pepper in a large bowl. Stir in 1 (8-oz.) block extra-sharp Cheddar cheese, finely shredded; and 1 (8-oz.) block sharp Cheddar cheese, shredded. Makes 3¼ cups

# Oyster and Bacon Po'Boy

———◆———

A high-voltage Cajun mayo amps up the flavor, but crisp, golden oysters are the real stars of this classic New Orleans po'boy. Frying at a high temp quickly browns the delicate cracker and cornmeal coating while keeping the oysters moist and tender inside. Armchair Travel Bonus: The taste is so authentic you'll swear you're having lunch in the French Quarter.

Serves 4   Hands-on 35 minutes   Total 35 minutes

4 bacon slices
⅓ cup chopped onion
¼ cup chopped green bell pepper
¼ cup chopped celery
1 garlic clove, minced
1 tomato, chopped and patted dry
2 tablespoons chopped fresh flat-leaf parsley
1½ teaspoons seasoned salt
⅓ cup mayonnaise
¼ teaspoon hot sauce

1 cup cracker meal
½ cup plain yellow cornmeal
⅛ teaspoon ground black pepper
1 (12-ounce) container fresh select oysters, drained
2 large eggs, beaten
Vegetable oil
4 (6- to 7-inch) French bread loaves, halved lengthwise and lightly toasted
Lettuce

1. Cook the bacon in a large skillet over medium-low until crisp; remove the bacon, reserving 1 tablespoon drippings in skillet.

2. Sauté the onion and next 3 ingredients in hot drippings 2 to 3 minutes. Add the tomato, parsley, and ½ teaspoon of the seasoned salt; drain and transfer onion mixture to a bowl. Stir in the mayonnaise and hot sauce.

3. Combine the cracker meal, cornmeal, pepper, and remaining 1 teaspoon seasoned salt in a medium bowl. Dip the oysters in the eggs; dredge in the cornmeal mixture.

4. Pour the oil to a depth of 3 to 4 inches in a Dutch oven; heat to 375°F. Fry the oysters, in batches, 1½ minutes or until golden, turning once. Drain on paper towels.

5. Spread the desired amount of the mayonnaise mixture on the cut sides of the bread. Place the bacon, lettuce, and oysters on the bottom half of the bread; cover with top half. Serve with remaining mayonnaise mixture.

1980s

# FRIED GREEN TOMATO PO'BOYS

New flavor combos trump traditional batter-fried shrimp and oyster po'boys. Topping the list? Sizzling fried green tomatoes and bacon with crisp, cold shreds of iceberg lettuce and spicy Rémoulade Sauce.

Serves 6   Hands-on 30 minutes
Total 40 minutes, including sauce and tomatoes

French bread baguettes | Cooked bacon
Rémoulade Sauce (see below) | Avocado slices
Shredded lettuce
Fried Green Tomatoes (see below)

Cut baguettes into 6-inch lengths. Split each lengthwise, cutting to but not through the other side; spread with Rémoulade Sauce. Layer with the lettuce, Fried Green Tomatoes, bacon, and avocado.

## RÉMOULADE SAUCE

1 cup mayonnaise
1/4 cup sliced green onions
2 tablespoons Creole mustard
1 tablespoon chopped fresh parsley
1 tablespoon minced fresh garlic
1 teaspoon horseradish

Stir together all ingredients; cover and chill. Makes 1 1/4 cups

## FRIED GREEN TOMATOES

1 large egg, lightly beaten
1/2 cup buttermilk
1/2 cup self-rising cornmeal mix
1/2 teaspoon table salt
1/2 teaspoon black pepper
1/2 cup all-purpose flour
3 medium-size, firm green tomatoes, cut into 1/3-inch-thick slices (about 1 1/4 pounds)
Vegetable oil

1. Whisk together the egg and buttermilk. Combine the cornmeal mix, salt, pepper, and 1/4 cup of the flour in a shallow dish. Dredge tomato slices in remaining 1/4 cup flour, dip in egg, and dredge in cornmeal mixture.

2. Pour 1/2 inch oil in a cast-iron skillet; heat to 375°F over medium-high. Fry the tomatoes, in batches, 2 minutes on each side or until golden. Drain on paper towels. Sprinkle hot tomatoes with salt to taste.

# Tacos al Carbon

—◇—

When Tex-Mex fever took hold in the 80s, tacos graduated from ground beef and jarred salsa to grilled flank steak and vibrant fresh salsas. Tacos al carbon ("over coal") were the hottest craze. Fresh cilantro was yet to go mainstream, so we offered an option for using dried in the pico de gallo. (Not a switch we'd make today.) But, if rain were in the forecast, we'd definitely pull out the stove-top grill pan.

Serves 4 to 6   Hands-on 30 minutes
Total 8 hours 45 minutes, including chill time and pico de gallo

2 pounds flank steak
½ cup vegetable oil
½ cup dry red wine
1 teaspoon table salt
1 teaspoon garlic powder
1 teaspoon freshly ground black pepper

½ lime
1 avocado, diced
10 (6-inch) corn tortillas
1 (8-ounce) container sour cream
Pico de Gallo (see below)

1. Place the steak in a large zip-top plastic freezer bag. Whisk together the oil, wine, salt, garlic powder, and pepper. Pour over steak; seal bag, and chill steak 8 to 24 hours, turning occasionally.

2. Preheat grill to 350° to 400°F (medium-high). Remove the steak from the marinade, discarding marinade. Grill, covered with grill lid, 4 to 7 minutes on each side or to desired degree of doneness. Let stand 10 minutes.

3. Squeeze the juice from the lime over the avocado; toss gently to coat.

4. Place the tortillas on a plate; cover with a paper towel. Microwave at HIGH 30 seconds to 1 minute or until warm.

5. Cut the steak diagonally across the grain into thin slices. Serve the steak in warm tortillas with the avocado, sour cream, and Pico de Gallo.

# Pico de Gallo

1 tomato, diced
2 serrano peppers, finely chopped

½ cup chopped onion
2 tablespoons chopped fresh cilantro

Stir together all ingredients. Cover and chill until ready to serve (up to 24 hours). Makes 1¼ cups

1980s

# POBLANO FISH TACOS

Wrapped in warm corn tortillas, the smoky char of a grilled poblano salsa with flash-marinated grouper offers a light, fresh take on the fried beer-battered fish tacos we loved in the 90s. Serve straight up, or crumble in some tangy queso fresco.

Serves 6   Hands-on 20 minutes   Total 40 minutes

1 large poblano pepper
½ English cucumber, coarsely chopped
1 cup grape tomatoes, quartered
2 tablespoons chopped red onion
1 garlic clove, minced
½ teaspoon table salt
3 tablespoons fresh lime juice
4 tablespoons olive oil

1 tablespoon mango-lime seafood seasoning
1½ pounds grouper or other firm white fish fillets
12 (6-inch) fajita-size corn tortillas, warmed
Lime wedges
Crumbled queso fresco (optional)

1. Preheat the grill to 350° to 400°F (medium-high). Grill the pepper, covered with grill lid, 3 to 4 minutes or until pepper looks blistered, turning once. Place the pepper in a large zip-top plastic freezer bag; seal and let stand 10 minutes to loosen skins. Peel the pepper; remove and discard seeds. Coarsely chop.

2. Combine the pepper, cucumber, next 4 ingredients, 2 tablespoons of the lime juice, and 2 tablespoons of the olive oil in a bowl.

3. Whisk together the seafood seasoning and remaining 1 tablespoon lime juice and 2 tablespoons olive oil in a large shallow dish or zip-top plastic freezer bag; add the fish, turning to coat. Cover or seal, and chill 5 minutes, turning once. Remove the fish from the marinade, discarding the marinade.

4. Grill the fish, covered with grill lid, 3 to 4 minutes on each side or just until fish begins to flake when poked with the tip of a sharp knife and is opaque in center. Cool 5 minutes. Flake fish into bite-size pieces.

5. Serve the fish and salsa in warm tortillas with lime wedges. Top with the queso fresco, if desired.

NOTE: We tested with Weber Mango Lime Seafood Seasoning.

# Warm Goat Cheese Salad

In the early 80s, Alice Waters put a simple salad of tender spring greens topped with warm medallions of local goat cheese on the menu at Chez Panisse in Berkeley, California. It didn't take long for the inspiration to migrate cross-country to upscale Southern restaurants. This stellar twist, that first ran in one of our "Holiday Dinners" features, is especially good paired with toasted black olive-walnut bread.

Serves 4   Hands-on 20 minutes   Total 20 minutes

⅓ cup extra virgin olive oil
3 tablespoons lemon juice
2 teaspoons thinly sliced green onions
1 teaspoon Dijon mustard
½ teaspoon table salt
¼ teaspoon ground black pepper
⅓ cup Italian-seasoned breadcrumbs
1 tablespoon grated Parmesan cheese
1 tablespoon sesame seeds

1 (10.5-ounce) goat cheese log, cut into
   8 slices
1 large egg, lightly beaten
2 tablespoons butter
1 tablespoon olive oil
1 (5-ounce) package mixed baby salad
   greens
8 pitted kalamata olives

1. Whisk together first 6 ingredients in a small bowl.

2. Combine the breadcrumbs, Parmesan cheese, and sesame seeds in a bowl.

3. Dip the goat cheese in the egg, and dredge in the breadcrumb mixture.

4. Melt the butter with 1 tablespoon olive oil in a large nonstick skillet over medium-high; add the goat cheese. Fry cheese 1 to 2 minutes on each side or until browned.

5. Toss the mixed greens with the vinaigrette in a serving bowl; add the olives, and top with the warm cheese.

1990s

# BABY BLUE SALAD

Mesclun, mache, and baby arugula fill our salad bowls
today. Pungent, ripe Gorgonzola and honey-sweet
balsamic vinaigrettes take center stage. Candied nuts
are the new crouton. Birmingham's former Homewood
Gourmet Chef Franklin Biggs' salad remains at the top
of our salad A-list.

Serves 2   Hands-on 30 minutes
Total 50 minutes, including pecans and vinaigrette

1 (5-ounce) bag mixed spring
   salad greens
2 ounces crumbled blue
   cheese
1 orange, peeled and sectioned
½ pint fresh strawberries,
   quartered

½ cup Sweet-and-Spicy Pecans
   (see below)
Balsamic Vinaigrette
   (see below)

Toss first 5 ingredients in a large bowl. Drizzle with ½ cup Balsamic
Vinaigrette; toss to coat. Serve with remaining vinaigrette.

# SWEET-AND-SPICY PECANS

¼ cup sugar
1 cup warm water
1 cup pecan halves
2 tablespoons sugar

1 tablespoon chili powder
⅛ teaspoon ground red
   pepper

1. Preheat the oven to 350°F. Stir together ¼ cup sugar and warm
water until sugar dissolves. Add the pecans; soak 10 minutes. Drain.

2. Combine 2 tablespoons sugar, chili powder, and red pepper.
Add the pecans; toss to coat. Arrange in a single layer on a lightly
greased baking sheet. Bake at 350°F for 10 minutes or until golden
brown, stirring once. Makes 1 cup

# BALSAMIC VINAIGRETTE

½ cup balsamic vinegar
3 tablespoons Dijon mustard
3 tablespoons honey
2 large garlic cloves, minced

2 small shallots, minced
¼ teaspoon table salt
¼ teaspoon black pepper
1 cup olive oil

Whisk together first 7 ingredients until blended. Gradually whisk
in the olive oil, blending well. Store leftover vinaigrette, covered, in
the refrigerator up to 2 weeks. Makes 1⅔ cups

# Shrimp Destin

◆

This sunny Florida-Panhandle twist on Shrimp Scampi is sautéed in garlic butter and served over toasted French rolls. Sent in by reader Frances Ponder of Destin, Florida, its enduring popularity landed it on the magazine's list of top 25 all-time-favorite recipes 20 years later.

Serves 6   Hands-on 20 minutes   Total 20 minutes

1 cup butter
¼ cup chopped green onions
2 teaspoons minced garlic
2 pounds unpeeled, large raw shrimp, peeled and deveined
1 tablespoon lemon juice
1 tablespoon dry white wine
½ teaspoon table salt

¼ teaspoon coarsely ground black pepper
1 tablespoon chopped fresh dill
1 tablespoon chopped fresh flat-leaf parsley
3 French rolls, halved lengthwise and toasted

1. Melt the butter in a large skillet over medium-high; add the green onions and garlic, and sauté 2 minutes or until onions are tender. Add the shrimp, lemon juice, wine, salt, and pepper; reduce heat to medium, and cook, stirring occasionally, 5 minutes. Stir in the dill and parsley.

2. Spoon shrimp mixture over toasted rolls, and serve immediately.

1980s

# SHRIMP DESTIN LINGUINE

Former Test Kitchen Pro Vanessa McNeil Rocchio developed this quick pasta riff on the classic, sautéing the shrimp in a 50-50 mix of butter and olive oil and tossing in hot cooked linguine with the buttery pan drippings. Turn up the heat by adding a squirt of Sriracha or dried crushed red pepper.

Serves 2 to 3   Hands-on 30 minutes   Total 30 minutes

1½ pounds unpeeled, large raw shrimp
1 (9-ounce) package refrigerated linguine
¼ cup butter
¼ cup olive oil
¼ cup chopped green onions
2 garlic cloves, minced

1 tablespoon dry white wine
2 teaspoons fresh lemon juice
½ teaspoon table salt
¼ teaspoon coarsely ground black pepper
1 tablespoon chopped fresh dill
1 tablespoon chopped fresh parsley

1. Peel the shrimp, leaving tails on, if desired. Devein, if desired.

2. Prepare the pasta according to package directions.

3. Meanwhile, melt the butter with oil in a large skillet over medium-high; add the green onions and garlic, and sauté 4 to 5 minutes or until onions are tender. Add the shrimp, wine, and next 3 ingredients. Cook over medium, stirring occasionally, 3 to 5 minutes or just until shrimp turn pink. Stir in the dill and parsley. Remove the shrimp with a slotted spoon, reserving sauce in skillet.

4. Add the hot cooked pasta to the sauce in skillet, tossing to coat. Transfer the pasta to a serving bowl, and top with the shrimp.

# Seafood Gumbo

———— ◇ ————

Gumbo is a source of great debate among Southerners. Some opt for seafood, others for chicken and andouille. Thicken with okra as it simmers, or toss in some filé at the finish? So many possibilities! Most agree the secret to a good gumbo is in the roux, but even then there's controversy over color. The magic of this recipe starts with a chocolate-colored roux. The next layer of flavor? The holy trinity of Cajun cooking: bell pepper, onion, and celery.

Serves 12 to 15   Hands-on 1 hour   Total 1 hour 45 minutes

1 bunch green onions
1/2 cup bacon drippings
1 cup all-purpose flour
1 green bell pepper, diced
1 large onion, diced
3 celery ribs, diced
2 garlic cloves, minced
1 large tomato, chopped
2 quarts plus 2 cups water
1/4 cup minced fresh flat-leaf parsley
2 teaspoons table salt

2 teaspoons ground black pepper
1/2 teaspoon ground red pepper
1 pound fresh lump crabmeat, drained
1 1/2 pounds unpeeled, medium-size raw
    shrimp, peeled and deveined
1 pint standard oysters, undrained
1 (12-ounce) package frozen sliced okra,
    thawed
1 tablespoon gumbo filé
Hot cooked rice

1. Slice the green onions, reserving green tops.

2. Heat the bacon drippings in a Dutch oven over medium; gradually whisk in flour. Cook, whisking constantly, until flour is chocolate colored (about 30 minutes).

3. Add the sliced green onions, bell pepper, onion, celery, garlic, and tomato to the roux, and cook 8 minutes or until vegetables are tender. Add 2 quarts plus 2 cups water, parsley, salt, black pepper, and red pepper; bring to a boil. Reduce heat, and simmer, uncovered, 30 minutes.

4. Pick the crabmeat, removing any bits of shell.

5. Increase heat to medium-high, and add the shrimp, oysters, okra, and green onion tops; simmer 10 minutes. Remove from heat, and stir in the crabmeat and gumbo filé; let stand 15 minutes. Add water, if necessary, for desired consistency. Serve over the rice.

1980s

# GRILLED SHRIMP GUMBO SALAD

A cure for hot-weather blues, spicy chargrilled okra, bell pepper, onion, and smoky-sweet Gulf shrimp create a colorful summer twist on seafood gumbo. Fresh Corn Vinaigrette ties it all together.

Serves 6 to 8   Hands-on 1 hour 10 minutes
Total 1 hour 40 minutes, including vinaigrette

6 (12-inch) wooden skewers
1 pound unpeeled, large raw shrimp
2 tablespoons olive oil
2½ teaspoons Cajun seasoning
1 pound fresh okra

6 (½-inch-thick) sweet onion slices
1 green bell pepper, quartered
2 (16-ounce) packages baby heirloom tomatoes, halved
Fresh Corn Vinaigrette (see below)

1. Soak the wooden skewers in water 30 minutes.

2. Preheat the grill to 350° to 400°F (medium-high). Peel the shrimp; devein, if desired. Drizzle the shrimp with 1 tablespoon of the olive oil, and sprinkle with ½ teaspoon of the Cajun seasoning. Thread the shrimp onto the skewers.

3. Drizzle the okra, onion, and bell pepper with remaining 1 tablespoon olive oil; sprinkle with remaining 2 teaspoons Cajun seasoning.

4. Grill the okra, covered with grill lid, 4 minutes on each side or until tender. Grill the onion slices and bell pepper, covered with grill lid, 6 minutes on each side or until tender. Grill the shrimp, covered with grill lid, 2 minutes on each side or just until the shrimp turn pink.

5. Cut the okra in half lengthwise. Coarsely chop the bell pepper. Toss together the okra, bell pepper, and onion in a large bowl.

6. Remove the shrimp from skewers, and toss with the okra mixture, tomatoes, and Fresh Corn Vinaigrette.

# FRESH CORN VINAIGRETTE

1 cup fresh corn kernels
⅔ cup olive oil
¼ cup fresh lemon juice
1 garlic clove, minced

2 tablespoons balsamic vinegar
1 tablespoon Creole mustard
1 teaspoon chopped fresh thyme

Whisk together all ingredients. Add table salt and freshly ground black pepper to taste. Makes 1½ cups

# Tarragon Pasta Chicken Salad

Early pasta salad recipes often featured a short list of familiar ingredients dressed with bottled vinaigrette. This one cleverly amps up the flavor of bottled Italian dressing with the addition of fresh tarragon and garlic. Cook the small pasta shells al dente (1 or 2 minutes less than package directions specify) so they keep their distinctive shape and texture when tossed with the chicken and dressing.

Serves 4 to 6   Hands-on 20 minutes   Total 4 hours 20 minutes

1 (8-ounce) bottle zesty Italian dressing
¼ cup white wine vinegar
2 tablespoons chopped fresh tarragon
1 garlic clove, minced
4 boneless, skinless chicken breasts
4 ounces uncooked medium-size shell pasta or elbow macaroni (about 1½ cups)
2 cups sliced celery
½ cup chopped red or green bell pepper
½ cup mayonnaise
¼ cup chopped green onions
1 tablespoon chopped fresh flat-leaf parsley

1. Combine the first 4 ingredients in a jar, and cover tightly with lid. Shake vigorously until well blended.

2. Place the chicken in an 11- x 7-inch baking dish; pour ¾ cup dressing mixture over the chicken; reserve remaining dressing mixture. Cover and chill the chicken and reserved dressing mixture 2 to 8 hours.

3. Preheat the oven to 350°F. Let the baking dish stand at room temperature 30 minutes.

4. Bake at 350°F for 30 to 35 minutes or until the chicken is done. Drain the chicken, and cool slightly; coarsely chop.

5. Meanwhile, cook the pasta to al dente; drain and cool slightly.

6. Toss together the chicken, reserved dressing mixture, pasta, celery, and next 4 ingredients in a large bowl. Cover and chill 1 hour before serving.

1980s

## FLASHBACK
### Pasta Salad Timeline

Macaroni salads, peppered with pickle relish and bits of leftover ham, had been around for decades, but it wasn't until the late 70s that those simple barbecue sides began transitioning into main-dish pasta salads. Story headlines in vintage issues of *Southern Living* offer a glimpse into the changing times.

**1979: Macaroni Makes the Salad**—For a change from the traditional tossed salad, serve macaroni instead.

**1982: Toss an Imaginative Pasta Salad**—So what was imaginative in '82? Spiral Macaroni Salad and layered Overnight Pasta Salad made with English peas and seashell pasta.

**1988: Pasta Makes the Perfect Salad**—even if you're not fluent in Italian!

# FARMERS' MARKET PASTA SALAD

Perfectly cooked pasta is a blank canvas for peak-season farmers' market finds. Slightly undercook it so it holds its shape when tossed with the vegetables and vinaigrette. Diced peaches are a surprising counterpoint to the smoky-rich flavor of the chicken. Parmesan Vinaigrette, spiked with cilantro and basil, ties it all together. Ripe for riffs, this dish also works with cheese-filled tortellini in place of the penne.

Serves 8 to 10   Hands-on 40 minutes   Total 55 minutes, including vinaigrette

2 cups halved baby heirloom tomatoes
2 small zucchini, thinly sliced into half
   moons
1 small red bell pepper, cut into thin strips
1 cup fresh corn kernels
1 cup sliced firm, ripe fresh peaches
   (about 2 medium)

½ cup thinly sliced green onions
Parmesan Vinaigrette (see below)
1 (8-ounce) package penne pasta*
2 cups shredded smoked chicken
   (about 10 ounces)
⅓ cup torn fresh basil
⅓ cup torn fresh cilantro

1. Toss together first 7 ingredients in a large bowl, and let stand 10 minutes.

2. Meanwhile, prepare the pasta according to package directions. Add the hot cooked pasta and chicken to the tomato mixture; toss gently to coat. Add table salt and ground black pepper to taste. Transfer to a serving platter, and top with the basil and cilantro.

*1 (20-ounce) package refrigerated cheese-filled tortellini may be substituted.

# PARMESAN VINAIGRETTE

½ cup grated Parmesan cheese
½ cup olive oil
2 teaspoons lemon zest
3 tablespoons fresh lemon juice
1 tablespoon balsamic vinegar

2 garlic cloves
2 teaspoons ground black pepper
½ teaspoon table salt
¼ cup chopped fresh basil
¼ cup chopped fresh cilantro

Process the first 8 ingredients in a blender or food processor until smooth. Add the herbs; pulse just until blended. Makes 1 cup

# She-Crab Soup

Local legend traces the origin of Charleston's iconic she-crab soup to a presidential dinner served at the home of Mayor Rhett in the early 1900s. Requested to create a special dish for the occasion, Rhett's genius butler conjured up a rich sherry-infused alchemy of freshly harvested crabmeat and cream. He then stirred in the coral-colored roe of the female crabs, which added a pale hue and umami depth of flavor that was way ahead of its time. In recent years, ecological efforts to preserve the supply of crabs banned the harvesting of roe from egg-bearing female crabs who carry the roe outside their shells. Only female crabs with the roe on the inside may be used. In *Charleston Receipts*, the spiral-bound classic published by the Junior League in 1950, Mrs. Henry Church suggests crumbling the yolks of hard-cooked eggs in the bottom of the soup plate as a substitute.

Serves 6 to 8   Hands-on 40 minutes   Total 45 minutes

3 tablespoons butter
1 medium onion, chopped
2 teaspoons all-purpose flour
1 quart whole milk
1 pound fresh lump crabmeat
¼ pound crab roe or hard-cooked
   egg yolk

⅛ teaspoon white pepper
⅛ teaspoon ground mace
2 cups half-and-half
½ cup sherry wine
1 tablespoon table salt
Garnishes: paprika, fresh parsley

1. Melt 1½ tablespoons of the butter in a saucepan over low; add the onion, and sauté 3 to 4 minutes or until softened.

2. Pour water to a depth of 1 inch in the bottom of a double boiler over medium heat; bring to a boil. Reduce heat, and simmer; place remaining 1½ tablespoons butter in top of the double boiler over simmering water. Cook until melted. Whisk in the flour.

3. Stir in the onion and milk, stirring constantly until blended. Stir in the crabmeat and roe; add pepper and mace, and cook 20 minutes. Stir in the half-and-half. Remove from heat, and stir in the wine and salt.

1960s

# CORN AND CRAB CHOWDER

South of Charleston, Savannahians are known for their fresh corn and crab chowder. Like she-crab soup, it's a simple but rich cream soup that gets its extraordinary flavor from local ingredients at their peak. The chowder is a summertime favorite, made when fresh Silver Queen corn is in season and at its sweetest. It's equally good made with shrimp or chicken.

Serves 6 to 8   Hands-on 1 hour 25 minutes
Total 1 hour 25 minutes

6 bacon slices
2 celery ribs, diced
1 medium-size green bell pepper, diced
1 medium onion, diced
1 jalapeño pepper, seeded and diced
1 (32-ounce) container chicken broth
3 tablespoons all-purpose flour
3 cups fresh corn kernels (about 6 ears)
1 pound fresh lump crabmeat, drained*
1 cup whipping cream
1/4 cup chopped fresh cilantro
1/2 teaspoon table salt
1/4 teaspoon ground black pepper
Oyster crackers
Garnish: fresh cilantro

1. Cook the bacon in a Dutch oven over medium 8 to 10 minutes or until crisp; remove the bacon, and drain on paper towels, reserving 2 tablespoons drippings in Dutch oven. Crumble the bacon.

2. Sauté the celery and next 3 ingredients in hot drippings 5 to 6 minutes or until tender.

3. Whisk together the broth and flour until smooth. Add to the celery mixture. Stir in the corn. Bring to a boil; reduce heat, and simmer, stirring occasionally, 30 minutes. Pick the crabmeat, removing any bits of shell. Gently stir in the crabmeat and next 4 ingredients; cook 4 to 5 minutes or until thoroughly heated. Serve warm with crumbled bacon and oyster crackers.

*1 pound peeled cooked shrimp or chopped cooked chicken may be substituted.

# Berry Gazpacho

◆

Fruit gazpacho wasn't trending below the Mason-Dixon Line 20 years ago. In fact, it wasn't even mentioned in the article when this recipe was first published. There's something remarkably versatile and very Southern (in a candy-sweet congealed salad sort of way) about a chilled soup that can make the leap from luncheon starter to light summer dessert simply by adding a scoop of sherbet.

Serves 6   Hands-on 15 minutes   Total 3 hours

1 (750-milliliter) bottle Riesling wine
1 vanilla bean, split
1 (1-ounce) package fresh mint
1 (10-ounce) package frozen
   strawberries, thawed
½ cup water
2 cups fresh raspberries

2 cups fresh blackberries
2 cups fresh blueberries
⅓ cup honey
2 tablespoons lemon juice
Raspberry sorbet
Garnishes: fresh mint sprigs,
   fresh berries

1. Bring first 3 ingredients to a boil in a large saucepan over medium-high; boil until reduced to 1½ cups (about 15 minutes). Cover and chill 2 to 24 hours.

2. Pour the wine mixture through a wire-mesh strainer into a large bowl; discard solids.

3. Process the strawberries and ½ cup water in a blender until smooth; pour through a strainer into the bowl with wine mixture; discard solids. Stir in the raspberries and next 4 ingredients; chill 30 minutes to 1 hour. Serve with raspberry sorbet.

1990s

# SUMMER GAZPACHO

It's everything delicious you'd expect from a classic gazpacho—plus a colorful confetti of diced watermelon and perfectly ripe summer fruits.

Serves 4 to 6   Hands-on 30 minutes   Total 30 minutes, including salad

1 medium-size red heirloom tomato
1 cup diced seedless watermelon
1 cup diced strawberries
1 Kirby cucumber, diced
1 cup diced peaches
1 jalapeño pepper, seeded and minced
1½ cups fresh orange juice
⅓ cup finely chopped sweet onion

1½ tablespoons chopped fresh basil
1½ tablespoons chopped fresh mint
2 tablespoons extra virgin olive oil
1 tablespoon red wine vinegar
½ teaspoon kosher salt
Avocado West Indies Salad (see below)
Whole grain crackers

1. Cut the tomato in half; gently squeeze to remove seeds. Discard seeds, and chop tomato. Combine the tomato and next 12 ingredients in a large pitcher. Serve immediately, or cover and chill up to 24 hours.

2. Meanwhile, make Avocado West Indies Salad. Spoon the gazpacho into bowls. Top with Avocado West Indies Salad. Serve with crackers.

## AVOCADO WEST INDIES SALAD

8 ounces fresh jumbo lump crabmeat, drained
1 medium avocado, chopped
⅓ cup diced sweet onion
2 tablespoons chopped fresh basil

3 tablespoons apple cider vinegar
3 tablespoons extra virgin olive oil
¼ teaspoon kosher salt
¼ teaspoon freshly ground black pepper

Pick the crabmeat, removing any bits of shell. Gently stir together the crabmeat, avocado, onion, basil, vinegar, olive oil, kosher salt, and freshly ground black pepper. Serve immediately, or chill up to 2 hours. Serves 4 to 6

# Smoked Pork Barbecue

---◆---

Hal Tyler of Richmond, Virginia, shared this recipe in a fall story that focused on men with a flair for cooking. His secret to perfectly smoked pork? Adding his special vinegar-based barbecue sauce to the water pan in the smoker. Sandwich the juicy pork butt in a soft white-bread bun, and douse with sauce. Topping with chowchow and a tangle of homemade coleslaw? Totally optional, but highly recommended.

Serves 10 to 12   Hands-on 20 minutes
Total 10 hours 50 minutes, including smoking time

Hickory wood chunks
2 cups ketchup
2 cups apple cider vinegar
1 cup butter
1 (5-ounce) bottle Worcestershire sauce
1 tablespoon table salt
1 tablespoon brown sugar
1 tablespoon dried minced onion
1 tablespoon hot sauce

2 small garlic cloves, minced
1/8 teaspoon ground red pepper
1/8 teaspoon ground black pepper
2 quarts water
1 (6- to 8-pound) bone-in pork shoulder
    roast or Boston butt
Hamburger buns (optional)
Garnishes: coleslaw, dill pickle slices

1. Soak the wood chunks in water 30 minutes.

2. Meanwhile, bring the ketchup and next 10 ingredients to a boil in a large saucepan; reduce heat, and simmer 10 minutes.

3. Prepare the smoker according to manufacturer's directions, using 1 cup barbecue sauce and 2 quarts water in water pan. Bring internal temperature to 225° to 250°F; maintain temperature for 15 to 20 minutes.

4. Drain the wood chunks, and place on coals. Place the roast on the upper cooking grate; baste generously with remaining barbecue sauce. Cover with smoker lid.

5. Smoke the roast, maintaining temperature inside smoker between 225° and 250°F, for 9 hours or until a meat thermometer inserted into thickest portion registers 195°F. (Refill water pan with a mixture of 1 cup barbecue sauce and 2 quarts water as needed.) Remove the roast from smoker, and wrap tightly in aluminum foil. Let stand 1 hour.

6. Shred the roast, and serve on buns, if desired.

1980s

# PORK GRIDDLE CAKES WITH CHERRY SALSA

Hearty, pork-rich griddle cakes topped with the sweet fiery heat of a fresh cherry salsa expand the classic white-bread-bun notion of a barbecue sandwich. Hungry for more? Add extra 'cue before spooning on the salsa!

Serves 8   Hands-on 55 minutes   Total 55 minutes

1½ cups self-rising white cornmeal mix
½ cup all-purpose flour
1 tablespoon sugar
1⅔ cups buttermilk
3 tablespoons butter, melted

2 large eggs, lightly beaten
2 cups chopped pulled barbecued pork (without sauce)
Cherry Salsa (see below)

1. Whisk together the cornmeal mix and next 5 ingredients just until moistened; stir in pulled pork.

2. Pour about ¼ cup batter for each griddle cake onto a hot, lightly greased griddle or large nonstick skillet. Cook for 3 to 4 minutes or until the tops are covered with bubbles and the edges look dry and cooked; turn and cook the other side 2 to 3 minutes or until done. Serve immediately with the salsa.

## CHERRY SALSA

½ cup red pepper jelly
1 tablespoon lime zest
¼ cup fresh lime juice
¼ teaspoon dried crushed red pepper

2 cups pitted, coarsely chopped fresh cherries
¾ cup diced fresh nectarines
⅓ cup chopped fresh cilantro
⅓ cup chopped fresh chives

Whisk together the red pepper jelly, lime zest, lime juice, and dried crushed red pepper in a small bowl. Stir in the cherries, nectarines, cilantro, and chives. Makes 2½ cups

## FLASHBACK
### Blizzard BBQ

Too cold and snowy to make it out to the grill? Turn your slow cooker into a countertop pit master! Many a wintry day, we've plugged into the comforts of this juicy fork-tender pork butt. We've tucked it into slider buns and taco shells, spooned it over twice-baked potatoes and cheese grits, and even paired it with pickled vegetables and Sriracha mayo for a down-South Vietnamese bánh mì.

**Slow Cooker Barbecue Pork:** Place 1 (3- to 4-lb.) boneless pork shoulder roast (Boston butt), trimmed, in a lightly greased 6-qt. slow cooker; pour 1 (18-oz.) bottle barbecue sauce and 1 (12-oz.) can cola soft drink over the roast. Cover and cook on LOW 8 to 10 hours or until meat shreds easily with a fork. Transfer the pork to a cutting board; shred with two forks, removing any large pieces of fat. Skim the fat from the sauce, and stir in the shredded pork. Serves 6

# Shrimp in Rémoulade Sauce

Shrimp rémoulade has deep, century-old roots in France, but it was made famous in the South by legendary restaurants in New Orleans. Its popularity gained momentum during the *Mad Men* era with the Francophile influences of Jackie Kennedy and Julia Child. There are two versions of rémoulade sauce: One is mayo-based similar to the French bistro classic, and the other is oil-based—but usually more spirited with horseradish and paprika than this vintage twist.

Serves 6   Hands-on 35 minutes   Total 2 hours 15 minutes

3 quarts water
3 pounds unpeeled, medium-size raw shrimp
1 (3.25-ounce) package boil-in-bag shrimp-and-crab boil
1 onion, quartered
1 lemon, sliced
1 tablespoon table salt
1 garlic clove
½ cup olive oil
6 tablespoons tarragon vinegar

3 tablespoons Creole mustard
3 tablespoons mayonnaise
4 green onions with tops, minced
1 celery rib, minced
Lettuce leaves
2 hard-cooked eggs, peeled and sliced
1 avocado, peeled and cut in wedges

1. Bring 3 quarts water to a boil; add next 6 ingredients. Cover and simmer 5 minutes or just until shrimp turn pink. Drain. Chill the shrimp 40 minutes.

2. Peel the shrimp, and devein, if desired.

3. Stir together the oil and next 5 ingredients. Pour over shrimp in a bowl, and toss shrimp to coat. Cover and chill 1 hour.

4. Toss the shrimp, and serve on the lettuce with the eggs and avocado.

1970s

# SHRIMP SALAD OVER ZESTY WATERMELON

Luncheon salads in scalloped tomato shells are totally old school. Perfectly poached shrimp, lightly dressed in a bright tarragon mayo, come to the table riding stylishly atop rectangular cuts of ice-cold watermelon. Baby arugula, tossed with a splash of fresh lemon juice and zest, adds a peppery citrus snap to the ensemble.

Serves 4   Hands-on 10 minutes   Total 30 minutes

2 lemons
4 (1-inch-thick) watermelon slices, rind removed
Kosher salt
Freshly ground black pepper
1 tablespoon finely chopped sweet onion

3 tablespoons mayonnaise
2 tablespoons finely chopped celery
1 pound peeled and deveined, large cooked shrimp
2 tablespoons chopped fresh tarragon
1 (5-ounce) package baby arugula

1. Grate the zest from the lemons to equal 1 tablespoon. Cut the lemons in half; squeeze the juice from the lemons into a measuring cup to equal 3 tablespoons.

2. Place each watermelon slice on a chilled plate. Season with desired amount of kosher salt and freshly ground pepper.

3. Microwave the onion in a medium-size microwave-safe bowl at HIGH 25 seconds or just until the onion is tender. Stir in the mayonnaise, celery, 1 teaspoon lemon zest, and 1 tablespoon lemon juice. Stir in the shrimp and tarragon. Add salt and pepper to taste.

4. Place the arugula in a medium bowl. Sprinkle with remaining 2 teaspoons lemon zest and 2 tablespoons lemon juice. Add salt and pepper to taste; toss to coat. Arrange the arugula mixture over the watermelon; top with the shrimp mixture. Serve immediately.

# Napoleon House Muffuletta

———◇———

In the early 90s, we traveled to New Orleans seeking the definitive muffuletta. We discovered lots of deliciously authentic twists. These small individual versions are served warm at the Napoleon House, an historic French Quarter eatery. Named for the unique bread used, the large round sesame-topped loaves were made by Sicilian bakers.

Serves 1 · Hands-on 10 minutes · Total 40 minutes, including salad plus chill time

2 ounces Genoa salami slices
2 ounces ham slices
2 ounces pastrami slices
¼ cup Italian Olive Salad (see below)

1 provolone cheese slice
1 Swiss cheese slice
1 (5-inch) sesame seed sandwich roll

1. Preheat the oven to 350°F. Layer first 6 ingredients on the bottom half of a roll; top with remaining roll half, and wrap in aluminum foil.

2. Bake at 350°F for 20 minutes or until thoroughly heated and the cheese is melted.

# Italian Olive Salad

Use leftovers as a pizza topping, in potato salad, or on a cheese plate.

4 cups pimiento-stuffed Spanish olives, drained and coarsely chopped
1 (15-ounce) can chickpeas, drained and coarsely chopped
1 (14-ounce) can artichoke hearts, drained and coarsely chopped
1 (7.75-ounce) jar cocktail onions, drained and coarsely chopped
1 cup olive oil

⅔ cup pickled vegetables, drained and coarsely chopped
½ cup red wine vinegar
¼ cup capers, drained
1 large green bell pepper, chopped
3 celery ribs, chopped
2 garlic cloves, minced
1½ tablespoons dried oregano
½ teaspoon ground black pepper

Stir together all ingredients; cover and chill 8 hours. Store, covered, in refrigerator up to 1 week. Makes 12 cups

1990s

# MUFFULETTA DOGS

Looking to bring a taste of New Orleans to your next cookout? This is just the ticket. Our latest muffuletta riff (we've also made muffuletta deviled eggs, sliders, and cocktail kabobs) lightens up the classic filling and turns it inside out for a chargrilled hot dog topping. It's light, fresh, and, quite frankly, delicious.

Serves 6   Hands-on 25 minutes
Total 25 minutes, plus chill time

2 cups chopped fresh cauliflower
½ cup grated carrot
3 reduced-fat provolone cheese slices, chopped
⅓ cup thinly sliced celery
⅓ cup chopped jarred marinated roasted red bell peppers
¼ cup chopped pimiento-stuffed Spanish olives
¼ cup chopped kalamata olives
¼ cup chopped fresh parsley
¼ cup bottled light olive oil vinaigrette
6 hot dogs
Rolls

Stir together the cauliflower, carrot, chopped provolone cheese, celery, chopped roasted red bell peppers, chopped stuffed olives, chopped kalamata olives, parsley, and vinaigrette. Cover and chill 2 hours. Grill the hot dogs according to package directions. Place the hot dogs in the rolls, and top with the cauliflower mixture.

## FLASHBACK
### Fat Tuesday Muffuletta-thons

Usually we scale down chef recipes for the home cook's use, but when 1994's February "Marvelous Muffulettas" story ran, it was Mardi Gras season. So we kept the behemoth restaurant yields of olive salad and recommended that readers host an impromptu Muffuletta-thon for their family and friends: Just multiply the sandwich ingredients to feed the extra folks. For those less inclined to stir up pitchers of Hurricane punch for a crowd, we offered the suggestion to creatively package the colorful olive salad and deliver it to friends as a gift along with instructions for making a muffuletta. Using it as a hot dog topping was a more recent stroke of inspired culinary brilliance.

# Hot Chicken Salad

———— ◇ ————

Facts are a little murky as to who first heated up chicken salad in a casserole dish, but by the 70s, it was the culinary high point of bridal shower luncheons. Toasted almonds or diced water chestnuts added extra crunch. Condensed cream soup was optional; mayo and a crushed potato chip topping were a must. This deluxe twist was the signature luncheon dish of the late Carolyn Flournoy, veteran food editor of *The Shreveport Times*. She also happened to be the mother of former *Southern Living* Associate Food Editor Kate Nicholson.

Serves 12   Hands-on 25 minutes   Total 1 hour

2 tablespoons butter
2 cups sliced celery
¼ cup chopped onion
1 (8-ounce) package sliced mushrooms
½ cup toasted slivered almonds
4 cups chopped cooked chicken
¼ cup chopped pimiento, drained
1 (8-ounce) can sliced water chestnuts, drained
½ teaspoon table salt

½ teaspoon freshly ground black pepper
1½ cups (6 ounces) shredded sharp Cheddar cheese
1 cup mayonnaise
½ cup sour cream
3 tablespoons fresh lemon juice
1 cup crushed potato chips
½ cup (2 ounces) finely shredded Parmesan cheese

1. Preheat the oven to 350°F.

2. Melt the butter in a large skillet over medium-high. Add the celery, onion, and mushrooms; cook, stirring often, 8 to 10 minutes or until mushrooms are tender and liquid evaporates. Cool slightly.

3. Stir together the almonds, mushroom mixture, chicken, and next 4 ingredients in a large bowl. Stir together 1 cup of the Cheddar cheese, the mayonnaise, sour cream, and lemon juice until blended; stir into the chicken mixture. Spoon into a lightly greased 13- x 9-inch baking dish; sprinkle with the remaining ½ cup Cheddar cheese, crushed potato chips, and Parmesan cheese.

4. Bake at 350°F for 30 minutes or until thoroughly heated.

1990s

# CHICKEN D'IBERVILLE

Say what you will, culinary elite, but down South, great casseroles are an art. Bubbling beneath its golden crumb topping, this is the quintessential chicken-and-wild-rice rendition. We've served it a hundred times, and we never have leftovers—a disappointment to those of us hoping to carry home a little post-party plate.

Serves 12 to 14   Hands-on 45 minutes   Total 3 hours 35 minutes

2 (3-pound) whole chickens
1 cup water
1 cup dry sherry
2 celery ribs
1 onion, quartered
1½ teaspoons table salt
½ teaspoon curry powder
¼ teaspoon ground black
   pepper
¼ teaspoon poultry seasoning
2 (6-ounce) packages long-
   grain and wild rice mix
½ cup butter
2 (8-ounce) packages sliced
   mushrooms

1 bunch green onions, chopped
   (about 1 cup)
1 (8-ounce) container sour
   cream
1 (10¾-ounce) can cream of
   mushroom soup
1 sleeve round buttery
   crackers, crushed (about
   1½ cups)
1 (6-ounce) can French fried
   onions, crushed
¼ cup butter, melted
¼ teaspoon paprika
⅛ teaspoon garlic powder

1. Bring the first 9 ingredients to a boil in a large Dutch oven; reduce heat, cover, and simmer 1 hour or until the chicken is done. Remove the chicken, reserving broth in Dutch oven. Let the chicken cool. Pour the broth through a fine wire-mesh strainer into an 8-cup liquid measuring cup; discard solids.

2. Cook the rice according to package directions, substituting 4¼ cups reserved chicken broth for water and omitting butter. (Add water to broth to equal 4¼ cups, if necessary.)

3. Skin, bone, and coarsely chop or shred the chicken.

4. Preheat the oven to 350°F. Melt the ½ cup butter in a large Dutch oven over medium; add the mushrooms and green onions, and sauté 10 minutes or until tender. Stir in the rice, chicken, sour cream, and soup. Spoon mixture into 8 (2-cup) casserole dishes, 8 (5½- x 3½-inch) mini loaf pans, 3 (8-inch or 9-inch) square baking dishes, or 1 (4-quart or 15- x 10-inch) casserole dish.

5. Stir together the crushed crackers and fried onions. Stir in the ¼ cup melted butter, paprika, and garlic powder. Sprinkle casserole evenly with cracker mixture.

6. Bake, covered, at 350°F for 20 to 30 minutes. Uncover and bake 5 to 10 more minutes or until bubbly.

## FLASHBACK

### Classic Chicken Tetrazzini

Rumored to have been created in Charleston in the early 1900s for visiting San Francisco soprano Luisa Tetrazzini, chicken tetrazzini is the doyenne of Southern casseroles.

**Classic Chicken Tetrazzini:** Preheat the oven to 350°F. Prepare 1½ (8-oz.) packages vermicelli, according to package directions. Melt ½ cup butter in a Dutch oven over low; whisk in ½ cup flour until smooth. Cook 1 minute, whisking constantly. Whisk in 4 cups milk and ½ cup dry white wine over medium, whisking constantly, 8 to 10 minutes or until mixture is thickened. Whisk in 2 Tbsp. bouillon granules, 1 tsp. seasoned pepper, and 1 cup Parmesan cheese. Remove from heat. Stir in 4 cups diced cooked chicken; 1 (6-oz.) jar sliced mushrooms, drained; and hot cooked pasta. Spoon mixture into a lightly greased 13- x 9-inch baking dish; sprinkle with ¾ cup slivered almonds and 1 cup Parmesan cheese. Bake at 350°F for 35 minutes or until bubbly. Serves 8 to 10

# Old-Fashioned Chicken Salad

This harkens back to our great-grandmother's day when a well-seasoned mix of chopped chicken and celery were bound together with homemade mayonnaise and a generous splash of fresh lemon juice. Boiled eggs and pickle relish were optional. Large hens, simmered until tender, yielded both white and dark meat for maximum flavor.

Serves 4 to 6   Hands-on 25 minutes   Total 2 hours 25 minutes

4 cups chopped cooked chicken
2 hard-cooked eggs, peeled and chopped
1 cup chopped celery
1/4 cup chopped onion
2 tablespoons fresh lemon juice
3/4 teaspoon table salt

1/2 teaspoon celery salt
1/8 teaspoon ground white pepper
Dash of ground red pepper
3/4 cup mayonnaise
1/2 teaspoon paprika
Garnish: fresh parsley sprigs

1. Gently toss together first 9 ingredients in a bowl. Fold in 1/2 cup of the mayonnaise; cover and chill 2 hours.

2. Stir in remaining 1/4 cup mayonnaise. Spoon chicken salad into a serving dish; sprinkle with paprika.

1980s

# CHICKEN SALAD EXOTIQUE

During the heyday of department-store tearooms, the makings of old-fashioned chicken salad took an adventurous turn. Innovative cooks stirred in fruits and nuts or curry and chutney. Recipes labeled exotic, glorified, and Polynesian came with a most popular addition: canned pineapple tidbits. Inspired by the many recipes from spiral-bound community cookbooks, we created four new cosmopolitan favorites of our own.

Serves 4 to 6   Hands-on 15 minutes
Total 50 minutes, plus chill time

½ cup mayonnaise
½ cup sour cream
2 tablespoons minced shallots
1 tablespoon chopped fresh tarragon
4 cups diced cooked chicken
2 cups halved seedless red grapes
1 cup diced celery
1 cup toasted slivered almonds
Garnish: fresh tarragon sprigs

Whisk together the first 4 ingredients in a large bowl; stir in the chicken and next 2 ingredients. Add table salt and ground black pepper to taste. Chill 3 hours. Stir in the almonds just before serving.

## VARIATIONS

**Curried Chicken Salad:** Omit shallots, tarragon, grapes, and almonds. Whisk ¼ cup finely chopped green onions, 1 Tbsp. grated fresh ginger, and 2 tsp. curry powder into mayonnaise mixture. Stir ¾ cup each golden raisins and diced yellow bell pepper into chicken mixture. Stir in ¾ cup toasted sweetened flaked coconut, and top with ½ cup chopped lightly salted roasted peanuts just before serving. Serves 4 to 6

**Poppy Seed Chicken Salad:** Omit tarragon and grapes. Whisk 2 Tbsp. chopped fresh basil, 1 Tbsp. orange zest, 3 Tbsp. honey, and 1 tsp. poppy seeds into mayonnaise mixture. Stir 1 cup sweetened dried cranberries into chicken mixture. Stir in 1 cup chopped toasted pecans just before serving. Serves 4 to 6

**Mango Chicken Salad:** Omit shallots, tarragon, grapes, and almonds. Whisk ¼ cup diced red onion; 2 jalapeño peppers, seeded and minced; 3 Tbsp. chopped fresh cilantro; and 1 Tbsp. lime zest into mayonnaise mixture. Stir 1½ cups diced fresh mango into chicken mixture before serving. Serves 4 to 6

# 3

# COCKTAIL HOUR

Cheers to comeback cocktails with a contemporary twist and tantalizing appetizers that look every bit as good as they taste.

# ◆ THE WAY WE DINE ◆

## 1980s Cocktail Party

With just a little bit of planning you can pull off the perfect party, complete with signature cocktails. Consider this your retro-fabulous blueprint.

# Mint Julep

Ingredients for this Kentucky Derby classic remain a constant but spirited debate ensues when it comes to proper technique. Some muddle the mint and sugar while others insist it's all about the mystical alchemy of bourbon, ice, and sugar—the mint should only be smelled and not tasted. Rule #1? Always chill the julep cups to keep the ice from melting too quickly.

Serves 4   Hands-on 10 minutes
Total 3 hours 10 minutes, plus freezing time

2 cups bourbon
2 teaspoons sugar
Fresh mint leaves

½ cup water
Finely crushed ice
Garnish: fresh mint sprigs

1. Place the bourbon in the freezer 24 hours prior to preparing mint juleps (the bourbon won't freeze, but it will acquire a syrup-like consistency).

2. Place ½ teaspoon of the sugar in a julep cup; add 10 fresh mint leaves and 2 tablespoons water. Stir gently until the sugar is dissolved. Gently stir in ½ cup bourbon. Add enough finely crushed ice to fill cup; stir gently. Repeat procedure 3 times.

3. Place the cups in the freezer, and freeze at least 3 hours.

4. Before serving, break the ice with a spoon.

1980s

## FLASHBACK
### Run for the Roses

A mint julep is more than a drink, it's a cup of tradition. That's the credo of former Associate Food Editor Cynthia Ann Briscoe—an authority on all things Derby. For decades, on the first Saturday in May, her parents hosted an annual Kentucky Derby party in Louisville. Back in 2000, they shared a few timeless favorites with our readers. Curried Chicken Pâté and Baby Hot Browns (a bite-size riff on the classic from Louisville's Brown Hotel) were on the menu, along with a horseshoe-shaped cheese spread topped with strawberry preserves and a beef tenderloin paired with Henry Bain Sauce (a century-old sauce created by the head waiter at Louisville's Pendennis Club). And for dessert? Bourbon Chocolate Pecan Tarts (page 347).

# MINT JULEP SWEET TEA

Pack up those silver julep cups and break out the tumblers. What could improve the thirst-quenching charms of a tall frosty pitcher of sweet iced tea? Fresh mint and bourbon, of course. Cheers to the latest trend of sweet tea-based cocktails. Simple, uncomplicated, and refreshingly easy to drink.

Makes 4 cups   Hands-on 10 minutes   Total 10 minutes

½ cup loosely packed fresh
  mint leaves
1 lemon, sliced
2 tablespoons sugar
3 cups cold sweetened tea

1 cup bourbon
Crushed ice
Garnishes: fresh mint leaves,
  lemon slices

Combine the first 3 ingredients in a 2-quart pitcher. Muddle ½ cup of the mint leaves in the pitcher to release flavors. Stir in the tea and the bourbon. Serve over crushed ice.

## VARIATION

**Sweet Tea Spritzer:** Stir together 2 cups cranberry juice, 1 cup sweet tea-flavored vodka, and ½ cup fresh lemon juice in a large pitcher. Stir in 5 cups ice cubes, and top with 1 (12-oz.) can lemon-lime soft drink. Gently stir. Serve immediately. Serves 4 to 6

## SOUTHERN HOSPITALITY

### Paper Doilies

In *The Southern Living Party Cookbook* we offered countless tips and sage entertaining advice to hostesses, like this ever-important suggestion: "In making out your shopping list, don't forget to include paper doilies for all trays you plan to use. About the only serving piece that requires no doily is a ceramic or pottery platter used for raw vegetables. Use white paper doilies, never plastic." Nowadays, we think a pretty linen does the trick quite nicely.

# Whiskey Sour Slush

Our favorite way to drink whiskey sours? With a summer-perfect arctic chill and a sunny mix of lemonade and sparkling citrus soda. They are big-batch, make-ahead, and stay safely tucked away in the pantry deep freeze until it is time to get the party started.

Makes 1 gallon   Hands-on 5 minutes   Total 8 hours 5 minutes

1 (12-ounce) can frozen lemonade
    concentrate, thawed
½ (12-ounce) can frozen orange juice
    concentrate, thawed

¾ cup lemon juice
2½ cups bourbon
1 (2-liter) bottle lemon-lime soft drink
Garnish: lemon slices

Stir together all ingredients. Freeze 8 hours. To serve, stir until mixture is slushy and well blended.

1980s

# BLACKBERRY PISCO SOURS

Old school simplicity rules, but Contributing Editor Marian Cooper Cairns, a mixologist extraordinaire, makes the switch from bourbon to a potent blend of fresh blackberries and pisco, a trendy South American grape brandy popular in Peru and Chile. What to sub if it's not stocked in your local liquor store? White tequila, grappa, or vodka.

Serves 4   Hands-on 15 minutes   Total 15 minutes

1 cup fresh blackberries
1 cup pisco, chilled
⅓ cup fresh lime juice
3 large pasteurized egg whites

5 tablespoons simple syrup
Angostura bitters (optional)
Garnishes: fresh basil leaves, fresh blackberries

1. Process the blackberries in a blender until smooth. Pour through a wire-mesh strainer into a 1-quart jar with a tight-fitting lid, discarding solids.

2. Add the pisco and next 3 ingredients to the jar. Cover with the lid, and shake vigorously for 30 seconds or until foamy. Pour the mixture into 4 (10-ounce) glasses filled with ice. Top each with a dash of bitters, if desired. Serve immediately.

## FRESH TAKE

### Addictive Nibble

A salty cocktail hour snack is always appreciated.

**Brown Butter–Rosemary Pecans:** Preheat oven to 350°F. Cook ¼ cup butter in a medium saucepan over medium, stirring constantly, 3 to 5 minutes until butter turns golden brown. Remove from heat, and stir in 4 cups pecan halves. Sprinkle with 2 tsp. kosher salt and 2 tsp. sugar. Bake at 350°F in a single layer on a baking sheet for 10 to 12 minutes or until toasted, stirring halfway through. Sprinkle with 1 Tbsp. chopped fresh rosemary. Bake at 350°F for 2 more minutes. Cool completely. Store in an airtight container. Makes 4 cups

# Chatham Artillery Punch

———— ◆ ————

Two hundred and fifty years ago, both Savannah and Charleston were stirring up potent champagne-and-green tea-based libations by the boozy bowlful. This notorious punch was originally concocted in the 1700s by Georgia's oldest military unit, the Chatham Artillery. We offered a scaled-down version of the original with a caveat: "Serve with caution." Plan ahead because the stock needs to ferment for two to six weeks—the longer the better.

Makes 2½ gallons   Hands-on 35 minutes   Total 35 minutes, plus chill time

4 ounces loose gunpowder green tea
2 quarts cold water
2¾ cups firmly packed light brown sugar
2¼ cups fresh orange juice (9 oranges)
1¼ cups fresh lemon juice (9 lemons)
2 (10-ounce) jars maraschino cherries, drained
2 (50.7-ounce) bottles Rhine or Catawba wine

1 (25.4-ounce) bottle brandy
1 quart light rum
1 quart rye whiskey
1 quart gin
½ cup Benedictine
1 (750-milliliter) bottle Champagne, chilled*
Garnishes: orange and lemon slices

1. Combine the tea and the water. Let stand at room temperature 8 to 24 hours.

2. Pour the tea through a fine wire-mesh strainer into a 3-gallon container; stir in the sugar and next 9 ingredients, stirring until sugar is dissolved. Cover and chill 8 to 24 hours.

3. Pour the mixture through a strainer into a bowl; discard solids. Pour the liquid into bottles. Chill for 2 to 6 weeks before serving.

4. When ready to serve, combine 1 gallon chilled punch mix with Champagne. Serve over ice.

*1 (1-liter) bottle club soda, chilled, may be substituted.

1980s

# MONTGOMERY PUNCH

Communal cocktails are making a comeback by the frosty bowlful. This festive punch is a holiday favorite of renowned writer and hostess Julia Reed, who discovered the recipe in a cookbook by the Junior League of Montgomery, Alabama. Rumored to be a town staple, the punch is bright and citrusy with a very merry nod to tradition.

Makes 14 cups   Hands-on 10 minutes
Total 9 hours 40 minutes, including Ice Ring

2 cups fresh lemon juice
1½ cups sugar
1 cup brandy
Ice Ring (see below)
2 (750-milliliter) bottles chilled
   sparkling wine

1 (375-milliliter) bottle chilled
   dessert wine (such as
   Sauternes)
Garnishes: orange slices,
   lemon slices, cranberries

Stir together the first 2 ingredients until the sugar dissolves. Stir in the brandy. Pour over the Ice Ring in a punch bowl. Stir in the sparkling and dessert wines.

# ICE RING

3 cups water
Sliced fruit, such as lemons
   and oranges

5 cups ice-cold water

Freeze 3 cups water in a tube pan or Bundt pan (that will fit into a punch bowl) 4 hours or until set. Place the sliced fruit in a single layer over the ice, and freeze 1 hour. Remove from the freezer; let stand 10 minutes. Add 5 cups ice-cold water; freeze 4 hours or until set. Let stand at room temperature 10 minutes before unmolding.

## FRESH TAKE

### Charcuterie Boards

Casual entertaining in 1981? *Have a Party with Fruit and Cheese*: Bring out the fruit and cheese, add a glass of wine, and even the simplest gathering becomes a festive occasion. The spirit is the same today, but the food focus has shifted to hearty charcuterie boards with a well-crafted selection of artisan meats and cheeses. Many local specialty grocers now carry an impressive array of hard sausages and country hams along with signature cheeses from Southern dairies. Ask to try samples when you're shopping for the building blocks of your board. Pick up a few loaves of rustic bread, some pickled fruits or vegetables, and a jar or two of a sweet-tart chutney and grainy mustard. Set it all out and you're ready to party.

# Frosted Margaritas

◆

The early 70s' frozen margarita craze set blenders whirring from Houston to Atlanta. The trick to a super-slushy mix? Scale up the margarita base and store in the freezer so it's totally frigid when it hits the ice. Taste of the South Trivia: The first frozen margarita machine, now in the Smithsonian National Museum of American History, was developed in the early 1970s by Dallas restaurateur Mariano Martinez.

Serves 2   Hands-on 10 minutes   Total 10 minutes

Lime wedges
Kosher salt
1 cup coarsely crushed ice
¼ cup plus 2 tablespoons tequila

¼ cup sifted powdered sugar
¼ cup fresh lime juice
2 tablespoons orange liqueur

1. Rub the rims of 2 cocktail glasses with the lime wedges. Place the salt in a saucer; spin or dip rims of the glasses in salt.

2. Process the ice and next 4 ingredients in a blender until mixture reaches desired consistency. Pour into prepared glasses.

Note: We tested with Triple Sec for orange liqueur.

1980s

# WATERMELON MARGARITA POPS

It's all about maximum summer coolness. Alcohol-fueled ice pops (aka poptails) are making a splash, especially at outdoor barbecues and poolside cocktail parties. Serve these icy spiked treats with a side of sea salt for sprinkling on top.

Makes 12 pops   Hands-on 15 minutes
Total 15 minutes, plus chill time

6 limes
4 cups chopped seedless
   watermelon
¾ cup tequila

½ cup sugar
12 (3-ounce) paper cups
12 (3½-inch) food-safe wooden
   ice-cream spoons

1. Grate the zest from 1 lime to equal 1 teaspoon. Squeeze the juice from the limes to equal ½ cup. Process the lime juice and watermelon in a blender until smooth. Pour through a fine wire-mesh strainer into a large measuring cup, discarding solids. Stir in the tequila, sugar, and 1 teaspoon lime zest, stirring until the sugar dissolves. Pour the mixture into paper cups.

2. Cover each cup with aluminum foil; make a small slit in the center, and insert 1 ice-cream spoon into each cup. Freeze 8 hours or until firm.

# Miss O'Grady's Cheese Straws

Cheese straws are the quintessential go-with-anything Southern party starter. Plus, they freeze so well they're perfect to keep on hand for impromptu guests—that is, if you don't eat them all while waiting for the doorbell. This vintage twist? A clever roll-and-fold technique incorporates the cheese into the buttery dough.

Makes 30   Hands-on 25 minutes   Total 2 hours 20 minutes

1½ cups all-purpose flour
¾ teaspoon table salt
½ cup cold shortening, cut into pieces
4 tablespoons ice-cold water
1 cup (4 ounces) shredded extra-sharp
   Cheddar cheese

Parchment paper
1 large egg, lightly beaten
30 pecan halves

1. Combine the flour and ¾ teaspoon of the salt in a medium bowl; cut in the shortening with a pastry blender until mixture is crumbly. Gradually add the ice-cold water, stirring until dry ingredients are moistened. Shape the dough into a 4-inch square (about 1 inch thick). Wrap in plastic wrap, and chill 1 hour.

2. Preheat the oven to 400°F. Roll the dough into a 14- x 10-inch rectangle (about ¼ inch thick). Sprinkle with ⅓ cup of the Cheddar cheese. Fold the dough over onto itself in 3 sections, starting with 1 short end. (Fold the dough rectangle as if folding a letter-size piece of paper.) Repeat entire process 2 more times, beginning with rolling into a ¼-inch-thick dough rectangle (about 14 x 10 inches).

3. Roll the dough to a ¼-inch thickness on a lightly floured surface; cut into 30 (2½- x 1½-inch) rectangles, and place on a parchment paper-lined baking sheet. Brush lightly with the egg. Place 1 pecan half in the center of each rectangle, pressing gently. Sprinkle lightly with table salt and red pepper to taste.

4. Bake at 400°F for 16 to 18 minutes or until lightly browned and crisp. Cool on baking sheet 5 minutes; transfer to a wire rack, and cool completely (about 15 minutes).

1970s

# PESTO SHORTBREAD

Start with an indulgent butter-flour-cheese template and amp it up with fresh basil, garlic, and toasted pine nuts. Swap out the Parmesan for pepper Jack, Cheddar, or crumbles of blue. Then pair those with jalapeño and pecans, toasted benne seeds, or walnuts. The results? A treasure trove of golden savory shortbreads that explode with flavor. Our latest favorite twist? Adding a barely there sprinkling of fine-grain sea salt just as the shortbreads are pulled from the oven.

Makes 14 dozen   Hands-on 40 minutes
Total 1 hour 40 minutes, plus chill time

1 cup butter, softened
1 (8-ounce) block Parmesan cheese, shredded
3 garlic cloves, pressed
½ cup pine nuts, finely chopped and toasted
1 tablespoon chopped fresh basil
¼ teaspoon ground red pepper
2 cups all-purpose flour
½ cup whole pine nuts

1. Beat the butter and Parmesan cheese at medium speed with an electric mixer until just blended. Add the garlic and the next 3 ingredients, beating just until blended. Gradually stir in the flour with a spoon (the mixture will become crumbly); stir until the mixture is blended and smooth (about 2 to 3 minutes). Or, instead of stirring the dough with a spoon after adding the flour, you can gently press mixture together with hands, and work until smooth.

2. Shape the shortbread dough into 8 (7-inch-long) logs. Wrap each log in plastic wrap, and chill for 8 hours.

3. Preheat the oven to 350°F. Cut logs into ⅓-inch-thick slices, and place on lightly greased baking sheets. Press 1 whole pine nut into the center of each dough slice.

4. Bake at 350°F for 15 to 18 minutes or until lightly browned. Remove shortbread to wire racks, and cool.

## FLASHBACK
### Crescent City Cocktails

From its punchy Hurricanes to its boozy Sazeracs, New Orleans claims to have birthed the cocktail. Apothecary Antoine Peychaud created a curative there in the 1830s. Mixed with brandy and absinthe and served in a French *coquetier*, or eggcup, Peychaud's Bitters drink was mispronounced "cocktail." Another bayou beverage said to cure what ails you was created by Henry C. Ramos at his bar in the late 1800s:

**The Ramos Gin Fizz:**
Combine 4 tsp. super-fine granulated sugar, ¼ tsp. orange flower water, 1½ Tbsp. lemon juice, 1 extra-large egg white, 2 Tbsp. cream, ⅛ tsp. vanilla extract, and 2 oz. gin in a blender; blend until frothy, about 1 minute. Pour mixture over crushed ice in a cocktail shaker to chill. Strain into 2 glasses. Top off each glass with club soda. Serves 2

# JALAPEÑO-PECAN SHORTBREAD

Substitute 1 (8-oz.) block Monterey Jack cheese with jalapeño peppers, shredded, for the 1 (8-oz.) block Parmesan cheese, shredded; and 1 cup finely chopped toasted pecans for the ½ cup finely chopped toasted pine nuts. Omit the garlic and basil. Shape the dough into 4 (7-inch-long) logs, and proceed as directed. Cut the chilled logs into ¼-inch-thick slices, and place on lightly greased baking sheets. Substitute 2½ cups pecan halves (about 65 to 75 halves) for the ½ cup pine nuts, pressing 1 pecan half into the center of each slice. Bake as directed. Makes about 9 dozen

# CAJUN BENNE SEED SHORTBREAD

Substitute 1 (8-oz.) block sharp Cheddar cheese, shredded, for the 1 (8-oz.) block Parmesan cheese, shredded; and ½ cup toasted sesame seeds for ½ cup finely chopped toasted pine nuts. Omit the garlic and basil, and add 2 Tbsp. Cajun seasoning. Shape the dough into 4 (5-inch-long) logs, and proceed with recipe as directed. Cut the chilled logs into ¼-inch-thick slices, and place on lightly greased baking sheets. Omit the pine nuts. Bake as directed. Makes about 6½ dozen

# Shrimp-in-a-Pickle

◆

Recipes for this Lowcountry treasure date back to the 1700s when shrimp was literally pickled with aromatics and herbs as a preservative. In later years, it evolved into a deliciously Southern cousin of ceviche: blanched shrimp layered with thinly sliced onions, bay leaves, and a sprinkling of briny capers chilled overnight in a flavorful marinade. Make this recipe faster by purchasing already peeled and deveined shrimp.

Serves 10 as an appetizer   Hands-on 1 hour 20 minutes
Total 1 hour 20 minutes, plus chill time

2½ pounds unpeeled, large raw shrimp
3 medium onions, sliced
1 cup vegetable oil
½ cup red wine vinegar
½ cup tarragon vinegar
2 tablespoons sugar
2½ tablespoons undrained capers
 (optional)

2 tablespoons fresh lemon juice
1 tablespoon Worcestershire sauce
1 teaspoon hot sauce
½ teaspoon table salt
8 bay leaves, broken

1. Peel and devein the shrimp.

2. Bring a large saucepan of water to a boil; add the shrimp, and cook 2 to 3 minutes or just until the shrimp turn pink. Drain well; rinse with cold water.

3. Layer the shrimp and onion in an airtight container. Stir together the oil and the remaining ingredients. Pour over the shrimp and onion. Cover and chill 24 hours, stirring occasionally. Discard the bay leaves before serving.

1980s

# CHIPOTLE SHRIMP COCKTAIL

A bright citrus-infused marinade spiked with fresh cilantro and the smoky heat of chipotles in adobo sauce takes the classic recipe south of the border. Crisp bell peppers add color and crunch. Like the classic, this is a do-ahead dream: Just layer the ingredients, then sit back and chill.

Serves 8   Hands-on 40 minutes
Total 50 minutes, plus chill time

1 large red onion
1 medium-size red bell pepper
1 medium-size yellow bell
  pepper
2 pounds peeled and deveined,
  large cooked shrimp with
  tails

1 cup ketchup
½ cup chopped fresh cilantro
½ cup fresh lime juice
3 tablespoons orange zest
½ cup fresh orange juice
2 to 3 canned chipotle peppers
  in adobo sauce, chopped

1. Cut the onion and the bell peppers into thin strips; layer with the shrimp in a large zip-top plastic freezer bag.

2. Whisk together the ketchup and next 5 ingredients; pour over shrimp mixture. Seal and chill 12 to 24 hours, turning the bag occasionally. Serve using a slotted spoon.

## FLASHBACK

### The Classic Shrimp Cocktail

From the 60s to the 80s, Shrimp Cocktail was the darling of suburban country club cuisine. It was the appetizer that got every party off to a great start, whether mounded in giant seashells with sauce on the side for a glitzy cocktail soirée or nestled artfully in crystal sherbet dishes for a formal seated dinner. Here we pay homage to our all-time favorite classic cocktail sauce.

**Cocktail Sauce:** Whisk together ½ cup chili sauce, ⅓ cup prepared horseradish, ⅓ cup ketchup, 2 Tbsp. fresh lemon juice, 1½ tsp. Worcestershire sauce, 1 tsp. hot sauce, and ¼ tsp. each of table salt and ground black pepper. Cover and chill. Makes a generous 1 cup

# Crab Cakes

A canapé-sized twist on crab cakes made the old-fashioned way—with the focus on the crab. A barely there binder of egg-soaked breadcrumbs holds it all together. Make ahead and chill on baking sheets, then pan-fry just before serving. Taste of the South Trivia: Backfin is a flavorful blend of broken pieces of jumbo lump and special grade crabmeat.

Serves 4    Hands-on 40 minutes    Total 40 minutes, plus chill time

1 pound fresh backfin crabmeat (or lump crabmeat)
1 large egg, lightly beaten
1 white bread slice, torn into small pieces
⅓ cup finely chopped onion
1 tablespoon mayonnaise
½ teaspoon table salt
½ teaspoon freshly ground black pepper
Ground red pepper
¼ cup butter
2 tablespoons olive oil

1. Pick the crabmeat, removing any bits of shell.

2. Combine the crabmeat, next 6 ingredients, and desired amount of red pepper in a medium bowl until well blended. Cover and chill 3 hours.

3. Shape the mixture into 8 (3½-inch) patties.

4. Melt 2 tablespoons of the butter with 1 tablespoon of the oil in a large skillet over medium-high. Add 4 patties; cook 2 to 3 minutes on each side or until browned. Repeat procedure with remaining butter, oil, and patties. Serve immediately.

1960s

# CRAB CAKE HUSH PUPPIES

Crab cakes go fish-fry casual. Bite-size, beer-laced cornmeal dumplings boast a crisp golden crust and tender center filled with jumbo lumps of crabmeat. It's a thrifty way to serve crabmeat to a crowd. Fry, in batches, and place hush puppies in a single layer on a baking sheet. Keep warm in a 200°F oven up to 30 minutes.

Serves about 32
Hands-on 25 minutes    Total 35 minutes

8 ounces fresh lump crabmeat
1 cup self-rising white cornmeal mix
1/2 cup self-rising flour
3 thinly sliced green onions
1/2 cup finely chopped red bell pepper
1 tablespoon sugar
1/4 teaspoon table salt
1 large egg
3/4 cup beer
Vegetable oil
White Rémoulade Sauce, Pineapple-Cucumber Salsa (both at left), or Cocktail Sauce (page 140)

1. Pick the crabmeat, removing any bits of shell. Stir together the cornmeal mix, flour, green onions, bell pepper, sugar, and salt in a large bowl. Stir in the crabmeat, egg, and beer until mixture is just moistened. Let stand 10 minutes.

2. Pour the oil to a depth of 2 inches in a Dutch oven; heat to 360°F. Drop the batter by tablespoonfuls into hot oil, and fry, in batches, 2 to 3 minutes or until golden brown, turning once. Serve with your favorite sauce.

# Pepper Jelly

Flashback 45 or 50 years to jewel-colored jellies distilled from an innovative brew of freshly picked garden peppers simmered with a potent blend of sugar and vinegar. They were easier than pie to make and ignited a frenzy of cream-cheese purchases by Southern hostesses, ever-at-the-ready to entertain guests at a moment's notice.

Makes 3 (½-pint) jars   Hands-on 25 minutes
Total 3 hours 25 minutes, including cool time

6 fresh jalapeño peppers, seeded and coarsely chopped (about 1½ cups)
1 green bell pepper, coarsely chopped (about 1 cup)
1 cup apple cider vinegar
5 cups sugar
½ (6-ounce) package liquid fruit pectin
¼ cup fresh lime juice

1. Puree the jalapeños, bell pepper, and vinegar in a blender until smooth. Pour through a fine wire-mesh strainer into a bowl, pressing the solids using a spoon; reserve liquid. Discard the solids.

2. Combine the pepper puree and the sugar in a large nonaluminum saucepan. Bring to a boil over medium-high, stirring constantly. Boil 6 to 8 minutes. Stir in the pectin and the lime juice. Boil, stirring constantly, 1 minute. Remove from the heat, and skim off foam with a metal spoon.

3. Pour into hot, sterilized jars, filling to ½ inch from top; wipe the jar rims. Cover at once with the metal lids, and screw on the bands; cool completely (about 3 hours). Store in the refrigerator.

1970s

# PEACH-PEPPER MOJITOS

Pop open a jar of pepper jelly and you've got way more than an easy appetizer to spoon over cream cheese at your fingertips. Use that tangy sweetness to jump-start salsas and vinaigrettes, glaze chargrilled pork chops and chicken, or upgrade roasted root vegetables. The latest trend? Pepper jelly-fueled cocktails.

Makes 8½ cups   Hands-on 5 minutes   Total 5 minutes

2 large unpeeled pitted peaches
½ cup Peach-Pepper Preserves (at left)
¼ cup fresh lemon juice
½ cup fresh mint leaves
4 cups club soda, chilled
2 cups white rum

1. Process the peaches, Peach-Pepper Preserves, and lemon juice in a blender or food processor until smooth.

2. Muddle the mint leaves against the bottom and sides of a pitcher to release their flavor. Add the club soda, white rum, and peach puree. Stir to combine. Serve immediately over ice.

## FRESH TAKE

### Shelf Life

Pepper jelly takes on a whole new dimension of sweet-and-spicy summer flavor when the spotlight is on fresh peaches. Bonus: It cooks in minutes in the microwave and keeps for weeks (not that it will last that long).

**Peach-Pepper Preserves:**
Stir together 4½ cups peeled and diced peaches (about 2½ lbs.); 1 jalapeño pepper, minced; ½ red bell pepper, finely chopped; 1½ cups sugar; 3 Tbsp. fresh lime juice; and 1 (1.75-oz.) pkg. powdered fruit pectin. Microwave at HIGH 8 minutes (mixture will boil). Stir the mixture, and microwave at HIGH 8 to 10 minutes or until thickened. (You're going for the viscosity of pancake syrup here. The mixture will thicken to soft-set preserves after it cools and chills.) Cool the mixture completely (about 2 hours). Serve immediately, or store the preserves in an airtight container in the refrigerator up to 3 weeks. Makes 3 cups

# Dainty Cucumber Sandwiches

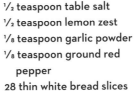

These diminutive, expertly trimmed pillows of geometric perfection, assembled from the soft white slices of a giant Pullman loaf, are party perfect. Extra-special occasions called for extra-thin bread slices rolled into pinwheels or wrapped around tender asparagus spears. Most popular fillings? Finely minced chicken salad with homemade mayo, pimiento cheese, and cucumber.

Makes about 2 dozen   Hands-on 30 minutes
Total 30 minutes

2 medium cucumbers, peeled
1 (8-ounce) package cream
   cheese, softened
2 tablespoons minced onion
2 tablespoons finely chopped
   fresh chives
1 tablespoon finely chopped
   fresh parsley

½ teaspoon table salt
½ teaspoon lemon zest
⅛ teaspoon garlic powder
⅛ teaspoon ground red
   pepper
28 thin white bread slices

1. Peel the cucumbers into long, thin ribbons using a vegetable peeler. Let stand, between paper towels, 10 minutes.

2. Meanwhile, combine the cream cheese and next 7 ingredients in a bowl.

3. Remove the crusts from the bread, and cut in half diagonally to make triangles. Spread 1½ teaspoons of the cream cheese mixture on 1 side of half of the bread triangles, and top with the cucumber ribbons (about ¼ cup each). Top with the remaining bread.

1980s

## SOUTHERN HOSPITALITY

### Tea Sandwich Tips

• Trim crusts after filling sandwiches, then cut into triangles, bow ties, or squares. Use a sharp serrated knife and gentle sawing motion to make neat, clean-cut edges.

• For rounds, cut straight down (without twisting!) using a small biscuit cutter.

• For a pretty flourish, spread a super-thin layer of softened butter over one or more cut edges of each tea sandwich, and dip in finely chopped fresh herbs, watercress, or finely chopped pecans.

• Prep tea sandwiches up to a day ahead, and refrigerate in an airtight container. To prevent the bread from drying out, cover the sandwiches with a sheet of wax paper and a damp paper towel. Uncover sandwiches just before serving.

# TEA SANDWICH TRIO

Creative fillings and flavorful breads are all the rage. Classic cucumber and cream cheese gets gussied up with fresh strawberries. Freshly grated ginger adds zing to curried shrimp or chicken salads. And goat cheese finds a stellar matchup in pepper jelly and pecans.

## GOAT CHEESE AND PECAN

These savory goat cheese and pecan tea sandwiches have a surprise layer of red pepper jelly.

Makes about 2 cups    Hands-on 20 minutes    Total 30 minutes

4 ounces cream cheese, softened
4 ounces goat cheese
1 cup (4 ounces) shredded white Cheddar cheese
½ cup finely chopped toasted pecans
2 tablespoons chopped fresh cilantro
Whole wheat bread slices
Red pepper jelly

Stir together the softened cream cheese, goat cheese, Cheddar cheese, pecans, and cilantro. Spread on whole wheat bread slices. Spread a thin layer of red pepper jelly on an equal number of whole wheat bread slices; sandwich cream cheese mixture slices with pepper jelly slices.

## CUCUMBER AND STRAWBERRY

Dainty cucumber tea sandwiches are given extra flair with diced fresh strawberries topping the filling.

Makes about 2 cups    Hands-on 20 minutes    Total 20 minutes

1 (8-ounce) package cream cheese, softened
½ cup peeled, seeded, and finely chopped cucumber
⅓ cup mayonnaise
¼ cup minced red onion
3 tablespoons finely chopped fresh basil
½ teaspoon freshly ground black pepper
¼ teaspoon table salt
Thin white bread slices
Fresh strawberries, diced

Stir together softened cream cheese, cucumber, mayonnaise, red onion, basil, freshly ground pepper, and salt. Spread on thin white bread; sandwich with diced fresh strawberries.

# CURRIED SHRIMP

Bet you can't eat just one of these curried shrimp tea sandwiches. Shrimp and curry are mixed together with toasted coconut, cream cheese, and ginger for a savory filling with a bite.

Makes about 3 cups · Hands-on 25 minutes · Total 40 minutes

2½ cups finely chopped peeled and deveined, cooked shrimp (about 1 pound of any size)

½ cup finely diced celery

½ cup toasted sweetened flaked coconut

1½ (8-ounce) packages cream cheese, softened

3 tablespoons minced green onions

1 tablespoon freshly grated ginger

1½ teaspoons curry powder

¼ teaspoon table salt

¼ teaspoon ground red pepper

Thin white bread slices

Stir together shrimp, celery, coconut, cream cheese, green onions, ginger, curry powder, salt, and red pepper until well blended. Spread on thin white bread.

**CURRIED CHICKEN:** Substitute 2½ cups finely chopped cooked chicken for the shrimp. Prepare recipe as directed. Spread on raisin bread.

# Best Deviled Eggs

Some believe a truly great deviled egg recipe never ventures beyond the mayo-mustard-pickle relish trinity. It's the formula preferred by purists such as Mississippian Jill Conner Browne, the once-famous Sweet Potato Queen whose love of deviled eggs was so renowned, fans would bring them by the dozen to her book signings. This vintage twist brightens the basics with a sprinkling of green olives and onion.

Serves 6 to 8 · Hands-on 10 minutes · Total 10 minutes

6 hard-cooked eggs, peeled
2 tablespoons mayonnaise
2 tablespoons finely chopped onion
1 tablespoon chopped green olives
1 teaspoon white vinegar

1 teaspoon yellow mustard
1/8 teaspoon table salt
Dash of ground black pepper
1/4 teaspoon paprika

Slice the eggs in half lengthwise, and carefully remove the yolks. Mash the yolks with mayonnaise. Stir in the onion and next 5 ingredients. Spoon or pipe yolk mixture into egg white halves. Sprinkle with the paprika.

1980s

# SIMPLY DEVILED EGGS

An updated list of lightened ingredients with full-on flavor, plus clever stir-ins, made these deviled eggs a favorite with the Food Staff the first time we tasted them.

Makes 2 dozen   Hands-on 30 minutes   Total 40 minutes

12 large eggs
⅓ cup fat-free Greek yogurt
2 ounces ⅓-less-fat cream cheese
1 tablespoon chopped fresh parsley
1 teaspoon Dijon mustard
⅛ teaspoon table salt

1. Place the eggs in a single layer in a stainless steel saucepan. (Do not use nonstick.) Add water to a depth of 3 inches. Bring to a rolling boil; cook 1 minute. Cover, remove from heat, and let stand 10 minutes. Drain.

2. Place the eggs under cold running water until just cool enough to handle. Tap the eggs on the counter until cracks form; peel.

3. Slice the eggs in half lengthwise, and carefully remove the yolks. Mash together the yolks, yogurt, and next 4 ingredients until smooth, using a fork. Spoon yolk mixture into egg white halves. Serve immediately, or cover and chill 1 hour before serving.

# Spicy Marinated Beef Tenderloin Rolls

---

It's been around for decades, but it's still the ultimate cocktail party trio: perfectly cooked beef tenderloin, sliced and served "tray-chic" on silver platters with a spicy side of horseradish sauce and a basket of buttery icebox rolls. Minimal effort is required on the part of the hostess, and yet the results are always extraordinary—very old school but never out of style. Horseradish gives the beef its spicy kick.

Serves 18 as an appetizer   Hands-on 35 minutes
Total 2 hours 45 minutes, including sauce (not including rolls), plus chill time

1 cup soy sauce
1 cup port wine
½ cup olive oil
1 teaspoon table salt
1 teaspoon freshly ground black pepper
1 teaspoon dried thyme

½ teaspoon hot sauce
4 garlic cloves, crushed
1 bay leaf
1 (5-pound) beef tenderloin, trimmed
Icebox Rolls (at right)
Horseradish Sour Cream (see below)

1. Combine first 9 ingredients in a 2-gallon zip-top plastic freezer bag; squeeze the bag until the mixture is well blended. Add the beef; seal bag, and chill 8 to 24 hours, turning occasionally.

2. Preheat the oven to 425°F. Remove the beef from the marinade; reserve the marinade. Place the beef on a rack in a roasting pan or jelly-roll pan. Bake at 425°F for 45 to 60 minutes or until a meat thermometer inserted into thickest portion registers 135°F (medium-rare), basting occasionally with reserved marinade. Let stand 10 minutes before thinly slicing.

3. Cut the rolls in half. Spread cut sides with Horseradish Sour Cream. Top bottom halves of the rolls with the beef, and cover with top halves of rolls, sour cream sides down.

Note: Bake tenderloin to an internal temperature of 135°F for medium-rare and 140°F for medium.

## Horseradish Sour Cream

1 (8-ounce) container sour cream
¼ cup mayonnaise
3 tablespoons prepared horseradish
2 tablespoons chopped fresh flat-leaf
   parsley

½ teaspoon table salt
¼ teaspoon freshly ground black pepper
Dried crushed red pepper (optional)

Stir together first 6 ingredients and the red pepper, if desired, in a medium bowl. Cover and chill until ready to serve. Makes 1¼ cups

# Icebox Rolls

1 (¼-ounce) envelope active dry yeast
2 tablespoons warm water (105° to 115°F)
1½ teaspoons sugar
½ cup boiling water
6 tablespoons shortening
6 tablespoons cold water

2 tablespoons sugar
1 teaspoon table salt
1 large egg, lightly beaten
3 cups all-purpose flour
¼ cup butter, melted
Parchment paper

1. Stir together the yeast, 2 tablespoons warm water, and 1½ teaspoons sugar in a small bowl, stirring until yeast is dissolved. Let stand 5 minutes.

2. Pour the boiling water over the shortening in a large heatproof bowl; stir until shortening is melted. Stir in the cold water, 2 tablespoons sugar, and salt. Stir in the egg and the yeast mixture. Gradually add the flour, stirring until blended. Cover and chill 24 hours.

3. Turn dough out on a lightly floured surface; knead 2 to 3 minutes. Shape the dough into 18 equal portions; roll into 1¾-inch balls. Dip the balls in melted butter, and place 2 to 3 inches apart on a large parchment paper-lined baking sheet. Cover rolls loosely with plastic wrap. Let rise in a warm place (80° to 85°F), free from drafts, 1 hour or until doubled in bulk.

4. Preheat the oven to 400°F. Uncover rolls. Bake at 400°F for 15 to 18 minutes or until lightly browned. Makes 1½ dozen

1980s

# BEEF TENDERLOIN CROSTINI

A powerhouse of fresh, new flavors updates the classic take on beef tenderloin. Crisp rounds of cornbread crostini deliver the perfect vehicle for thinly sliced chargrilled fillets topped with mango-onion relish and a vibrant green cilantro sauce. It's a thrifty but impressive way to serve a pricey party favorite. Bonus: Most of the components are make-ahead.

Makes 3 dozen    Hands-on 45 minutes    Total 1 hour 35 minutes

## CILANTRO SAUCE
2 teaspoons cumin seeds
1½ cups firmly packed fresh
    cilantro leaves
⅓ cup olive oil
1 garlic clove
2 tablespoons fresh lime juice
½ teaspoon kosher salt
2 tablespoons water

## MANGO-RED ONION RELISH
½ cup diced red onion
1 teaspoon olive oil
1 large mango, diced
¼ cup diced red bell pepper
1 jalapeño pepper, seeded and
    minced
1 tablespoon Champagne
    vinegar

## BEEF TENDERLOIN
1 pound beef tenderloin fillets
1 tablespoon olive oil
1 teaspoon kosher salt
½ teaspoon freshly ground
    black pepper
⅛ teaspoon garlic powder
Herbed Cornbread Crostini
    (at right)

1. Make the Cilantro Sauce: Place a small skillet over medium-high until hot; add cumin seeds, and cook, stirring constantly, 1 to 2 minutes or until toasted. Cool 10 minutes. Process the cilantro, next 5 ingredients, and toasted cumin seeds in a blender until smooth, stopping to scrape down sides as needed. Cover and chill until ready to serve.

2. Make the Relish: Sauté the onion in 1 teaspoon hot olive oil in a small skillet over medium-high 6 to 8 minutes or until onion is tender. Transfer to a medium bowl, and stir in the mango, next 3 ingredients, and table salt and ground black pepper to taste.

3. Make the Beef Tenderloin: Rub the steaks with 1 tablespoon olive oil. Sprinkle with 1 teaspoon salt and next 2 ingredients. Place a grill pan over medium-high until hot; cook the steaks 8 minutes on each side or to desired degree of doneness. Let stand 5 minutes. Thinly slice the steaks.

4. Assemble: Top the flat sides of Herbed Cornbread Crostini with the relish and steak; drizzle with the Cilantro Sauce.

# HERBED CORNBREAD CROSTINI

2 cups self-rising white
   cornmeal mix
2 tablespoons sugar
2 large eggs
½ cup sour cream
½ cup buttermilk

½ cup butter, melted
2 tablespoons chopped fresh
   chives
2 tablespoons chopped fresh
   parsley

Preheat the oven to 450°F. Stir together the cornmeal mix and
sugar in a large bowl; make a well in the center of the mixture.
Whisk together the eggs, sour cream, buttermilk, and melted
butter in a medium bowl. Add to the cornmeal mixture, stirring just
until dry ingredients are moistened. Fold in the chives and parsley.
Spoon batter into 3 lightly greased 12-cup muffin pans (about
1 tablespoon per cup), spreading the batter to cover the bottoms
of the cups. Bake at 450°F for 8 minutes or until set. Immediately
remove from pans to wire racks. Serve warm. Makes 3 dozen

# Texas Caviar

Helen Corbitt, famed 1950s Neiman Marcus food director, first served "pickled black-eyed peas" on New Year's Eve at the Houston Country Club. Marinated in a garlic-and-onion vinaigrette, they were a huge hit and were later christened "Texas Caviar." As the recipe made its way across the South, bell peppers, corn, and other ingredients were added. The big surprise here? Green tomatoes bring a bright, almost citrusy note to the mix.

Makes 8 cups   Hands-on 20 minutes   Total 20 minutes, plus chill time

2 (14-ounce) cans black-eyed peas, drained
1 (15½-ounce) can white hominy, drained
2 medium tomatoes, chopped
2 green tomatoes, chopped
1 medium-size green bell pepper, chopped

2 jalapeño peppers, chopped
½ cup chopped onion
½ cup chopped fresh cilantro
2 garlic cloves, minced
1 (8-ounce) bottle zesty Italian dressing
Tortilla chips

Stir together the first 9 ingredients in a large bowl. Add the dressing to the black-eyed pea mixture, stirring until combined. Cover and chill 2 hours. Drain. Serve with the tortilla chips.

1980s

# LUCKY BLACK-EYED PEA SALAD

Texas Caviar gets a flavor makeover with diced fresh peaches, tender watercress leaves, and a tangy-sweet vinaigrette spiked with jalapeño peppers and cilantro. Like the classic, it doubles as an appetizer and salad. Trade the tortilla chips for crisp mini cornsticks baked in cast-iron pans, and serve in small whiskey rocks glasses.

Serves 6   Hands-on 1 hour 5 minutes
Total 10 hours 5 minutes, including chill time

1 (16-ounce) package frozen black-eyed peas
¼ cup chopped fresh cilantro
¼ cup red pepper jelly
¼ cup red wine vinegar
2 tablespoons olive oil
1 jalapeño pepper, seeded and minced

¾ teaspoon table salt
¼ teaspoon freshly ground black pepper
1 cup diced red bell pepper
⅓ cup diced red onion
2 large fresh peaches, peeled and diced
2 cups torn watercress

1. Prepare the peas according to package directions, simmering only until al dente; drain and let cool 1 hour.

2. Whisk together the cilantro and next 6 ingredients in a large bowl. Add the cooked black-eyed peas, bell pepper, and onion, tossing to coat; cover and chill 8 hours. Stir the peaches and watercress into pea mixture just before serving.

## FRESH TAKE

### Herbaceous Cocktails

Inspired by the farm-to-table movement, mixologists are garnishing drinks with aromatic sprigs of fresh herbs. Our five favorite ways to add an herbaceous kick to cocktails? With these custom-picked pairings. Rosemary brings out the woodsy notes of a gin and tonic. Cilantro complements the peppery flavor of tequila in a margarita. Basil is a natural partner for the peach puree in a bellini. And tarragon? The sweet licorice undertones are a perfect match for the Herbsaint in a Sazerac. If you prefer a mocktail, try pairing the floral softness of fresh lavender with the citrusy lemonade sharpness of a refreshing Arnold Palmer.

# Oysters Rockefeller

Created by Jules Alciatore at the famed New Orleans restaurant Antoine's, Oysters Rockefeller dates back to 1899. The original recipe remains a mystery (a spinach-watercress debate still persists), but a true Rockefeller riff is bold and vibrant with freshly blended herbaceous ingredients and a splash of anise-flavored liqueur. The name? Inspired by the buttery richness of Alciatore's dish.

Serves 36 as an appetizer   Hands-on 30 minutes   Total 35 minutes

Rock salt
4 bacon slices, finely chopped
¼ cup butter, melted
½ cup all-purpose flour
2 cups frozen chopped spinach, thawed (undrained)
½ cup finely chopped green onions
½ cup finely chopped fresh flat-leaf parsley

½ cup oyster liquor (reserved oyster liquid)*
2 garlic cloves, minced
⅛ teaspoon ground red pepper
¼ cup absinthe
3 dozen oysters in the half shell, drained, reserving oyster liquid

1. Put a ½-inch layer of the rock salt in 2 large jelly-roll pans.

2. Cook the bacon in a large skillet over medium 4 to 6 minutes or until crisp; drain, reserving drippings in skillet.

3. Add the butter and the flour to hot drippings; cook, stirring constantly, 3 to 5 minutes or until golden brown. Add the spinach and the next 5 ingredients. Bring to a simmer. Cook, stirring occasionally, 10 minutes or until very thick. Remove from heat. Stir in the absinthe and bacon, and add table salt to taste.

4. Preheat the broiler with oven rack 6 inches from heat. Arrange 18 oysters on salt in prepared pans; top with the spinach mixture. Broil 4 to 6 minutes or until lightly browned.

*Water may be substituted, if desired.

1960s

# GRILLED OYSTERS ON THE HALF SHELL

It's a chargrilled homage to Gulf oyster houses, with a garlic-and-herb butter nod to Oysters Rockefeller. Cooking over coals adds a sweet campfire smokiness and intensifies the oysters' briny flavor. Want to make the shells easier to shuffle around on the grates? Nestle them on a rimmed baking sheet lined with rock salt. Bonus: A salt bed evenly distributes the heat, and the oysters are less likely to tip so you won't lose that flavorful oyster liquor.

Serves 4 to 6   Hands-on 25 minutes   Total 25 minutes

1 pound (2 cups) butter, softened
1/2 cup finely grated Parmesan cheese
1/4 cup finely chopped parsley
2 garlic cloves, minced
1 tablespoon Worcestershire sauce
1 teaspoon paprika
1/2 teaspoon ground red pepper
1/2 teaspoon hot sauce
2 dozen large fresh oysters on the half shell
Garnish: fresh flat-leaf parsley sprigs

1. Preheat the grill to 450°F. Pulse first 8 ingredients in a food processor until well combined.

2. Arrange the oysters in a single layer on the grill. Carefully spoon 2 teaspoons of the butter mixture into each oyster; grill, without a grill lid, 7 minutes or until the edges curl.

**BROILED OYSTERS**: Preheat the broiler with the oven rack 3 inches from heat. Prepare the recipe as directed, placing the oysters in a single layer in a jelly-roll pan. Broil 4 minutes or until the edges curl and the butter drips over the shell.

## FRESH TAKE

### NOLA Revival

What's old is new: Classic cocktails are making a comeback. Topping the list of favorites? New Orleans Vieux Carré, Pimm's Cup, and the Sazerac, which was originally served at the Sazerac Coffee House in the French Quarter.

**Sazerac:** Pour 1 Tbsp. anise liqueur (such as Herbsaint or Pernod) into a 6- to 8-oz. glass, and swirl to coat the inside of the glass; discard any excess liqueur. Fill the glass with ice cubes. Combine 3 Tbsp. rye whiskey, 1/2 tsp. simple syrup, 4 or 5 dashes of Peychaud's bitters, and 2 dashes of Angostura bitters in a cocktail shaker filled with ice cubes. Cover with lid, and shake vigorously until thoroughly chilled (about 30 seconds). Remove ice from glass, and discard; strain mixture in the cocktail shaker into the chilled glass. Rub glass rim with 1 lemon peel, and add to drink. Serve immediately. Serves 1

# Hot Artichoke Spread

Almost every post-60s spiral-bound Southern cookbook boasts a twist on this perennial party favorite. It's a classic four-ingredient recipe. Later versions amped up the original combo with a flourish of toasted almonds or fresh tarragon—or better still, something more extravagant like shrimp or crabmeat.

Makes 2½ cups   Hands-on 15 minutes   Total 35 minutes

1 (14-ounce) can whole
   artichoke hearts, drained
   and chopped
1 cup mayonnaise
1 cup grated Parmesan cheese

½ teaspoon garlic powder
Assorted crackers
Garnishes: paprika, fresh
   parsley sprig

**1.** Preheat the oven to 350°F. Stir together the first 4 ingredients until well blended. Spoon into a lightly greased 3-cup baking dish.

**2.** Bake at 350°F for 20 minutes or until bubbly and hot. Serve with the assorted crackers.

1970s

## FRESH TAKE

### Magnificent Mergers

Popular spinach dips and California onion dip, made with packaged dry soup mix, were both dethroned on the 70s party circuit by hot artichoke dip. This recipe, minus the soup mix, merges the best of spinach and artichoke dips. If you want to go retro, bake it in a hollowed-out bread bowl.

**Spinach-Artichoke Dip:** Stir together 1 (14-oz.) can artichoke hearts, drained and chopped; 1 (10-oz.) package frozen chopped spinach, thawed and drained; 1 (8-oz.) package cream cheese, softened; 1 cup freshly grated Parmesan cheese; 1 cup chopped toasted pecans; ½ cup sour cream; ½ cup mayonnaise; 2 garlic cloves, pressed; and ½ tsp. ground red pepper. Spoon spinach mixture into a shallow 1½-qt. baking dish; top with an additional ½ cup freshly grated Parmesan cheese. Bake at 375°F for 25 to 30 minutes or until golden. Serve with pita chips. Serves 8 as an appetizer

# HOMEMADE BUTTERMILK RICOTTA DIP

In 1980, we advised readers looking for an elegant appetizer to "Dip in with an Artichoke" and recommended pairing the steamed leaves with lemon mayo or a chafing dish of warm anchovy butter. Today, we'd opt for this versatile (and impressive) homemade ricotta dip for dipping steamed artichoke leaves or fresh raw vegetables.

Makes 1½ cups  Hands-on 40 minutes
Total 13 hours 10 minutes

3 cups whole milk (preferably organic)
1½ cups whole buttermilk (preferably organic)
1 cup heavy cream (preferably organic)
¼ teaspoon kosher salt
Cheesecloth
Extra virgin olive oil
Sea salt and dried crushed red pepper

1. Bring the first 4 ingredients to a simmer, without stirring, in a heavy nonaluminum Dutch oven (about 9½ inches in diameter) over medium; cook, without stirring, 20 to 25 minutes or just until bubbles appear and temperature reaches 175° to 180°F. (Do not boil.)

2. Stir gently, and return to a simmer. Cook, without stirring, 5 to 6 minutes or until temperature reaches 190°F. (Do not boil or stir. Mixture will look curdled.) Remove from heat, and let stand 30 minutes.

3. Line a fine wire-mesh strainer with 3 layers of cheesecloth, and place over a bowl. Spoon mixture into the strainer. Cover with cheesecloth; chill 12 to 24 hours. Remove the cheese, discarding strained liquid.

4. Spoon the cheese into a serving bowl; drizzle with the olive oil, and sprinkle with the salt and crushed red pepper. Refrigerate the dip in an airtight container up to 2 days.

# Country Ham on Angel Biscuits

Salty and robust, dry-cured country ham sliced tissue-paper thin and tucked into bite-size angel biscuits is hog heaven. The sweet mustard sauce is optional. These featherlight baking powder, biscuit-yeast roll hybrids were the latest craze on 70s cocktail buffets.

Serves 30   Hands-on 20 minutes

Total 5 hours, 30 minutes, not including biscuits, mustard, or peaches

1 (15-pound) sugar-cured country ham
1 (16-ounce) package light brown sugar
Whole cloves
Angel Biscuits (at right)

Peach Chutney Halves (see below)
Honey mustard, warmed
Fresh curly-leaf parsley sprigs (optional)

1. Preheat the oven to 350°F. Scrub the ham thoroughly with a stiff brush (do not soak). Pour water to 1½ inches in a very large, deep roasting pan. Place the ham, skin side down, in pan; coat exposed portion generously with brown sugar.

2. Bake at 350°F for 4 hours, basting with pan juices every 30 minutes.

3. Carefully remove the ham from the water (do not discard water). Remove the skin from the ham. Place the ham, fat side up, on a cutting board; score the fat in a diamond pattern, and stud with the cloves. Return ham to pan, fat side up; coat top generously with brown sugar.

4. Bake, uncovered, 1 hour. Let stand 10 minutes. Thinly slice.

5. Serve the ham in the biscuits with Peach Chutney Halves, honey mustard, and, if desired, parsley.

Note: A larger or smaller ham may be substituted. Bake at 350°F for 20 minutes per pound; uncover during the last hour of baking, after the fat is scored and studded with cloves.

## Peach Chutney Halves

1 (9-ounce) jar hot mango chutney        1 (29-ounce) can peach halves, drained

Preheat the broiler with the oven rack 4 inches from heat. Spoon about 1 teaspoon chutney into the center of each peach half on a jelly-roll pan. Broil 3 to 5 minutes. Serves 8 to 10

# Angel Biscuits

1 (1/4-ounce) envelope active dry yeast
2 tablespoons warm water (105° to 115°F)
2 cups buttermilk
5 cups all-purpose flour
1/4 cup sugar
1 tablespoon baking powder
1 teaspoon baking soda
1 teaspoon table salt
1 cup shortening

1. Preheat the oven to 475°F. Combine the yeast and warm water in a 4-cup measuring cup; let stand 5 minutes or until bubbly. Stir in buttermilk.

2. Combine the flour and next 4 ingredients in a large bowl; cut in shortening until mixture is crumbly. Add yeast mixture, stirring with a fork until dry ingredients are moistened.

3. Turn the dough out on a lightly floured surface, and knead lightly 3 or 4 times. Roll dough to a 3/4-inch thickness; cut into rounds using a 2 1/2-inch cutter, rerolling dough scraps once. Place on lightly greased baking sheets.

4. Bake at 475°F for 12 to 15 minutes. Makes 1 1/2 dozen

1970S

## FRESH TAKE

### City Ham, Country Ham

Country hams are hand-rubbed with salt, sugar, and spice; sometimes smoked; and then air-dried for ages at cool temperatures. This preservation method dehydrates the meat, concentrating its flavor. Smithfield Ham is dry-cured country ham from Smithfield, Virginia. Virginia Ham is a country ham similar to Smithfield Ham but not from the protected designation of origin. (Note: Smithfield Foods, a pork-producing company founded in Smithfield, also makes hams, most of which are wet-cured city hams.) Skip the labor-intensive steps of scrubbing and soaking a country ham by buying a precooked one. City hams are wet-cured in a salty brine. Spiral-cut hams are wet-cured and precooked. Harry J. Hoenselaar, who invented the spiral-slicing machine also founded HoneyBaked Ham in Michigan in 1957. It wasn't until the patent expired in 1981 that spiral-cut hams were available in grocery stores.

# HAM BISCUITS WITH CHUTNEY AND BLUE CHEESE BUTTER

Gingery spiral-cut ham stacks up with Blue Cheese Butter and jarred chutney inside this cream cheese twist on classic angel biscuits.

Makes about 18 biscuits   Hands-on 30 minutes
Total 5 hours 45 minutes, including ham and butter

1 (¼-ounce) envelope active dry yeast
¼ cup warm water (105° to 115°F)
5 cups all-purpose flour
2 tablespoons sugar
1 tablespoon baking powder
1 teaspoon baking soda
1 teaspoon table salt
1 (8-ounce) package cold cream cheese, cut into pieces

½ cup cold butter, cut into pieces
1¼ cups buttermilk
Parchment paper
2 tablespoons butter, melted
Blue Cheese Butter (at right)
Ginger Ale-Brown Sugar Smoked Ham, sliced (see below)
Jarred fruit chutney (optional)

1. Preheat oven to 400°F. Combine yeast and warm water in a small bowl; let stand 5 minutes.

2. Meanwhile, whisk together the flour and next 4 ingredients in a large bowl; cut the cream cheese and cold butter into flour mixture with a pastry blender or fork until crumbly.

3. Combine the yeast mixture and buttermilk, and add to the flour mixture, stirring just until dry ingredients are moistened. Turn the dough out onto a lightly floured surface, and knead lightly 6 to 8 times (about 30 seconds to 1 minute), sprinkling with up to ¼ cup additional flour as needed to prevent sticking.

4. Roll the dough to ¾-inch thickness. Cut with a 2½-inch round cutter. Arrange biscuits on parchment-lined baking sheets. Bake 13 to 15 minutes. Brush with melted butter.

5. Layer biscuits with Blue Cheese Butter, slices of Ginger Ale-Brown Sugar Smoked Ham, and fruit chutney, if desired.

# GINGER ALE-BROWN SUGAR SMOKED HAM

1 (8-pound) smoked bone-in ham
2 (12-ounce) bottles spicy ginger ale
½ cup bourbon
¼ cup firmly packed dark brown sugar

2 teaspoons coarsely ground black pepper
½ teaspoon kosher salt
½ teaspoon dry mustard
¼ teaspoon ground red pepper

1. Preheat the oven to 325°F. Remove the skin from ham; trim fat to ¼-inch thickness. Make shallow cuts in the fat 1 inch apart in a diamond pattern. Place the ham, fat side up, in a roasting pan; add the ginger ale and bourbon to pan. Cover loosely with foil.

2. Bake, covered, at 325°F for 4½ hours or until a thermometer registers 140°F, basting with pan juices every 30 minutes. Stir together brown sugar and next 4 ingredients. Remove from oven, uncover, and sprinkle sugar mixture over ham, pressing mixture into fat.

3. Bake, uncovered, at 325°F for 25 minutes or until crust is browned and a meat thermometer registers 145°F. Transfer to a cutting board, and let stand 15 minutes before carving. Serves 16

# BLUE CHEESE BUTTER

1 (5-ounce) wedge soft ripened blue cheese, rind removed

½ cup butter

1 green onion, minced

2 tablespoons chopped fresh parsley

1 teaspoon Dijon mustard

¼ teaspoon freshly ground black pepper

Let the cheese and butter come to room temperature. Stir together the cheese, butter, and remaining ingredients with a fork until thoroughly blended. Serve immediately. Store, covered, in refrigerator up to 1 week. Makes 1 cup

# Okra Fries

There's nothing "medi-okra" about these golden fries. Reader Catherine O'Quin's secret? Tender new okra from her Tylertown, Mississippi, garden. The tiny pods are dredged and deep-fried whole for an extra-crisp cornmeal crunch. Says Catherine: "They taste just like popcorn." That translates into perfect pub fare for the cocktail hour.

Serves 4   Hands-on 15 minutes   Total 15 minutes

20 small fresh okra pods, trimmed
1 cup buttermilk
Vegetable oil
¾ cup all-purpose flour

¼ cup plain yellow cornmeal
1 teaspoon baking powder
½ teaspoon kosher salt
⅛ teaspoon ground black pepper

1. Place the okra and buttermilk in a shallow container. Let stand.

2. Meanwhile, pour the oil to a depth of 1½ inches in a Dutch oven; heat over medium-high to 375°F.

3. Stir together the flour, cornmeal, baking powder, salt, and pepper. Remove each okra pod from the buttermilk, letting excess drip off, and dredge in cornmeal mixture.

4. Fry the okra, in batches, in the hot oil 3 to 4 minutes or until golden brown, turning once. Drain on paper towels. Sprinkle lightly with salt.

1980s

# SMASHED FRIED OKRA

Imagine a summer-fresh okra pod splintered and deep-fried like a sweet onion blossom. Pair that crisp, cornmeal-crusted thought with Mississippi's legendary Comeback Sauce, first developed in the 30s as a house dressing for the Mayflower Cafe in Jackson. Eighty years later it still keeps fans coming back for more.

Serves 4 to 6   Hands-on 40 minutes
Total 1 hour 10 minutes, including sauce

1 pound fresh okra
1½ cups buttermilk
2 cups fine plain yellow cornmeal

Kosher salt and freshly ground black pepper
Canola oil

1. Use a meat mallet to smash the okra, starting at the tip of the pod and working toward the stem end. Place the buttermilk in a shallow dish, and place the cornmeal in another shallow dish. Stir desired amount of salt and pepper into the buttermilk and cornmeal. Dip the okra in the buttermilk; dredge in cornmeal, shaking off excess.

2. Pour the oil to depth of 2 inches into a large Dutch oven; heat to 350°F. Fry the okra, in batches, 2 to 3 minutes or until browned and crisp, turning once. Remove the okra, using a slotted spoon; drain on paper towels. Add the salt and pepper; serve immediately.

## COMEBACK SAUCE

1 cup mayonnaise
¼ cup chili sauce
2 tablespoons ketchup
1 tablespoon lemon juice
1 teaspoon smoked paprika
2 teaspoons Worcestershire sauce

1 teaspoon hot sauce
½ teaspoon kosher salt
½ teaspoon garlic powder
½ teaspoon onion powder
½ teaspoon dry mustard
¼ teaspoon freshly ground black pepper

Stir together the mayonnaise, chili sauce, ketchup, lemon juice, paprika, Worcestershire sauce, hot sauce, salt, garlic powder, onion powder, dry mustard, and pepper. Cover and chill 30 minutes before serving. Refrigerate, covered, up to 1 week. Makes 1½ cups

# 4

# DINNERTIME

From down-home chicken pot pies to pork grillades
that call out for the good china, these memorable
main dishes hit all the right comfort notes.

## 1990s Dinner Party

Meet your new dinner party menu:
six great 90s-inspired recipes that will
never go out of style.
Trust us: You'll swear by these
Southern favorites for years to come.

**Sparkling Charleston Cosmopolitans**
(page 213)

**Baby Blue Salad with Sweet-and-Spicy Pecans
and Balsamic Vinaigrette** (page 82)

**Beef Tenderloin with Five-Onion Confit**
(page 213)

**Skillet Green Beans** (page 281)

**Fennel-and-Potato Gratin** (page 284)

**Lemon Bar Cheesecake** (page 302)

# Chicken Fried Steak

Historians are divided on the origins of chicken fried steak—some trace it to German settlers in the Texas Hill Country, others to trailblazing chuckwagon cooks. Most agree authentic versions involve tenderized beef steak that's breaded, fried, and blanketed with a peppery cream gravy. This recipe ticks all the right boxes, including a golden cracker crumb crust that considerably ups the crunch factor.

Serves 4   Hands-on 30 minutes   Total 30 minutes

¼ cup plus 3 tablespoons all-purpose flour
½ teaspoon table salt
½ teaspoon ground black pepper
4 (4-ounce) cubed beef steaks
1 large egg, lightly beaten

½ cup plus 2 tablespoons milk
1 cup saltine cracker crumbs
2 cups vegetable oil
1¼ cups chicken broth
Dash of Worcestershire sauce
Dash of hot sauce

1. Combine ¼ cup of the flour and next 2 ingredients; sprinkle both sides of steaks with flour mixture.

2. Combine the egg and 2 tablespoons of the milk in a shallow dish. Dip the steaks in egg mixture; dredge in cracker crumbs.

3. Cook the steaks in hot oil in a large heavy skillet over medium 2 minutes on each side or until browned. Cover, reduce heat, and simmer, turning occasionally, 15 minutes or until tender. Remove the steaks, and drain on paper towels, reserving 3 tablespoons drippings in the skillet. Keep the steaks warm.

4. Whisk remaining 3 tablespoons flour into the hot drippings until smooth. Cook 1 minute, whisking constantly. Gradually add the broth and remaining ½ cup milk; cook over medium, whisking constantly, 3 minutes or until thickened and bubbly. Stir in the Worcestershire sauce and hot sauce; add salt and pepper to taste. Serve gravy with steaks.

1990s

# DAVID'S CHICKEN FRIED STEAK

Texas Chef David Bull, of Second Bar + Kitchen in Austin, opts for tender well-marbled rib-eye steaks, pounded with the textured side of a meat mallet to mimic the look of cubed steak. A triple dip-and-dredge in buttermilk, egg, and peppered flour accounts for the extra-crisp crust. Redeye gravy made with smoked bacon and ham replaces the traditional cream gravy, but you definitely won't hear us complaining.

Serves 4   Hands-on 45 minutes
Total 2 hours 30 minutes, including gravy

| | |
|---|---|
| 4 (4-ounce) rib-eye steaks | 2 cups buttermilk |
| 3 cups all-purpose flour | 1/2 teaspoon hot sauce |
| 1 teaspoon baking powder | 1 teaspoon table salt |
| 1/2 teaspoon baking soda | 1/4 teaspoon freshly ground |
| 1/4 teaspoon ground red | black pepper |
| pepper | 3 cups vegetable oil |
| 2 large eggs | Redeye Gravy (at right) |

1. Place the steaks between 2 sheets of heavy-duty plastic wrap, and flatten to 1/4-inch thickness, using the flat side of a meat mallet. Lightly pound the steak, using the textured side of the meat mallet. Wrap tightly with plastic wrap, and chill 1 hour.

2. Combine the flour and next 3 ingredients in a bowl. Whisk together the eggs and next 2 ingredients in a separate bowl. Sprinkle both sides of the steaks with salt and black pepper.

3. Dip the steaks in the egg mixture, and dredge in the flour mixture, shaking off excess. Repeat procedure 2 more times.

4. Fry the steaks, 1 at a time, in hot oil in a nonstick skillet over medium-high 4 to 6 minutes on each side or until golden. Drain on a wire rack in a jelly-roll pan. Serve with the gravy.

# REDEYE GRAVY

¼ cup butter
1½ thick smoked bacon slices, diced
½ cup chopped smoked ham
1 small onion, diced
2 garlic cloves, minced
2 teaspoons finely chopped fresh sage
2 tablespoons all-purpose flour

1 cup milk
1 cup beef broth
¾ cup brewed coffee
1 tablespoon chopped fresh chives
2 teaspoons cracked black pepper
Garnish: chopped fresh chives

1. Melt the butter in a large saucepan over medium; add the bacon, and cook, stirring occasionally, 5 to 7 minutes or until done. Add the ham and next 3 ingredients; sauté 3 to 4 minutes or until the onion is translucent. Reduce heat to medium-low. Add the flour. Cook, stirring constantly, 3 to 5 minutes or until golden brown.

2. Slowly whisk in the milk and next 2 ingredients; bring to a boil over high, stirring occasionally. Reduce heat to low. Simmer, stirring often, 14 to 18 minutes or until thickened. Remove from heat. Stir in the 1 tablespoon chives and pepper. Makes about 4 cups

# Heavenly Smoked Brisket

———◇———

Brisket is the legendary low-and-slow-cooked cut of the Lone Star State, but its fame extends far beyond Texas borders. This recipe came to us from a reader in Alexandria, Louisiana. Hickory-smoked with a bold brown sugar-Cajun spice rub, it topped our annual list of favorites in 1995. There's no barbecue sauce. None needed. The heavenly flavor of the brisket simply speaks for itself.

Serves 12   Hands-on 10 minutes
Total 13 hours 20 minutes, including chill and smoking time

½ cup firmly packed dark brown sugar
2 tablespoons table salt
2 tablespoons Cajun seasoning
1 tablespoon lemon-pepper seasoning
2 tablespoons Worcestershire sauce
1 (5- to 6-pound) beef brisket
Hickory wood chunks

1. Combine the first 5 ingredients. Place the brisket in a large shallow dish. Spread the sugar mixture on both sides of brisket. Cover and chill 8 hours.

2. Soak the wood chunks in water to cover 1 hour. Prepare the smoker according to manufacturer's directions, bringing the internal temperature to 225° to 250°F; maintain temperature for 15 to 20 minutes.

3. Drain the wood chunks, and place on coals. Remove the brisket from the marinade, reserving marinade. Place the brisket on lower cooking grate. Pour reserved marinade over brisket. Cover with the smoker lid.

4. Smoke the brisket, maintaining a low temperature inside smoker between 225° and 250°F, for 5 hours or until a meat thermometer inserted into thickest portion registers 180°F. Remove from the smoker, wrap in aluminum foil, and let stand 10 to 15 minutes. Cut against the grain into thin slices.

Note: We tested with Prudhomme's Blackened Beef Magic Cajun seasoning.

1990s

# SMOKED BEEF BRISKET

Champion Texas pitmaster Christopher Prieto's brisket is smoky perfection. He opts for a whole brisket to feed a crowd and uses a fiery dry rub, a seductively sweet sauce, and a judicious use of smoke. His takeaway? Avoid oversmoking and masking other flavors by waiting until the intense early smoke clears before adding the meat.

Serves 12   Hands-on 40 minutes
Total 12 hours 45 minutes, including rub and sauce

1 (12- to 14-pound) beef brisket, trimmed
½ cup Worcestershire sauce
1 cup Beef Rub (see below)
3 to 4 pecan, hickory, or oak wood chunks

15 pounds charcoal briquettes
El Sancho Barbecue Sauce, optional (at left)

1. Brush or rub the brisket generously with the Worcestershire sauce. Coat the entire brisket with Beef Rub, and chill 1 to 4 hours.

2. Remove the brisket from the refrigerator, and let stand 1 hour.

3. Prepare a fire using wood chunks in a smoker according to manufacturer's directions. Place a water pan in the smoker; add water to fill line. Regulate temperature to 250° to 260°F for 15 to 20 minutes.

4. Place the brisket, fat side down, on top cooking grate and close the smoker. Smoke 5 hours or until a meat thermometer inserted into the center where the point and flat meet registers 165°F.

5. Remove the brisket from the smoker, and wrap tightly in wax-free butcher paper; return brisket to the smoker. Cook 3 to 5 more hours, checking temperature each hour until meat thermometer inserted into the center of the brisket registers 200°F.

6. Remove the brisket; open the butcher paper, and let steam escape for 4 minutes. Rewrap and let brisket stand in butcher paper 2 hours.

7. Remove the brisket from the butcher paper; place on a cutting board, reserving ¼ cup drippings in paper. Slice meat across the grain into ¼-inch-thick slices. Combine reserved drippings and El Sancho Barbecue Sauce, if desired, and serve immediately.

## FRESH TAKE

### To Sauce or Not To Sauce...

The debate rages on. Barbecue purists balk at sauces that blanket the flavorful crust or "bark" of perfectly smoked brisket, while other 'cue fans think sauceless brisket is as good as naked. There is no right answer, so try it both ways. Christopher Prieto's Favorite Sauce?

**El Sancho Barbecue Sauce:** Stir together ⅓ cup tomato paste, ½ cup ketchup, 1 cup apple cider vinegar, ¼ cup yellow mustard, ¼ cup Worcestershire, 1 Tbsp. hot sauce, 1 Tbsp. granulated onion, 1 Tbsp. granulated garlic, 1 Tbsp. kosher salt, 2 tsp. hickory liquid smoke, and 1 tsp. coarse tellicherry black pepper in a medium saucepan over medium. Add 1 cup sugar and 1 cup honey; bring to a boil. Reduce and simmer, stirring occasionally, for 30 minutes. Makes 3 cups

## BEEF RUB

Stir together 1 cup kosher salt, 1 cup coarse tellicherry black pepper, 3 tablespoons granulated garlic, and 2 teaspoons red pepper until well blended. Store in an airtight container up to 1 month. Makes 2 ¼ cups

# Lowcountry Seafood Boil

A Lowcountry Boil is one-pot cooking at its peak-of-summer best: a seasonal celebration of local seafood simmered with smoked sausage, fresh-picked corn, and new potatoes. There are no hard and fast rules when it comes to a recipe, but we highly recommend foregoing a serving platter in favor of a newspaper-covered picnic table.

Serves 8 to 12   Hands-on 20 minutes   Total 1 hour

6 baby red potatoes (about 4 pounds), quartered if large
3 large sweet onions, peeled and halved
2 tablespoons table salt
1 dozen live blue crabs
2 (3-ounce) packages crab boil
3 garlic bulbs, peeled
4 to 6 lemons, halved

1 cup apple cider vinegar
1 dozen ears fresh corn, husks removed (about 4 pounds)
1½ pounds smoked sausage, cut into 2-inch pieces
5 pounds unpeeled, large raw shrimp
Melted butter
Cocktail sauce

1. Fill a 5- or 6-gallon pot about two-thirds full of water; bring to a boil. Add the potatoes, onions, and salt; cover and cook on high 20 minutes.

2. Stir in the crabs, crab boil, garlic, lemons, and vinegar; cook 10 minutes. Reduce the heat, and add the corn and sausage; simmer 5 minutes. Remove from the heat, and add the shrimp; let stand 5 minutes.

3. Drain; arrange the crab, shrimp, corn, sausage, and potatoes on a serving platter. Serve with the melted butter and cocktail sauce.

Note: To remove the meat from a crab, pry off the apron flap on the underside of the crab with your thumb or a knife. Lift off the top shell, using your thumb or a knife. Then break off the large claws, and set aside. Peel off the spongy substance on both sides of the crab body. Remove the digestive organs and other parts of the center body. This will expose a hard, semitransparent membrane covering the edible crabmeat. On each half, use a knife to remove the membrane covering the meat, or slice lengthwise through each half without removing the membrane. Large chunks of the meat will be exposed; remove the meat with a knife or your fingers. Crack the claws with a mallet, nutcracker, or knife handle, and remove the meat.

1980s

# SHRIMP-BOIL POTATO SALAD

Iconic Southern dishes are reinventing themselves in surprisingly delicious new ways. Turns out all those fabulously fresh coastal flavors found in a Lowcountry Boil play together extremely well in a cool main-dish salad. The downside of the transformation? You can still serve it at a communal table but you'll definitely want to pass out forks.

Serves 6   Hands-on 40 minutes   Total 1 hour 20 minutes

10 cups water
1 (3-ounce) package boil-in-bag shrimp-
   and-crab boil
3 pounds baby red potatoes, halved
1 pound smoked link sausage, cut into
   $\frac{1}{2}$-inch pieces
4 ears fresh corn, husks removed
2 pounds peeled and deveined jumbo raw
   shrimp with tails

$\frac{1}{2}$ cup fresh lemon juice
$\frac{1}{3}$ cup olive oil
$\frac{1}{4}$ cup chopped fresh flat-leaf parsley
3 tablespoons Creole mustard
4 green onions, sliced
1 garlic clove, pressed
1 teaspoon paprika
1 teaspoon prepared horseradish
Garnish: fresh flat-leaf parsley leaves

1. Bring 10 cups water to a boil in a Dutch oven over high; add the crab boil, potatoes, and sausage; return to a boil, and cook 10 minutes. Add the corn, and return to a boil. Cook 3 minutes or until the potatoes are tender. Add the shrimp; cover, remove from heat, and let stand 5 minutes or just until the shrimp turn pink.

2. Meanwhile, whisk together the lemon juice and next 7 ingredients in a medium bowl.

3. Drain the shrimp mixture. Cut kernels from the cobs. Discard the cobs. Stir together the corn kernels, shrimp mixture, and lemon juice mixture in a large bowl. Serve immediately, or cover and chill up to 24 hours.

NOTE: We tested with Conecuh Original Smoked Sausage.

# Chicken Pot Pie

Chicken pot pie may have roots elsewhere in the world, but its soul-satisfying comforts are definitely not lost in the Southern kitchen. Baked family-style in a shallow casserole dish, this old-fashioned favorite hits all the right notes with a rich and creamy chicken filling and golden egg-washed lattice crust.

Serves 6   Hands-on 25 minutes   Total 2 hours 5 minutes, including pastry

⅓ cup butter
½ cup chopped celery
½ cup chopped onion
⅓ cup all-purpose flour
2¾ cups chicken broth
½ teaspoon table salt
½ teaspoon freshly ground black pepper

3½ cups chopped cooked chicken
1 (10-ounce) package frozen mixed
  vegetables, thawed
3 hard-cooked eggs, peeled and chopped
Pastry (see below)
1 large egg, lightly beaten

1. Preheat the oven to 400°F. Melt the butter in a large heavy saucepan over medium-high; add the celery and onion, and sauté 6 minutes. Add the flour, and cook, stirring constantly, 1 minute. Gradually add the broth; cook over medium, stirring constantly, until mixture is thickened and bubbly.

2. Stir in the salt and pepper. Stir in the chicken, vegetables, and eggs. Spoon into a lightly greased 11- x 7-inch (2-quart) baking dish.

3. Roll out the Pastry into a large rectangle (about ⅛ inch thick) on a lightly floured surface. Cut the Pastry into ¾-inch-wide strips using a fluted pastry wheel. Arrange the strips in a lattice-fashion across the top of the baking dish. Lightly brush the Pastry with the egg.

4. Bake at 400°F for 35 to 40 minutes or until golden brown and bubbly.

# Pastry

1½ cups all-purpose flour
¾ teaspoon table salt

½ cup plus 1½ tablespoons shortening
4 to 5 tablespoons ice-cold water

Combine the flour and salt; cut in the shortening with a pastry blender until mixture is crumbly. Sprinkle the cold water, 1 tablespoon at a time, over the surface of the mixture; stir with a fork until all ingredients are moistened. Shape the dough into a flat rectangle; wrap in plastic wrap, and chill 1 hour. Makes 1 (11- x 7-inch) lattice crust

# SKILLET CHICKEN POT PIE

A few well-chosen shortcuts trim the prep time but not the made-from-scratch flavor. Rotisserie chicken jump-starts the creamy filling (one bird yields the perfect amount of meat). Frozen hashbrowns get meltingly tender when baked and matchstick carrots add a crisp fresh snap. Bonus: The steady even heat of a cast-iron skillet beautifully browns the bottom crust.

Serves 6 to 8   Hands-on 30 minutes
Total 1 hour 30 minutes

CHICKEN PIE FILLING
1/3 cup plus 2 tablespoons butter
1/3 cup all-purpose flour
1½ cups chicken broth
1½ cups milk
1½ teaspoons Creole seasoning
1 large sweet onion, diced
1 (8-ounce) package sliced fresh mushrooms
4 cups shredded cooked chicken

2 cups frozen cubed hash browns
1 cup matchstick carrots
1 cup frozen small sweet peas
1/3 cup chopped fresh parsley

PASTRY CRUST
1 (14.1-ounce) package refrigerated piecrusts
1 large egg white

1. Make the Filling: Preheat the oven to 350°F. Lightly grease a 10-inch cast-iron skillet. Melt 1/3 cup of the butter in a large saucepan over medium; add the flour, and cook, whisking constantly, 1 minute. Gradually add the chicken broth and milk, and cook, whisking constantly, 6 to 7 minutes or until thickened and bubbly. Remove from heat, and stir in the Creole seasoning.

2. Melt remaining 2 tablespoons butter in a large Dutch oven over medium-high; add the onion and mushrooms, and sauté 10 minutes or until tender. Stir in the chicken, next 4 ingredients, and the sauce.

3. Make the Crust: Place 1 piecrust in prepared skillet. Spoon the chicken mixture over the piecrust, and top with the remaining piecrust.

4. Whisk the egg white until foamy; brush the top of the piecrust with the egg white. Cut 4 or 5 slits in the top of the pie for steam to escape.

5. Bake at 350°F for 1 hour to 1 hour and 5 minutes or until golden brown and bubbly.

# Barbecued Spareribs

Some say the secret to great barbecue is less about what you put on the meat than what you leave off. This vintage recipe serves up no-frills spareribs at their smoky backyard best—grilled and basted with a finger-lickin' barbecue sauce until just tender enough to tug cleanly off the bone.

Serves 3 to 4   Hands-on 20 minutes   Total 2 hours 20 minutes

3 to 4 pounds pork spareribs
1 medium onion, grated
1 cup ketchup
¼ cup lemon juice
2 tablespoons brown sugar

2 tablespoons apple cider vinegar
1 tablespoon Worcestershire sauce
1 teaspoon ground black pepper
½ teaspoon table salt
½ cup water

1. Preheat the grill to 250° to 300°F (low). Remove the thin membrane from the back of each slab by slicing into it and pulling it off. (This will make the ribs more tender.)

2. Stir together the next 8 ingredients and ½ cup water in a saucepan. Bring to a boil, and simmer 10 minutes.

3. Grill the ribs, covered with grill lid, 50 minutes to 1 hour, basting with the barbecue sauce every 10 minutes during last 30 minutes of grilling.

4. Preheat the oven to 325°F. Remove the ribs from the grill. Baste with any remaining barbecue sauce, and wrap tightly in aluminum foil. Place on a baking sheet.

5. Bake at 325°F for 1 hour. Let stand, covered with foil, 10 minutes. Cut into individual ribs before serving.

1970s

# ULTIMATE SMOKY, SWEET RIBS

A meaty rack of St. Louis-style ribs is elevated with a triple hit of flavor from a perfectly seasoned rub, a tangy-sweet sauce, and the slow, steady heat of applewood smoke. When the Test Kitchen was challenged, these moist delectable ribs (with a Memphis accent) smoked the competition.

Serves 4 to 6   Hands-on 45 minutes   Total 7 hours 10 minutes, including rub, braising liquid, and sauce, plus chill time

2 (2½- to 3-pound) slabs
 St. Louis-style pork ribs
Smoky Dry Rub (see below)
1 cup applewood smoking chips

Rib Braising Liquid (at right)
Sweet-and-Spicy Barbecue Sauce
 (at right)

1. Rinse the slabs, and pat dry. Remove the thin membrane from back of each slab by slicing into it and pulling it off. (This will make the ribs more tender.) Rub both sides of the slabs with Smoky Dry Rub (about 3 to 4 tablespoons per slab), pressing gently to adhere. Wrap each slab in plastic wrap, and chill 8 to 12 hours. Soak the wood chips in water 30 minutes.

2. Prepare the smoker according to the manufacturer's directions, bringing the internal temperature to 225° to 250°F; maintain temperature 15 to 20 minutes.

3. Drain the wood chips, and place on coals. Place the slabs, meat sides up, on the cooking grate; cover with the smoker lid.

4. Smoke the slabs, maintaining temperature inside the smoker between 225° and 250°F for 3½ hours.

5. Remove the slabs from the smoker. Place each slab, meat side down, on a large piece of heavy-duty aluminum foil. (Foil should be large enough to completely wrap the slab.) Bring up the edges of the foil to contain the liquid. Pour half of the Rib Braising Liquid over each slab. Tightly wrap each slab in foil. Return the slabs, meat sides down, to the smoker. Cook, covered, 1 to 1½ hours, checking for tenderness after 1 hour.

6. Remove the slabs; unwrap and discard the foil. Generously brush both sides of the slabs with Sweet-and-Spicy Barbecue Sauce.

7. Return the slabs to the smoker, and smoke 20 more minutes or until caramelized.

## SMOKY DRY RUB

Stir together ¼ cup firmly packed dark brown sugar, 2 Tbsp. smoked paprika, 1 Tbsp. kosher salt, 2 tsp. garlic salt, 2 tsp. chili powder, 2 tsp. ground black pepper, 1 tsp. onion salt, 1 tsp. celery salt, 1 tsp. ground red pepper, and 1 tsp. ground cumin. Store in an airtight container at room temperature up to 1 month. Makes ½ cup

## RIB BRAISING LIQUID.

Stir together 1 cup apple juice, 1 Tbsp. Smoky Dry Rub, 2 tsp. balsamic vinegar, and 1 minced garlic clove. Refrigerate in an airtight container up to 1 week. Makes 1 cup

## SWEET-AND-SPICY BARBECUE SAUCE

Sauté ½ cup chopped sweet onion, 2 minced garlic cloves, and 1 seeded and minced jalapeño pepper in 1 Tbsp. hot olive oil in a large saucepan over medium-high 4 to 5 minutes or until tender. Stir in 1 (32-oz.) bottle ketchup (such as Heinz), 1 cup firmly packed dark brown sugar, 1 cup apple cider vinegar, ½ cup apple juice, ½ cup honey, 1 Tbsp. Worcestershire sauce, 1 tsp. kosher salt, 1 tsp. freshly ground black pepper, 1 tsp. celery seeds, and ½ tsp. dried crushed red pepper. Bring to a boil, stirring occasionally. Reduce heat to low; simmer, stirring occasionally, 30 minutes. Use immediately, or refrigerate in an airtight container up to 1 month. Makes 5 cups

### FLASHBACK
#### Pork Rib Primer

The near-sacred rituals for turning out tender mouthwatering ribs are as varied as the 'cue-loving regions of the South, and every backyard pitmaster is equally passionate about his preferred cut. Meaty, well-marbled St. Louis-style ribs (aka country-style ribs) are hearty enough to eat with a knife and fork. They're sold both as "slabs" and cut into individual ribs. A Memphis favorite, succulent baby back ribs are lean and tender with lots of meat between their short bones. Larger spareribs are considered by many to be the most flavorful cut, but they're less meaty and less tender than baby backs and take longer to cook.

# Burk's Farm-Raised Catfish Fry

In 1980, Rome, Georgia, reader Bessie Burk won the National Catfish Fry with her buttermilk-marinated, cornmeal-crusted catfish fillets expertly fried two at a time in hot peanut oil. The ultimate cookware for such crisp golden brown perfection? A deep cast-iron Dutch oven that evenly holds the heat and is wide enough to fry without overcrowding.

Serves 6   Hands-on 25 minutes   Total 8 hours 25 minutes

6 (³/₄- to 1-pound) farm-raised
  catfish fillets
1 cup buttermilk
1 tablespoon ground black pepper
1½ teaspoons table salt
2 cups self-rising cornmeal mix
1½ to 2 quarts peanut oil

1. Cut shallow diagonal slices 2 inches apart into thickest portion of the sides of the fish. Place the fish in a large shallow dish.

2. Combine the buttermilk, pepper, and salt; pour over the fish. Cover and chill 8 to 24 hours, turning the fish occasionally.

3. Remove the fish from the marinade; discard the marinade. Dredge the fish in the cornmeal mix, pressing to adhere.

4. Pour the peanut oil to a depth of 1½ inches in a large deep skillet; heat to 370°F. Fry the fish, 2 fillets at a time, in the hot oil 6 minutes or until golden. Drain on a wire rack over paper towels. Serve immediately.

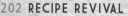

1990s

# FRIED CATFISH WITH PICKLED PEPPERS

Ready to move beyond the predictable catfish and tartar sauce combo? We thought so. Our new condiment of choice: the addictive sweet-and-sour bite of pickled peppers. We used a mix of banana peppers and jalapeños, but feel free to sub in serranos, Fresno, Thai, or poblanos.

Serves 4   Hands-on 20 minutes   Total 20 minutes

1½ cups all-purpose flour
2¼ teaspoons table salt
2 teaspoons freshly ground
  black pepper
4 large eggs
2 tablespoons water

1½ cups plain yellow cornmeal
4 (6-ounce) catfish fillets
Vegetable oil
Pickled mild banana pepper
  rings
Pickled jalapeño pepper rings

Combine the flour and 1 teaspoon each of the salt and pepper in a shallow dish. Whisk together the eggs and 2 tablespoons water in another dish. Combine the cornmeal, 1 teaspoon of the salt, and the remaining 1 teaspoon pepper in a third dish. Sprinkle the catfish with remaining ¼ teaspoon salt. Dredge the fillets, 1 at a time, in the flour mixture, shaking off excess; dip in the egg mixture, and dredge in the cornmeal mixture, shaking off excess. Place on a wire rack in a jelly-roll pan. Pour the oil to a depth of 2 inches in a cast-iron Dutch oven. Heat over medium-high to 350°F. Fry the fillets, 2 at a time, in the hot oil 6 minutes or until done. Drain on a wire rack over paper towels. Serve with the pickled pepper rings.

## FRESH TAKE

### The Light Side of Southern Fried

The challenge: Rethink fried catfish without losing the golden crunch. The two-part solution we discovered? Lightly coating the fillets, rather than the skillet, with vegetable cooking spray allows the oil to evenly cover the surface of the fish. The natural sugars found in paprika caramelize with yellow cornmeal, producing a crisp, golden brown crust.

**Light and Crispy Pan-fried Catfish:** Sprinkle 4 (6-oz.) catfish fillets evenly with ½ tsp. salt and ¼ tsp. pepper. Stir together ⅓ cup yellow cornmeal and 1 Tbsp. paprika in a shallow dish. Dredge fillets in cornmeal mixture; coat lightly with vegetable cooking spray. Cook in a hot nonstick skillet over medium 3 to 4 minutes on each side or until fish begins to flake and is opaque throughout. Serves 4

# Bourbon-Braised Pork Chops

———— ◇ ————

The beauty of this (almost) hands-off method? None of the luscious flavor is lost as the bourbon-infused braising liquid reduces and melds with the natural juices from the citrus and pork.

Serves 4   Hands-on 25 minutes   Total 1 hour 25 minutes

⅓ cup all-purpose flour
½ teaspoon table salt
¼ teaspoon ground black pepper
4 (1-inch-thick) pork chops
1 tablespoon vegetable oil
4 orange slices
2 tablespoons brown sugar

2 tablespoons cornstarch
⅛ teaspoon ground allspice
1 cup hot water
¼ cup orange juice
2 tablespoons bourbon
¼ cup currants or raisins

1. Combine the flour, salt, and pepper; dredge pork chops in flour mixture.

2. Heat the oil in a large skillet over medium; brown the pork chops on both sides. Place an orange slice on top of each chop.

3. Combine the brown sugar, cornstarch, and allspice in a small saucepan; gradually stir in the water. Cook over medium, stirring constantly, until mixture thickens and comes to a boil. Cook 1 minute, stirring constantly. Remove from heat; stir in the orange juice, bourbon, and currants. Spoon over the pork chops. Cover, reduce heat, and simmer 1 hour or until the pork chops are tender.

1980s

# PORK GRILLADES

Quick-cooking pork cutlets topped with a pepper jelly-laced peach sauce offer a summery riff on classic New Orleans grillades braised in a spicy gravy. The oil in the skillet should shimmer before adding the cutlets—the pork should sizzle and hiss as soon as it hits the pan.

Serves 4   Hands-on 1 hour 25 minutes
Total 2 hours 30 minutes, including grits

1 pound (¼-inch-thick) pork loin cutlets
½ teaspoon kosher salt
¼ teaspoon freshly ground black pepper
1 tablespoon olive oil
2 tablespoons finely chopped shallots or onion
1 to 2 teaspoons chopped fresh thyme
¼ cup dry white wine
3 tablespoons red pepper jelly
1 large peach, peeled and chopped
1 medium tomato, diced
Summer Corn Grits (see below)
Garnish: fresh thyme leaves

1. Preheat the oven to 200°F. Sprinkle the pork with the salt and pepper. Cook, in batches, in hot oil in a large skillet over medium-high 3 minutes on each side or until done. Transfer the pork to a wire rack in a jelly-roll pan, and keep warm in a 200°F oven.

2. Add the shallots and thyme to the skillet; sauté 1 minute or until tender. Stir in the wine and pepper jelly until smooth. Stir in the peach and tomato, and cook, stirring often, 2 to 3 minutes or until thoroughly heated. Add salt and pepper to taste. Pour the sauce over the pork, and serve immediately with the grits.

# SUMMER CORN GRITS

1½ cups fresh corn kernels (about 3 ears)
1 garlic clove, minced
2 teaspoons olive oil
4 cups water
1 cup uncooked stone-ground grits
1 teaspoon kosher salt

Sauté the corn kernels and garlic in hot olive oil in a medium saucepan over medium-high 2 to 3 minutes or until the corn is tender. Transfer the mixture to a small bowl. Add the water to the saucepan, and bring to a boil over medium-high. Stir in the uncooked grits and 1 teaspoon kosher salt; return to a boil, stirring occasionally. Cover, reduce heat to low, and cook, stirring occasionally, 30 to 35 minutes or until tender. Stir in the corn mixture, and add salt to taste. Serves 4 to 6

# Coconut Fried Shrimp

Extra-crispy, beer-battered, and deep-fried. Does it get any better? We think not. Okay, maybe. But only because of that addictive spicy-sweet mustard and marmalade dipping sauce that's always served on the side. Small wonder the novelty of coconut shrimp created as many waves inland as it did on the coast.

Makes about 3 dozen   Hands-on 45 minutes
Total 50 minutes, including dip

1 pound unpeeled, medium-
   size raw shrimp
¾ cup all-purpose baking mix
¾ cup beer
1 tablespoon sugar

¾ cup all-purpose flour
3 cups sweetened flaked
   coconut
Vegetable oil
Orange-Lime Dip (see below)

1. Peel the shrimp, leaving the tails intact; devein, if desired.

2. Stir together the baking mix, beer, and sugar until smooth.

3. Coat the shrimp in the flour; dip in the beer mixture, allowing excess to drain. Roll the coated shrimp in the coconut, pressing to adhere.

4. Pour the oil to a depth of 3 inches in a large saucepan; heat to 350°F. Cook the shrimp, a few at a time, 1 to 2 minutes or until golden; drain on paper towels, and serve immediately with Orange-Lime Dip.

Note: We tested with Blue Moon Wheat Ale and Bisquick all-purpose baking mix.

## Orange-Lime Dip

1 (10-ounce) jar orange
   marmalade
3 tablespoons spicy brown
   mustard

2 tablespoons fresh lime juice

Combine all ingredients in a small saucepan; cook over medium, stirring constantly, until marmalade melts. Remove from heat; cool. Store, covered, in refrigerator up to 1 week. Makes 1¼ cups

1990s

---

## FRESH TAKE

### Oven-Fried Coconut Shrimp

Preheat the oven to 425°F. Peel 1½ lb. large raw shrimp, leaving tails on; devein, if desired. Place a wire rack coated with vegetable cooking spray in a 15- x 10-inch jelly-roll pan. Whisk 2 large egg whites just until foamy. Stir together ¼ cup cornstarch and 1 Tbsp. Caribbean jerk seasoning in a shallow dish. Stir together 1 cup sweetened flaked coconut, 1 cup panko (Japanese breadcrumbs), and 1 tsp. paprika in another shallow dish. Dredge shrimp, 1 at a time, in cornstarch mixture; dip in egg whites, and dredge in coconut mixture, pressing gently to adhere. Lightly coat the shrimp on each side with cooking spray; arrange the shrimp on wire rack. Bake at 425°F for 10 to 12 minutes or just until the shrimp turn pink, turning once after 8 minutes.

# SPICY MANGO SHRIMP

A quick and colorful skillet sauté garnished with toasted coconut offers
a light, innovative take on the sweet-hot flavors of the classic coconut
shrimp-and-dip pairing. Served over Coconut-Lime Rice, it makes a
weeknight-easy one-dish meal almost as good as a tropical island retreat—
in an armchair-travel sort of way.

Serves 6 to 8   Hands-on 45 minutes   Total 1 hour 30 minutes, including rice

Coconut-Lime Rice (see below)
1½ pounds peeled, large raw shrimp
3 tablespoons olive oil
1 cup chopped green onions
1 cup diced red bell pepper
2 garlic cloves, minced
1 tablespoon grated fresh ginger
½ to 1 teaspoon dried crushed red pepper

1 cup chopped fresh mango
¼ cup chopped fresh cilantro
¼ cup soy sauce
2 tablespoons fresh lime juice
Topping: toasted sweetened flaked
    coconut
Garnish: fresh cilantro

1. Make the Coconut-Lime Rice; keep warm.

2. Sauté half of the shrimp in 1 tablespoon of the hot oil in a large skillet over medium-
high 2 to 3 minutes or just until the shrimp turn pink. Remove the shrimp from the skillet.
Repeat procedure with 1 tablespoon of the hot oil and the remaining shrimp.

3. Sauté the onions and next 4 ingredients in the remaining 1 tablespoon hot oil over
medium-high 1 minute. Stir in the mango and next 3 ingredients, and cook 1 minute; stir in
the shrimp. Serve over the hot cooked Coconut-Lime Rice; top with the toasted coconut.

# COCONUT-LIME RICE

2 cups water
1 cup light coconut milk
½ teaspoon table salt

1½ cups uncooked jasmine rice
1 teaspoon lime zest
1½ tablespoons fresh lime juice

Bring 2 cups water, coconut milk, and salt to a boil in a saucepan over medium. Stir in
the rice; cover, reduce heat to low, and simmer, stirring occasionally to prevent scorching,
20 to 25 minutes or until liquid is absorbed and the rice is tender. Stir in the lime zest and
juice. Serves 6

# Beef Tenderloin with Five-Onion Confit

This is tenderloin perfection: browned to a crisp char on the outside, baked to a juicy medium-rare within, and guaranteed to impress the most discerning guest. Caramelized in cognac and pan drippings, the five-onion confit with garlic and shallots makes it all the more sublime.

Serves 8   Hands-on 40 minutes   Total 1 hour 20 minutes

1 (3½-pound) beef tenderloin, trimmed
1½ teaspoons table salt
1 teaspoon ground black pepper
Kitchen string
2 tablespoons canola oil
3 tablespoons butter
2 yellow onions, cut into rings
2 large red onions, cut into rings
2 bunches green onions, chopped
2 cups chopped shallots (about 8 large shallots)
5 garlic cloves, minced
½ cup cognac
½ cup beef broth
1 tablespoon chopped fresh thyme
Garnish: fresh thyme

1. Preheat the oven to 400°F. Sprinkle the beef with ½ teaspoon of the salt and ½ teaspoon of the pepper. Tie with the kitchen string at 1-inch intervals. Brown the beef on all sides in hot oil in a heavy roasting pan or an ovenproof Dutch oven. Remove beef, reserving drippings in the pan.

2. Add the butter to hot drippings, and cook over medium-high until melted. Add yellow and red onion rings and remaining 1 teaspoon salt and remaining ½ teaspoon pepper; sauté 5 minutes.

3. Add the green onions, shallots, and garlic, and sauté 10 minutes. Remove from heat. Stir in the cognac and broth; return to heat, and cook over high, stirring constantly, 5 minutes or until liquid evaporates. Return the beef to the pan, placing on top of the onions. Sprinkle with the 1 tablespoon thyme.

4. Bake, covered, at 400°F for 30 to 40 minutes or until a meat thermometer inserted into thickest portion of the beef registers 130° to 135°F (medium-rare).

5. Remove the beef from the pan, reserving the onion mixture in the pan; cover the beef loosely, and let stand 10 minutes.

6. Meanwhile, cook the onion mixture over medium, stirring constantly, 3 to 5 minutes or until the liquid evaporates. Add salt and pepper to taste. Slice the beef, and serve with the onion mixture.

1990s

# MOLASSES GRILLED FLANK STEAK

Dinner parties these days are more casual, and the juxtaposition of flavors is more dynamic. Tenderloin remains timeless, but lesser bistro steaks such as hanger, skirt, and flank are becoming more popular. A marinade, a hot grill, and a quick turn of the tongs are all it takes to bring this latest favorite to the table. Well, that and a little prep for the sassy nectarine and watermelon salsa—worth every slice and dice.

Serves 6 to 8   Hands-on 30 minutes
Total 5 hours 25 minutes, including salsa

¾ cup molasses
⅓ cup soy sauce
¼ cup canola oil
¼ cup fresh lemon juice
2 tablespoons Worcestershire sauce
2 tablespoons grated fresh ginger

3 garlic cloves, minced
1 teaspoon dried crushed red pepper
1 (2-pound) flank steak
Watermelon Salsa (see below)
Garnish: fresh cilantro

1. Place the first 8 ingredients in a 2-gallon zip-top plastic freezer bag; squeeze the bag to combine. Add the steak; seal the bag, and chill 4 to 12 hours. Remove the steak from the marinade, discarding the marinade.

2. Preheat the grill to 400° to 450°F (high). Grill the steak, covered with grill lid, about 9 minutes on each side or to desired degree of doneness. Remove from the grill, and let stand 10 minutes. Cut diagonally across the grain into thin slices. Season with salt and pepper to taste; serve with Watermelon Salsa.

## WATERMELON SALSA

1 cup diced unpeeled nectarine
2 jalapeño peppers, seeded and minced
1 tablespoon sugar
3 tablespoons fresh lime juice
2 teaspoons orange zest

2 teaspoons grated fresh ginger
2 cups seeded and diced watermelon
½ cup chopped fresh cilantro
⅓ cup diced red onion

Stir together the first 6 ingredients in a large bowl; let stand 15 minutes. Add the watermelon and next 2 ingredients, and gently toss to coat. Serve immediately, or cover and chill up to 24 hours. Makes 4 cups

# Fried Chicken
# with Cream Gravy

This is old-school fried chicken at its simplest and best—flawlessly seasoned with a cocoa-hued crust so crisp it shatters with the first bite. The slightly sweet, caramel-like taste of evaporated milk tempered with Worcestershire sauce is the key to the extra-tender juicy meat and richly flavored cream gravy.

Serves 4   Hands-on 50 minutes   Total 9 hours

1 (12-ounce) can evaporated milk
1 tablespoon Worcestershire sauce
1 (2½- to 3-pound) whole chicken, cut up
¾ cup plus 2 tablespoons all-purpose flour
¾ cup plain yellow cornmeal

1¼ teaspoons table salt
Dash of ground black pepper
⅓ to ½ cup vegetable oil
1 tablespoon butter
½ cup water
¼ teaspoon ground black pepper

1. Stir together the evaporated milk and Worcestershire sauce. Place the chicken in a shallow dish, and pour the milk mixture over the chicken. Cover and chill 8 to 24 hours.

2. Stir together ¾ cup of the flour, cornmeal, ¾ teaspoon of the salt, and dash of pepper in a large shallow bowl. Drain chicken, reserving ½ cup milk mixture; dredge chicken in the flour mixture, shaking off the excess. Let stand 5 minutes.

3. Cook the chicken in hot oil in a large, deep cast-iron skillet over medium-high 30 to 35 minutes, turning once. Drain the chicken well on paper towels, reserving 1½ tablespoons drippings in skillet.

4. Add the butter to hot drippings; melt over low. Stir in remaining 2 tablespoons flour, stirring until smooth. Cook, stirring constantly, 1 minute. Gradually add reserved ½ cup milk mixture and ½ cup water; cook over medium, stirring constantly, 1 minute or until the mixture is thickened and bubbly. Stir in ¼ teaspoon pepper and remaining ½ teaspoon salt. Serve the gravy with the chicken.

1980s

# MAN-CATCHING FRIED CHICKEN

Reader Leah Stacey: "I borrowed the recipe name from a former First Lady of Alabama who claimed her fried chicken had such powers."

Serves 6 to 8   Hands-on 1 hour 35 minutes
Total 2 hours 35 minutes

4½ pounds chicken pieces
2 cups buttermilk
1 large egg
Vegetable oil
2 cups self-rising flour
1 tablespoon table salt
½ teaspoon ground red pepper
¼ teaspoon garlic powder
¼ teaspoon ground black pepper
½ cup butter
¼ cup plus 2½ tablespoons honey
½ cup pecans, coarsely chopped
Pickled okra, halved lengthwise

1. Preheat the oven to 200°F. Place the chicken in a 13- x 9-inch baking dish. Whisk together the buttermilk and egg until blended; pour over the chicken. Cover; chill 1 to 8 hours, turning the chicken after 30 minutes.

2. Pour the vegetable oil to a depth of 1½ inches in a Dutch oven; heat over medium to 340°F. Whisk together the flour and the next 4 ingredients in a shallow dish. Dredge the chicken in the flour mixture, shaking off the excess.

3. Fry the chicken in batches in hot oil 20 minutes or until done, turning occasionally. Drain on a wire rack over paper towels in a jelly-roll pan; keep warm in a 200°F oven. Melt the butter in a small saucepan over medium; whisk in the honey until blended. Stir in the pecans; bring the mixture to a boil, whisking often. Reduce the heat to low, and cook, stirring occasionally, 8 to 10 minutes or until thickened. Drizzle over the chicken; serve immediately with pickled okra.

## FRESH TAKE

### The Golden Standard

Southern fried chicken comes to the table pan-fried, deep-fried, Korean-spiced, sweet-tea brined, and Nashville-hot. It's even drizzled with honey and passed around cocktail parties in bite-size waffle cones. And that's just for starters. When our travel editors hit the big cities and back roads in search of the latest fine-feathered trends, they discovered hip new joints with old-school flavor, rural cafes with global inspirations, and fine-dining pantheons that reveled in plating up down-home fried chicken and waffles with an after-sundown vibe. Their high-low conclusions? There's no better pairing than Champagne and fried chicken—regardless of who's cooking.

# Crawfish Étouffée

In Louisiana, crawfish season signals the arrival of spring. This classic Cajun étouffée starts with a simply seasoned roux. Enriched with crawfish fat, the recipe closely resembles the original 20s dish created by Mrs. Charles Hebert at the eponymous Breaux Bridge Hebert Hotel. A longtime Lenten favorite, crawfish étouffée has inspired dozens of variations including Creole versions that add tomatoes. Mrs. Hebert did not.

Serves 12   Hands-on 45 minutes   Total 50 minutes

4 (1-pound) packages peeled crawfish
   tails with fat
1 tablespoon hot sauce
About 1 teaspoon ground red pepper
½ cup vegetable oil
½ cup all-purpose flour
4 celery ribs, chopped
2 large onions, chopped

3 large green bell peppers, chopped
1 bunch green onions with tops, chopped
½ cup water
1 teaspoon table salt
½ teaspoon black pepper
½ cup chopped fresh flat-leaf parsley
¼ cup heavy cream
Hot cooked rice

1. Sprinkle the crawfish with the hot sauce and ¼ to ½ teaspoon of the red pepper.

2. Stir together the oil and flour in a 4-quart Dutch oven. Cook over medium, stirring constantly, 10 to 15 minutes or until the roux is the color of a penny.

3. Stir in the celery and next 3 ingredients; cook, stirring often, 8 minutes or until vegetables are tender. Add the crawfish and ½ cup water; cook over low, stirring occasionally, 15 minutes.

4. Stir in the salt, black pepper, and the remaining ½ teaspoon ground red pepper; simmer 5 minutes. Stir in the parsley and cream. Serve over the rice.

1980s

# CRAWFISH CAKES

Lucky leftovers from crawfish boils inspire a myriad of clever dishes. This spicy Louisiana riff on crab cakes strikes the perfect balance between filler and crawfish. Lightly bound with soft breadcrumbs and mayo, the cakes cook up crisp and golden and tender inside. A creamy sauce cools down the fiery Cajun seasoning. And, might we add, these also make fabulous sliders.

Serves 4 to 6   Hands-on 40 minutes
Total 40 minutes, including cream

1 pound cooked, peeled
   crawfish tails*
3 cups soft breadcrumbs
1/2 cup mayonnaise
1/2 cup chopped green onions
2 garlic cloves, pressed
1 tablespoon lemon juice
1 tablespoon Worcestershire
   sauce
1 teaspoon Cajun seasoning

1/4 teaspoon ground red
   pepper
1 large egg, lightly beaten
3 tablespoons vegetable oil
Cilantro-Lime Cream
   (see below)
Garnishes: fresh cilantro
   leaves, crawfish tails, lemon
   wedges

1. Stir together the crawfish, 2 cups of the breadcrumbs, and next 8 ingredients. Shape into 12 patties. Coat with the remaining 1 cup breadcrumbs.

2. Cook the patties, in batches, in hot oil in a large skillet 3 to 4 minutes on each side or until golden. Drain on paper towels; serve with Cilantro-Lime Cream.

*Substitute 1 pound frozen cooked crawfish tails, thawed and drained, or 1 pound cooked and peeled shrimp for fresh crawfish, if desired.

# CILANTRO-LIME CREAM

1/2 cup sour cream
2 tablespoons chopped fresh
   cilantro

1 tablespoon lime juice
1/4 teaspoon table salt

Stir together all ingredients in a bowl. Makes 1/2 cup

Don't live on the bayou? Chances are you may still find yourself invited to a rowdy spring crawfish boil. If so, you'll definitely want to be armed with the proper know-how for cracking open a Louisiana lobster and getting to the tasty morsels inside the shell. Start by holding the crawfish on both sides of the tail joint, thumbs on one side of the shell and index fingers on the other. With a quick twisting motion, snap the head away from the tail. (Optional step for diehards: Suck the juice from the crawfish head.) Use your thumbs to peel away the shell from the widest part of the tail, pulling back from the center, just as you'd peel a shrimp. Hold the tip of the tail and gently tug out the tender meat.

# Peppered Pot Roast

◇

Pot roast was once synonymous with midday Sunday dinner—a thrifty one-pot meal that could be slipped into the oven before breakfast and left to simmer effortlessly until fall-apart tender and ready to serve when the family returned home from church.

Serves 8 to 10   Hands-on 20 minutes   Total 2 hours 50 minutes

1 teaspoon beef bouillon granules
1 cup water
1 (4- to 5-pound) boneless chuck roast, trimmed
2 teaspoons table salt
1 teaspoon ground black pepper
3 tablespoons vegetable oil
1 cup dry red wine
¼ cup chopped onion

2 tablespoons brown sugar
½ teaspoon garlic salt
¼ teaspoon dried thyme
Dash of ground nutmeg
1½ tablespoons cornstarch
¼ cup water
2 tablespoons cracked peppercorns
¼ cup chopped fresh flat-leaf parsley (optional)

1. Preheat the oven to 350°F. Whisk together the bouillon and 1 cup water.

2. Sprinkle the roast with table salt and black pepper. Brown the roast in hot oil in a Dutch oven 5 minutes on each side. Add the wine, bouillon mixture, onion, sugar, garlic salt, thyme, and nutmeg.

3. Bake, covered, at 350°F for 2½ hours. Remove the roast from the Dutch oven, reserving 2 cups cooking liquid. Thinly slice the roast; place on a serving platter.

4. Whisk together the cornstarch and ¼ cup water. Strain the fat from reserved cooking liquid. Whisk the cornstarch mixture and peppercorns into the liquid.

5. Bring the mixture to a rolling boil over medium-high, whisking constantly. Boil 1 minute. Serve the gravy over the sliced roast. Sprinkle with parsley, if desired.

1980s

# ITALIAN POT ROAST

The inspiration may be Italian but the taste is pure Southern comfort. Countertop cooking is in again, but today's slow cookers are plugged into more sophisticated flavors—dinners worthy of weekend company.

Serves 6   Hands-on 18 minutes   Total 9 hours

1 (8-ounce) package sliced fresh mushrooms

1 large sweet onion, cut in half and sliced

1 (3- to 4-pound) boneless chuck roast, trimmed

1 teaspoon ground black pepper

2 tablespoons olive oil

1 (1-ounce) envelope dry onion soup mix

1 (14-ounce) can beef broth

1 (8-ounce) can tomato sauce

3 tablespoons tomato paste

1 teaspoon dried Italian seasoning

2 tablespoons cornstarch

2 tablespoons water

1. Place the mushrooms and onion in a lightly greased 5- to 6-quart slow cooker.

2. Sprinkle the roast with pepper. Cook the roast in hot oil in a large skillet over medium-high 2 to 3 minutes on each side or until browned.

3. Place the roast on top of the mushrooms and onion in the slow cooker. Sprinkle the onion soup mix over the roast; pour the beef broth and tomato sauce over the roast. Cover and cook on LOW 8 to 10 hours or until the meat shreds easily with a fork.

4. Transfer the roast to a cutting board; cut into large chunks, removing any large pieces of fat. Keep the roast warm.

5. Skim the fat from the juices in the slow cooker; stir in the tomato paste and Italian seasoning. Stir together the cornstarch and 2 tablespoons water in a small bowl until smooth; add to the juices in the slow cooker, stirring until blended. Increase the heat to HIGH. Cover and cook 40 minutes or until the mixture is thickened. Stir in the roast.

# Lemonade Chicken

Frozen lemonade concentrate was introduced in the late 50s and soon
became a favorite ingredient in both sweet and savory dishes. Here it
teams up with bottled soy sauce for a quick-fix basting sauce that amps up
the smoky flavors of charcoal-grilled chicken with a sweet-and-sour Asian
twist. Feel free to sub in an equal amount of frozen limeade or orange
juice concentrate.

Serves 8  Hands-on 15 minutes  Total 40 minutes

½ (12-ounce) can frozen lemonade
   concentrate, thawed (about ¾ cup)
½ cup soy sauce
1 teaspoon seasoned salt

½ teaspoon celery salt
⅛ teaspoon garlic powder
2 (2½- to 3-pound) whole chickens, cut up
Garnish: lemon slices

1. Preheat the grill to 350° to 400°F (medium-high).

2. Stir together first 5 ingredients.

3. Grill the chicken, covered with grill lid, 5 to 7 minutes or until the skin begins to brown.
Brush with the sauce, and grill 20 to 25 more minutes or until done (a meat thermometer
inserted into the thickest portion should register at least 165°F), basting with the sauce and
turning often.

1980s

# SWEET TEA-BRINED CHICKEN

## FLASHBACK

### The French Bread Basket

New Orleans is famous for its French bread—in particular Leidenheimer's crusty loaves. In 1980, we featured a scaled-down version of their century-old recipe so readers could experience the fresh-baked flavor at home. A decade later, artisan breads were trending in neighborhood bakeries and upscale restaurants where they were often paired with olive oil dipping sauces.

**Olive Oil Dipping Sauce:** Stir together 1 cup olive oil; 2 garlic cloves, minced; 2 Tbsp. each of chopped fresh parsley and basil; 2 tsp. each of chopped fresh oregano, rosemary, and freshly ground black pepper; and ½ tsp. each of dried crushed red pepper and table salt. Bonus: The garlic-and-fresh herb mix is equally good stirred into a cup of softened butter.

It's a bold claim, but this just might be the finest, most flavorful chicken to ever come off the Test Kitchen grill. Steeped with fresh citrus and rosemary, the tea creates a brine with remarkable flavor. Molasses-tinged brown sugar lends a subtle sweetness that caramelizes as the chicken slowly cooks over indirect heat. Taste of the South Trivia: The tannins found in tea are natural tenderizers.

Serves 6 to 8   Hands-on 30 minutes
Total 2 hours 35 minutes, plus chill time

4 cups water
2 family-size tea bags
½ cup firmly packed light brown sugar
¼ cup kosher salt
1 small sweet onion, thinly sliced
1 lemon, thinly sliced

3 garlic cloves, halved
2 (6-inch) fresh rosemary sprigs
1 tablespoon freshly cracked black pepper
2 cups ice cubes
1 (3½- to 4-pound) cut-up whole chicken

1. Bring 4 cups water to a boil in a 3-quart heavy saucepan; add the tea bags. Remove from heat; cover and steep 10 minutes.

2. Discard the tea bags. Stir in the sugar and next 6 ingredients, stirring until the sugar dissolves. Cool completely (45 minutes); stir in the ice. (Mixture should be cold before adding the chicken.)

3. Place the tea mixture and chicken in a large zip-top plastic freezer bag; seal. Place the bag in a shallow baking dish, and chill 24 hours. Remove the chicken from the marinade, discarding the marinade; pat the chicken dry with paper towels.

4. Light 1 side of the grill, heating to 300° to 350°F (medium); leave other side unlit. Place the chicken, skin side down, over the unlit side, and grill, covered with grill lid, 20 minutes. Turn the chicken, and grill, covered with a grill lid, 40 to 50 minutes or until done. Transfer the chicken, skin side down, to lit side of the grill, and grill 2 to 3 more minutes or until the skin is crispy. Let stand 5 minutes before serving.

# King Ranch Chicken

Texans claim bragging rights for King Ranch Chicken, but its tortilla-layered origins are unclear. The legendary King Ranch politely declines ownership. Whether it's a riff on chilaquiles or an indulgent chile con queso twist on chicken à la king, one thing's for certain—it's one of the few casseroles whose mainstream popularity transcends both age and gender.

Serves 6   Hands-on 15 minutes   Total 1 hour 35 minutes

1 (3-pound) whole chicken, cut up
1 medium onion, sliced
1 celery rib, cut into 3-inch pieces
2½ teaspoons table salt
1 (10¾-ounce) can cream of
    chicken soup

1 (10-ounce) can diced tomatoes with
    green chiles
8 (6-inch) fajita-size flour tortillas, cut
    into 2-inch strips
2 cups (8 ounces) grated sharp Cheddar
    cheese

1. Preheat the oven to 350°F. Lightly grease a 2-quart baking dish. Place the chicken, onion, celery, and salt in a large saucepan with water to cover. Bring to a boil; cover, reduce heat to medium, and cook 30 minutes or until the chicken is done. Remove the chicken, reserving the broth. Discard the skin and bones, and cut the chicken into cubes.

2. Pour 1 cup reserved broth through a fine wire-mesh strainer into a saucepan, discarding solids. Stir in the cream of chicken soup and tomatoes. (Discard remaining broth.)

3. Cook the broth mixture over medium-high until thoroughly heated.

4. Layer equal amounts of the tortilla strips, cubed chicken, broth mixture, and Cheddar cheese in the prepared baking dish, repeating the layers until all ingredients are used.

5. Bake at 350°F for 40 minutes.

1960s

# KING RANCH CHICKEN MAC & CHEESE

This magical melding of King Ranch Chicken and creamy mac and cheese is guaranteed to satisfy cravings when seasonal temperatures drop. Twists of pasta stand in for corn tortillas with tasty results.

Serves 6   Hands-on 20 minutes   Total 45 minutes

½ (16-ounce) package cellentani pasta

2 tablespoons butter

1 medium onion, diced

1 green bell pepper, diced

1 (10-ounce) can diced tomatoes and green chiles

1 (8-ounce) package pasteurized prepared cheese product, cubed

3 cups chopped cooked chicken

1 (10¾-ounce) can cream of chicken soup

½ cup sour cream

1 teaspoon chili powder

½ teaspoon ground cumin

1½ cups (6 ounces) shredded Cheddar cheese

1. Preheat the oven to 350°F. Lightly grease a 10-inch cast-iron skillet or an 11- x 7-inch baking dish. Prepare the pasta according to package directions.

2. Meanwhile, melt the butter in a large Dutch oven over medium-high. Add the onion and bell pepper, and sauté 5 minutes or until tender. Stir in the tomatoes and green chiles and prepared cheese product; cook, stirring constantly, 2 minutes or until cheese melts. Stir in the chicken, next 4 ingredients, and hot cooked pasta until blended. Spoon the mixture into prepared skillet or baking dish; sprinkle with the shredded Cheddar cheese.

3. Bake at 350°F for 25 to 30 minutes or until bubbly.

# Chicken with White BBQ Sauce

The roots of Alabama's legendary white barbecue sauce stretch back to 1925 and a smoking pit that Big Bob Gibson dug beneath a sycamore tree in his backyard. Big Bob's must-try specialty? Hickory-smoked chicken with a tangy white barbecue sauce.

Serves 4   Hands-on 15 minutes
Total 40 minutes, plus 24 hours for marinating

2 cups mayonnaise
⅓ cup apple cider vinegar
¼ cup lemon juice
2 tablespoons sugar
2 tablespoons cracked black pepper

2 tablespoons white wine Worcestershire sauce
1 (2½- to 3-pound) whole chicken, quartered

1. Whisk together the first 6 ingredients in a small bowl. Reserve 1 cup sauce; cover and chill remaining sauce.

2. Place the chicken in a shallow dish. Pour reserved 1 cup sauce over chicken, turning to coat. Cover and chill 24 hours, turning chicken once.

3. Preheat the grill to 300° to 350°F (medium). Remove the chicken from the marinade, discarding the marinade. Grill the chicken, covered with grill lid, 25 to 30 minutes or until done (a meat thermometer inserted into the thickest portion should register at least 165°F), turning the chicken occasionally. Serve the chicken with remaining sauce.

1990s

# GRILLED CHICKEN THIGHS

Tender, juicy chicken thighs rule the roost—especially grilled, dry-rubbed, perfectly charred, and dripping with sauce. White 'cue sauce purists insist there are only four ingredients: mayo, vinegar, salt, and black pepper. Others defy tradition with equally delicious results.

Serves 5  Hands-on 35 minutes  Total 4 hours 35 minutes, including the sauce

1 tablespoon dried thyme
1 tablespoon dried oregano
1 tablespoon ground cumin
1 tablespoon paprika
1 teaspoon onion powder

1/2 teaspoon table salt
1/2 teaspoon ground black pepper
10 skin-on, bone-in chicken thighs
    (about 3 pounds)
White Barbecue Sauce (see below)

1. Combine the first 7 ingredients until blended. Rinse the chicken, and pat dry; rub the seasoning mixture over the chicken. Place the chicken in a zip-top plastic freezer bag. Seal and chill 4 hours.

2. Preheat the grill to 350° to 400°F (medium-high). Remove the chicken from the bag; discard marinade.

3. Grill the chicken, covered with grill lid, 8 to 10 minutes on each side or until a meat thermometer inserted into thickest portion registers 180°F. Serve with the White Barbecue Sauce.

## WHITE BARBECUE SAUCE

1 1/2 cups mayonnaise
1/4 cup white wine vinegar
1 garlic clove, minced
1 tablespoon coarse ground black pepper
1 tablespoon spicy brown mustard

1 teaspoon sugar
1 teaspoon table salt
2 teaspoons prepared
    horseradish

Stir together the mayonnaise, vinegar, minced garlic, pepper, mustard, sugar, salt, and horseradish until blended. Cover and chill 2 to 4 hours. Store, refrigerated, in an airtight container up to 1 week. Makes 1 3/4 cups

# 5
# SIDEBOARD

As passionate as we are about smoky barbecue
and crisp fried chicken, it's what's served alongside
the main event that always steals the show.

# 2000s Potluck

Celebrate summer's bounty with a farm-to-table feast where everyone feels at home. Smoky sweet-tea grilled chicken anchors a potluck supper of harvest-fresh favorites just made for sharing.

# A Mess O' Peas

Coaxed to tenderness in a pork-laced broth, field peas shine in this heirloom recipe from Peggy Smith, charter member of The Southern Living Test Kitchen. The secret is a wisp of vinegar from the pickled hot peppers her grandmother added to the pot.

Serves 10 to 12   Hands-on 10 minutes   Total 1 hour 5 minutes

2 quarts water
1 (8- to 10-ounce) smoked ham hock
6 cups shelled fresh field peas
4 to 6 hot peppers in vinegar, drained

1 large garlic clove, smashed and peeled
1 teaspoon sugar
1½ teaspoons table salt
1 teaspoon ground black pepper

1. Bring 2 quarts water and the ham hock to a boil in a large Dutch oven over medium-high. Reduce heat to low, and simmer 30 minutes.

2. Stir in the peas and remaining ingredients; cover and simmer 25 to 30 minutes or until peas are done. Serve with a slotted spoon.

1990s

# FIELD PEAS, OKRA, AND ANDOUILLE SAUSAGE

Mississippi cookbook author Whitney Miller uses spicy andouille sausage and baby okra to transform a medley of Southern field peas into a garden-fresh gumbo of Cajun flavor. It's a perfect companion for Grilled Chicken Thighs with White Barbecue Sauce (page 233).

Serves 8 to 10   Hands-on 5 minutes   Total 35 minutes

½ pound andouille sausage, cut into ¼-inch-thick slices

6 cups assorted fresh or frozen field peas

½ pound small, fresh whole okra

12 fresh basil leaves, torn

1. Sauté the andouille in a Dutch oven over medium 5 minutes or until lightly browned.

2. Add the field peas and water to cover 1 inch above peas; bring to a boil. Cover, reduce heat to medium-low; simmer 20 minutes. Add the okra; cover and simmer 5 minutes or until the okra and peas are tender. Stir in the basil, and add salt and pepper to taste. Transfer to a serving dish; serve with a slotted spoon.

## FLASHBACK
### Field Pea Primer

Southern farmers' markets in midsummer brim with field pea varieties, each with a taste and texture as unique as their markings. Plump crowders crowd so closely inside the pod that the peas begin to square off. Brown crowders and speckled Whipporwills are revered for their meaty flavor and rich "pot likker." Pink-eyed peas boast a colorful purple hull and a less earthy taste than their black-eyed cousins. Lady peas, prized for their sweet flavor, are considered the doyenne of cream cultivars. They remain pale green or white when cooked and, like butter peas, yield a bright "potlikker."

# Tee's Corn Pudding

Perhaps a more delicious recipe for corn pudding exists somewhere, but we seriously doubt it. A perfect ratio of sweet summer corn to creamy custard puts this at the top of our side-dish list for over 20 years. Who is this marvelous Tee? The maternal grandmother of Kathy Cary, Louisville chef and owner of Lilly's Bistro, who shared her family recipes in "A Bluegrass Christmas to Remember." Also featured in that holiday story was a spectacular triple-layer lemon-coconut cake that was so popular with readers it inspired the now decades-long tradition of white cakes on our December covers.

Serves 10 to 12   Hands-on 20 minutes   Total 1 hour 5 minutes

12 to 13 ears fresh corn, husks removed
$\frac{1}{4}$ cup sugar
3 tablespoons all-purpose flour
2 teaspoons baking powder
1$\frac{1}{2}$ teaspoons table salt
6 large eggs
2 cups whipping cream
$\frac{1}{2}$ cup butter, melted

1. Preheat the oven to 350°F. Cut the kernels from the cobs into a large bowl (about 7 cups). Scrape the milk and the remaining pulp from the cobs into the bowl; discard the cobs.

2. Combine the sugar and the next 3 ingredients. Whisk together the eggs, whipping cream, and butter in a large bowl. Gradually add the sugar mixture to the egg mixture, whisking until smooth; stir in the corn. Pour into a lightly greased 13- x 9-inch baking dish.

3. Bake at 350°F for 40 to 45 minutes or until set. Let stand 5 minutes.

1990s

# FRESH CORN-ASIAGO BREAD PUDDING

Savory bread puddings are stealing the spotlight on Southern sideboards. Seasonally inspired by fresh farmers' market finds, they have the same custard-like richness as their whiskey-sauced cousins. Here, aged Asiago imparts a salty umami depth—a perfect counterpoint to fresh corn and cream's milky sweetness.

Serves 12 Hands-on 5 minutes
Total 1 hour 20 minutes, including stand time

1½ cups milk
1 cup whipping cream
3 large eggs
½ teaspoon table salt
½ teaspoon freshly ground
   black pepper

1 (12-ounce) French bread loaf,
   cut into 1-inch cubes (8 cups)
4 cups fresh corn kernels
1½ cups (6 ounces) shredded
   Asiago cheese

1. Whisk together the first 5 ingredients in a large bowl; add the bread, tossing to coat. Let stand 30 minutes.

2. Preheat the oven to 375°F. Stir the corn and Asiago cheese into the bread mixture; spoon into a well-buttered 13- x 9-inch baking dish. Bake at 375°F for 45 minutes or until set and golden brown.

# Yellow Squash Casserole

From foolproof soufflés feathered with finely grated breadcrumbs to wonderfully rich gratins, squash casseroles are a summer ritual. This still-popular 70s treasure is doubled down on the herb-seasoned stuffing mix, creating a summery riff on cornbread dressing.

Serves 10 to 12   Hands-on 20 minutes   Total 1 hour

2 ⅔ to 3 pounds yellow squash, sliced
1 (10 ¾-ounce) can cream of chicken soup
1 (8-ounce) container sour cream
1 (5-ounce) can water chestnuts, drained
    and sliced
1 (2-ounce) jar pimiento, drained
2 cups finely chopped onions

½ cup butter, melted
1 teaspoon table salt
½ teaspoon ground black pepper
1 (8-ounce) package herb-seasoned
    stuffing mix
Garnish: fresh curly-leaf parsley sprigs

1. Preheat the oven to 350°F. Cook the squash in boiling water to cover in a saucepan 10 minutes or until tender; drain and return to pan, reserving 1½ cups liquid. Mash squash.

2. Stir together the reserved 1½ cups liquid from the squash, soup, and next 7 ingredients in a large bowl. Stir in all but ½ cup of the stuffing mix until blended; stir in the squash.

3. Pour the mixture into a lightly greased 13- x 9-inch baking dish. Crush remaining stuffing mix in a zip-top plastic freezer bag. Sprinkle over the squash mixture in the baking dish.

4. Bake at 350°F for 30 minutes or until golden brown and set.

# ZUCCHINI, SQUASH, AND CORN CASSEROLE

Our latest (and perhaps best) contribution to the summer casserole hall of fame takes full advantage of seasonal abundance, layering the flavors and textures of sautéed zucchini and yellow squash with sweet corn and onions. Soft white breadcrumbs double as a barely there binder and buttery crumb topping.

Serves 8 to 10   Hands-on 40 minutes   Total 1 hour 40 minutes

1 1/2 pounds yellow squash, cut into 1/4-inch-thick slices
1 1/2 pounds zucchini, cut into 1/4-inch-thick slices
1/4 cup butter
2 cups diced sweet onion
2 garlic cloves, minced
3 cups fresh corn kernels
1 1/2 cups (6 ounces) freshly shredded white Cheddar cheese
1/2 cup sour cream
1/2 cup mayonnaise
2 large eggs, lightly beaten
2 teaspoons freshly ground black pepper
1 teaspoon table salt
1 1/2 cups soft, fresh breadcrumbs
1 cup freshly grated Asiago cheese, divided
Garnish: fresh flat-leaf parsley leaves

1. Preheat the oven to 350°F. Bring the first 2 ingredients and water to cover to a boil in a Dutch oven over medium-high, and boil 5 minutes or until crisp-tender. Drain; gently press between paper towels.

2. Melt 2 tablespoons of the butter in a skillet over medium-high; add onion, and sauté 10 minutes or until tender. Add the garlic, and sauté 2 minutes.

3. Stir together the squash, onion mixture, corn, next 6 ingredients, and 1/2 cup each of the breadcrumbs and the Asiago cheese just until blended. Spoon the mixture into a lightly greased 13- x 9-inch baking dish.

4. Melt the remaining 2 tablespoons butter. Stir in remaining 1 cup breadcrumbs and 1/2 cup Asiago cheese. Sprinkle over the casserole.

5. Bake at 350°F for 45 to 50 minutes or until golden brown and set. Let stand 15 minutes before serving.

## FLASHBACK
### Panning for Gold

The makings of squash casserole also came to the summer table in a number of deep-fried guises—from Cheddar-rich fritters to fat croquettes with béchamel bindings and cracker-crumb coatings. Not to be forgotten is the delectable hush-puppy twist that stole the fish fry show.

**Squash Puppies:**
Combine 3/4 cup self-rising cornmeal, 1/4 cup all-purpose flour, 1/2 tsp. salt, 1/4 tsp. black pepper, and 1/8 tsp. ground red pepper in a large bowl. Stir together 6 cooked and mashed yellow squash; 1/2 cup buttermilk; 1 small minced onion; and 1 large egg; add to the cornmeal mixture. Stir to blend. Heat 1/2 inch vegetable oil in a deep cast-iron skillet to 350°F. Drop batter by tablespoonfuls, in batches, into oil; fry 3 minutes on each side or until golden. Drain on paper towels; sprinkle evenly with 1/2 tsp. table salt.

# Broccoli Salad

◇

The 80s broccoli salad boom wasn't about trendy hard-to-find ingredients but rather familiar flavors tossed together in a novel coleslaw sort of way, all sassed up with a sweet-tart spark of creamy mayo dressing. Taste of the South Trivia: Broccoli may seem like a relative newcomer to the roster of Southern sides, but it was growing in Thomas Jefferson's Monticello garden in 1767. Recipes featuring steamed broccoli can be found in many early cookbooks, including Mary Randolph's 1824 *The Virginia Housewife*.

Makes 6 cups  Hands-on 20 minutes  Total 2 hours 20 minutes

4 medium-size heads broccoli (about 2¼ pounds)
10 bacon slices, cooked and crumbled
5 green onions, sliced
½ cup raisins
1 cup mayonnaise
2 tablespoons sugar
2 tablespoons red wine vinegar

1. Trim the stems from the broccoli; cut the florets into bite-sized pieces. Place in a large bowl. Add the bacon, green onions, and raisins; toss.

2. Stir together the mayonnaise and remaining ingredients until well blended. Add to the broccoli mixture, and toss gently. Cover and chill 2 to 3 hours.

1980s

# BROCCOLI, GRAPE, AND PASTA SALAD

What's better than broccoli salad? Broccoli and pasta salad, of course. We kept everything we love about the classic but traded the raisins for seedless red grapes. We guarantee you'll go back for seconds. And thirds.

Serves 6 to 8   Hands-on 25 minutes
Total 3 hours 30 minutes, including chill time

1 cup chopped pecans
½ (16-ounce) package farfalle (bow-tie) pasta
1 pound fresh broccoli
1 cup mayonnaise
⅓ cup sugar
⅓ cup diced red onion
⅓ cup red wine vinegar
1 teaspoon table salt
2 cups seedless red grapes, halved
8 cooked bacon slices, crumbled

1. Preheat the oven to 350°F. Toast the pecans on a baking sheet 7 minutes, stirring halfway through.

2. Prepare the pasta according to package directions.

3. Meanwhile, cut the broccoli florets from the stems, and separate the florets into small pieces using the tip of a paring knife. Peel away the tough outer layer of the stems, and finely chop the stems.

4. Whisk together the mayonnaise and next 4 ingredients in a bowl. Add the broccoli, hot cooked pasta, and grapes; stir to coat. Cover and chill 3 hours. Stir the bacon and pecans into the salad just before serving.

## FRESH TAKE

### Choosing Sides

Find bagged broccoli slaw in the produce section, but you can just as easily toss together this homemade twist made with the sweet crunch of shredded napa cabbage. Why? Because it's so tasty.

**Broccoli Slaw with Candied Pecans:** Cut 1 lb. broccoli florets from stems; separate florets into small pieces using a paring knife. Peel away tough outer layer of stems; finely chop stems. Whisk together 1 cup mayonnaise, ½ cup thinly sliced green onions, ⅓ cup sugar, ⅓ cup red wine vinegar, 1 tsp. table salt, 1 tsp. lemon zest, and ¼ tsp. ground red pepper in a large bowl; add ½ small head napa cabbage, thinly sliced; ½ cup golden raisins; and broccoli, and stir to coat. Cover and chill 1 hour. Stir in 1 (3.5-oz.) package roasted glazed pecan pieces just before serving.

# Macaroni and Cheese

For a brief and shining moment in the eighties, sour cream and cottage cheese were the brilliant stir-ins—amping up the creamy comforts of classic Cheddar-and-elbow macaroni blends. This deluxe twist, spiked with smoky bits of diced ham and topped with buttered breadcrumbs, appeared in our stellar collection of five-star recipes.

Serves 6   Hands-on 20 minutes   Total 50 minutes

1 (8-ounce) package elbow macaroni
2 cups (8 ounces) shredded sharp
   Cheddar cheese
2 cups cottage cheese
1 (8-ounce) container sour cream
1 cup diced cooked ham
2 tablespoons minced onion
1 large egg, lightly beaten

¼ teaspoon kosher salt
¼ teaspoon ground black pepper
Vegetable cooking spray
1 cup soft, fresh breadcrumbs
2 tablespoons butter, melted
¼ teaspoon paprika
Garnishes: sliced cherry tomatoes, fresh
   parsley sprigs

1. Preheat the oven to 350°F. Prepare the macaroni according to package directions.

2. Gently stir together the macaroni, Cheddar cheese, and next 7 ingredients in a large bowl. Spoon into a 2-quart baking dish coated with cooking spray.

3. Stir together the breadcrumbs, butter, and paprika in a small bowl. Sprinkle the breadcrumb mixture diagonally across the top of the casserole, forming stripes.

4. Bake at 350°F for 30 to 35 minutes or until golden brown.

1980s

# HUGH'S SOUTHERN MAC AND CHEESE

Atlanta Chef Hugh Acheson swaps elbow macaroni for cavatappi pasta—a tubular twist that captures the creamy goodness of béchamel, bacon, and leeks bound in a gooey mix of aged Cheddar and Gruyère. Baking in a cast-iron skillet seriously ups the crispy edge factor.

Serves 4 to 6   Hands-on 45 minutes   Total 1 hour 35 minutes

¼ pound thick bacon slices, diced (about 4 slices)
2 medium leeks, cut into ½-inch rounds (about 1 cup)
⅓ (16-ounce) package uncooked cavatappi pasta
1½ tablespoons butter
1½ tablespoons all-purpose flour
1 cup milk, warmed
½ teaspoon dry mustard
¼ teaspoon table salt

¼ teaspoon ground black pepper
Pinch of ground red pepper
1 cup (4 ounces) freshly grated 2-year-old aged Cheddar cheese
1 large egg yolk
½ cup freshly grated Gruyère cheese
2 tablespoons heavy cream
¼ cup toasted soft, fresh breadcrumbs

1. Preheat the oven to 375°F. Cook the bacon in a skillet over medium, stirring, 7 minutes or until crisp. Remove and drain on paper towels. Reserve the drippings for another use.

2. Cook the leeks in boiling water in a Dutch oven 5 minutes. Remove with a slotted spoon, reserving water. Plunge the leeks into ice water to stop the cooking process; drain.

3. Add the pasta to boiling water. Cook al dente, 10 minutes. Drain.

4. Melt the butter in a large skillet over medium. Reduce heat to medium-low, and whisk in flour until smooth. Cook, whisking constantly, 2 minutes or until golden brown. Slowly whisk in the milk. Cook, whisking constantly, 3 minutes or until thickened. Whisk in the dry mustard, next 3 ingredients, and ½ cup of the Cheddar cheese, stirring until melted. Remove from heat. Season with salt and pepper to taste.

5. Gently stir together the pasta, cheese sauce, half each of the cooked bacon and leeks, and egg yolk. Stir in the Gruyère cheese and remaining ½ cup Cheddar cheese. Spoon the pasta mixture into a buttered 8-inch cast-iron skillet, and sprinkle with the remaining bacon and leeks. Drizzle with the cream; sprinkle with the breadcrumbs.

6. Bake at 375°F for 35 minutes or until golden and bubbly. Let stand 15 minutes before serving.

# Deviled Potato Salad

The marvelous thing about potato salad is the fact that it's endlessly and brilliantly adaptable to one's personal preferences—which is why every good cook south of the Mason-Dixon Line has a special recipe. You may be reluctant to try a new twist, but honestly, what's not to love about a potato salad that throws the makings of deviled eggs into the mix?

Serves 6 to 8   Hands-on 35 minutes   Total 1 hour 50 minutes

6 medium-size baking potatoes, peeled
   and cubed (4½ cups)
8 hard-cooked eggs, peeled
2½ tablespoons yellow mustard
2 tablespoons apple cider vinegar
1 tablespoon prepared horseradish
1 cup mayonnaise
1 cup sour cream

½ teaspoon celery salt
1 teaspoon table salt
1 cup chopped celery
¼ cup chopped onion
2 tablespoons chopped green bell pepper
2 tablespoons chopped pimiento
Garnishes: tomato wedges, cucumber
   slices

**1.** Bring the potatoes and salted water to cover to a boil in a Dutch oven over medium-high, and cook 15 to 20 minutes or until tender. Drain.

**2.** Slice the eggs in half lengthwise; carefully remove the yolks. Mash the yolks with the mustard, vinegar, and horseradish in a bowl. Stir in the mayonnaise, sour cream, celery salt, and table salt.

**3.** Chop the egg whites. Gently stir together the egg whites, potatoes, celery, onion, bell pepper, and pimiento. Fold in the egg yolk mixture. Cover and chill 1 hour.

1960s

# BIG DADDY'S BLUE CHEESE AND BACON POTATO SALAD

The notion of firing up the grill for side dishes pushes the potato salad envelope into a whole new territory of ridiculously delicious possibilities. Drizzled with olive oil and wrapped in a foil packet, thin-skinned baby red potatoes take on a subtle note of smoky flavor plus get extra-crispy and brown at the edges. It's best served warm—tossing in the blue cheese and bacon table side with a certain amount of Caesar-salad showmanship.

*Serves 6   Hands-on 30 minutes   Total 35 minutes*

3 pounds baby red potatoes, cut in half
2 tablespoons olive oil
1 teaspoon table salt
1 teaspoon freshly ground black pepper
1 cup mayonnaise
¼ cup chopped fresh parsley
¼ cup white balsamic vinegar*

2 teaspoons sugar
2 teaspoons Dijon mustard
1 cup thinly sliced red onion
4 ounces crumbled blue cheese
6 bacon slices, cooked and crumbled
Garnish: fresh flat-leaf parsley leaves

1. Preheat the grill to 350° to 400°F (medium-high). Place the potatoes in a single layer in the center of a large piece of heavy-duty aluminum foil. Drizzle with the olive oil; sprinkle with the salt and pepper. Bring up the foil sides over the potatoes; double fold the top and side edges to seal, making 1 large packet.

2. Grill the potatoes, in the foil packet, covered with grill lid, 15 minutes on each side. Remove the packet from grill. Carefully open the packet, using tongs, and let potatoes cool 5 minutes.

3. Whisk together the mayonnaise and next 4 ingredients in a large bowl; add the potatoes, tossing gently to coat. Stir in the onion, blue cheese, and bacon.

*Balsamic vinegar may be substituted but will darken the color of the dressing.

## FLASHBACK
### Family Feuds

One of the tasting table's most impassioned debates was not about barbecue or football but Southern potato salad. We argued about the type of potato, peeled versus unpeeled, the brand of mayo, and spicy brown versus yellow mustard. Sweet pickle, dill pickle, or no pickle? Toss the warm potatoes with a vinaigrette? The debate was heated but never was settled to anyone's full satisfaction. In the end, we decided on Fipps Family Potato Salad—the salt and pepper basics made with russets and grated hard-boiled egg, bound simply but deliciously with the perfect amount of mayo and spicy brown mustard. It was a recipe that just happened to be very similar to then Editor in Chief John Floyd's mother's recipe. Because all potato salads have their virtues, we also offered a slew of optional stir-ins.

# Favorite Tomato Aspic

Once upon a time, tomato aspics were the brilliant red centerpieces of luncheon buffets. They were peppered with pimiento-stuffed olives or crisp bits of celery, chilled in ring-shaped molds, turned out onto lettuce-lined trays, and filled with the hostess's signature blend of chicken or shrimp salad.

Serves 8 to 10   Hands-on 30 minutes
Total 6 hours 35 minutes, including chill time

2 envelopes unflavored gelatin (2 tablespoons)
¼ cup cold water
½ cup boiling water
4 cups tomato juice
1 tablespoon minced onion
1 teaspoon sugar
1 teaspoon table salt
1 teaspoon seasoned salt

1 teaspoon Worcestershire sauce
½ teaspoon celery seeds (or several minced celery tops)
2 bay leaves
2 whole cloves
3 tablespoons fresh lemon juice
Garnish: fresh parsley

1. Sprinkle the gelatin over the cold water in a bowl; let stand 5 minutes. Whisk in the boiling water until the gelatin is dissolved.

2. Stir together the tomato juice and next 8 ingredients in a large saucepan; bring to a boil over medium-high. Reduce heat, and simmer, stirring occasionally, 15 minutes. Pour through a wire-mesh strainer into a bowl; stir in the lemon juice and gelatin.

3. Pour into a 10-inch ring mold coated with cooking spray or 6 individual molds; chill 6 hours or until set.

1970s

## SOUTHERN HOSPITALITY

### Ashtray Tip

Yes, we said it! In *The Southern Living Party Cookbook* from the 70s, we offered a clever tip that exemplifies the times: "If you own large decorative ashtrays, which aren't easily identifiable as ashtrays, before guests come, take a puff or two of a cigarette, extinguish it and leave it on the tray."

Of course, we assumed every consummate host or hostess had a pack of cigarettes lying around, smoker or not, and wouldn't mind lighting up for the sake of party guests.

# HEIRLOOM
# TOMATO SALAD

It's all about fresh. Tomato aspics are relegated to the back of the recipe box while the genius pairing of heirloom tomatoes with a tangy-sweet field pea salsa captures the best flavors of summer on one cool platter. Try it with a variety of colorful heirlooms—Pink Brandywine and Cherokee Purple for their rich, meaty flavor; sweet and fruity Sun Gold or Snow White cherry tomatoes; and a more tart variety such as Green Zebra.

Serves 8   Hands-on 15 minutes   Total 50 minutes

4 pounds assorted heirloom tomatoes
2 small Kirby cucumbers, sliced
1 small red onion, sliced

Lady Pea Salsa (see below)
Fresh basil leaves
Grilled shrimp (optional)

Cut the tomatoes into wedges or in half, depending on size. Gently toss the tomatoes with the cucumbers and onion. Top with the Lady Pea Salsa and the basil. Add the grilled shrimp, if desired, for a heartier salad.

# LADY PEA SALSA

1 cup diced unpeeled nectarine
2 jalapeño peppers, seeded and minced
1 tablespoon sugar
3 tablespoons fresh lime juice
2 teaspoons orange zest

2 teaspoons grated fresh ginger
2 cups cooked fresh lady peas
$\frac{1}{2}$ cup chopped fresh cilantro
$\frac{1}{3}$ cup diced red onion

Stir together the first 6 ingredients in a large bowl; let stand 15 minutes. Add the peas and next 2 ingredients, and gently toss to coat. Serve immediately, or cover and chill up to 24 hours. Makes 4 cups

# Favorite Three-Bean Salad

Post-war canned convenience reached a crescendo with marinated bean salads. Ours featured green beans, yellow wax beans, and kidney beans, along with the crunch of diced bell pepper and onion. Later five-bean salads upped the pantry ante with the addition of garbanzos and pinto beans.

Serves 6 to 8   Hands-on 15 minutes   Total 8 hours 15 minutes, including chill time

1 (14.5-ounce) can green beans, drained
1 (14.5-ounce) can wax beans, drained
1 (15.5-ounce) can kidney beans, drained and rinsed
1 medium-size green bell pepper, sliced
1 medium onion, sliced

¾ cup sugar
½ cup canola oil
½ cup apple cider vinegar
1½ teaspoons table salt
½ teaspoon ground black pepper

1. Gently stir together the first 5 ingredients.

2. Whisk together the sugar and next 4 ingredients; pour over the vegetables, stirring gently until well blended. Cover and chill 8 to 24 hours.

1960s

# PEAR AND GREEN BEAN SALAD

Canned green beans surrender to the seductive snap of tender-crisp haricots verts paired with fresh fruit and tender baby lettuces. Kentucky Chef Ouita Michel's bourbon-spiked sorghum vinaigrette ties it all together with the same sweet-and-tangy vibe of retro bean salads but in a new way.

Serves 8    Hands-on 15 minutes    Total 30 minutes, including vinaigrette

8 ounces haricots verts (French green beans), trimmed
1 (5-ounce) package gourmet mixed salad greens
2 red Bartlett pears, cut into thin strips
½ small red onion, sliced
1 (4-ounce) package crumbled Gorgonzola cheese
1 cup toasted pecans
Sorghum Vinaigrette (see below)

Cook the beans in boiling salted water to cover 3 to 4 minutes or until crisp-tender; drain. Plunge the beans into ice water to stop the cooking process; drain. Toss together the salad greens, next 4 ingredients, and beans. Serve with the Sorghum Vinaigrette.

## SORGHUM VINAIGRETTE

½ cup sorghum syrup
½ cup malt or apple cider vinegar
3 tablespoons bourbon
2 teaspoons grated onion
1 teaspoon table salt
1 teaspoon freshly ground black pepper
½ teaspoon hot sauce
1 cup olive oil

Whisk together the first 7 ingredients until blended. Add the oil in a slow, steady stream, whisking until smooth. Makes 2 cups

# Angel Corn Sticks

Inspired by the angel biscuit craze of the 70s, we gave classic buttermilk cornbread batter a featherlight lift simply by stirring a packet of yeast into the batter. Sizzling hot cast-iron corn stick pans deliver a crisp, nutty, all-around crust with a tender moist crumb inside.

Makes 2 dozen   Hands-on 15 minutes   Total 30 minutes

1½ cups plain yellow cornmeal
1 cup all-purpose flour
1 (¼-ounce) envelope active dry yeast
1 tablespoon sugar
1½ teaspoons baking powder

1 teaspoon table salt
½ teaspoon baking soda
2 large eggs, beaten
2 cups buttermilk
½ cup vegetable oil

1. Preheat the oven to 450°F. Stir together the first 7 ingredients in a large bowl. Combine the eggs, buttermilk, and oil; add to the dry ingredients, stirring until the batter is smooth. Spoon the batter into 2 well-greased cast-iron corn-stick pans, filling half full.

2. Bake at 450°F for 12 to 15 minutes or until golden brown.

1980s

# CORNBREAD MADELEINES

Is it possible to trump the cast-iron crispness of a corn stick? These shell-shaped madeleines are every bit the exquisite pleasure of Proust's sweet remembrances. Tinged with sweetness, they make a welcome addition to the Southern breadbasket. Shiny madeleine pans yield the best results.

Makes 4 dozen   Hands-on 10 minutes   Total 1 hour 14 minutes

2 cups self-rising white
   cornmeal mix
½ cup all-purpose flour
¼ cup sugar

2 cups buttermilk
½ cup butter, melted
2 large eggs, lightly beaten

1. Preheat the oven to 400°F. Whisk together the cornmeal mix, flour, and sugar in a large bowl. Combine the buttermilk, butter, and eggs, and add to dry ingredients whisking together just until blended.

2. Spoon the batter into lightly greased shiny madeleine pans, filling three-fourths full. Bake at 400°F, in batches, 16 to 18 minutes or until golden brown. Remove from the pans immediately.

3. Serve hot, or cool completely on wire racks (about 20 minutes), and freeze in zip-top plastic bags up to 1 month.

4. To serve, arrange madeleines on a baking sheet, and bake at 350°F for 5 to 6 minutes or until thoroughly heated.

## FRESH TAKE

### The Savory Side of Jam

Savory pepper jellies have had a prime spot on our pantry shelves for years, but few equal the flavor bomb of Atlanta Chef Linton Hopkins' bacon marmalade. It's insanely delicious with cornbread or sweet potato biscuits, but also try it on paninis and burgers.

**Bacon Marmalade:** Dice ½ (16-oz.) package thick hickory-smoked bacon slices. Cook bacon in a skillet over medium-high, stirring often, 4 minutes or just until dark golden brown; drain on paper towels. Wipe skillet clean; return bacon to skillet. Add 1 cup sorghum syrup; cook, stirring constantly, 1 minute. Add 1½ cups apple cider vinegar; cook, stirring often, 8 minutes or until liquid is reduced by half. Add ½ cup chicken broth and 1 bay leaf; cook 5 minutes or until slightly thickened. Add kosher salt and cracked pepper to taste.

# Turnip Greens with Pot Liquor Dumplings

A tangle of fresh turnip greens are cooked the old-fashioned way—simmered low and slow until meltingly tender and glistening with pot liquor. The hot water cornmeal dumplings are a delicacy that needs sufficient room to cook properly, so be sure to use a widemouthed lidded pot with plenty of space for the steam to rise. The tale about greens tasting sweeter after the first frost? Totally true. Hardy greens respond to colder temperatures by moving water from the leaves to the roots, which concentrates the sugars in the leaves.

Serves 3 to 4   Hands-on 30 minutes   Total 1 hour 30 minutes

## Greens:

¼ pound salt pork (or desired amount of bacon drippings)
2 garlic cloves, smashed
1 teaspoon table salt
2 pounds fresh young turnip greens, trimmed

## Pot Liquor Dumplings:

1 cup self-rising cornmeal mix
½ teaspoon table salt
⅔ cup boiling water

1. Make the Greens: Combine the salt pork, garlic, salt to taste, and 6 cups water in a 3-quart saucepan. Cover and bring to a simmer. Add the greens; cover and simmer 20 minutes or until the greens are tender. Transfer the greens to a serving platter, reserving boiling pot liquor; keep the greens warm.

2. Make the Dumplings: Combine the cornmeal and ½ teaspoon salt in a bowl. Stir in ⅔ cup boiling water until well blended. Shape into 12 balls (1 heaping tablespoonful each).

3. Place the dough balls in boiling pot liquor. Cover and simmer 20 to 30 minutes or until done. Remove from heat, and let stand 10 minutes.

4. Arrange the dumplings on a serving platter with the greens; pour desired amount of pot liquor over the greens and dumplings to keep them moist and hot. Serve immediately.

1960s

# KALE AND COLLARDS SALAD

Belle Chevre cheesemaker Tasia Malakasis takes a fresh approach to traditionally long-simmered greens by slicing collards and kale into thin ribbons and tossing with a fresh garlicky Lemon Dressing. Left to chill for an hour before adding the avocados and pears, the dressing acts as a marinade, tenderizing the uncooked greens.

Serves 8 to 10   Hands-on 35 minutes
Total 1 hour 35 minutes, including dressing

1 bunch fresh collard greens (about 8 ounces)
1 bunch Tuscan kale (about 8 ounces)
3/4 cup sweetened dried cranberries
Lemon Dressing (see below)
3 Bartlett pears, sliced

2 avocados, peeled and diced
1 tablespoon fresh lemon juice
1 small head radicchio, shredded
3/4 cup chopped toasted pecans
6 cooked bacon slices, crumbled

1. Trim and discard the tough stalks from the centers of the collard and kale leaves; stack the leaves, and roll up, starting at 1 long side. Cut into 1/4-inch-thick slices. Toss the collards and kale with the cranberries and Lemon Dressing in a large bowl. Cover and chill 1 hour.

2. Toss together the pears and next 2 ingredients just before serving. Toss the pear mixture, radicchio, pecans, and bacon with the collard mixture. Serve immediately.

## LEMON DRESSING

1/4 cup fresh lemon juice
2 garlic cloves, minced
2 teaspoons Dijon mustard
1 teaspoon kosher salt

1/2 teaspoon freshly ground black pepper
1/2 cup olive oil

Whisk together the lemon juice and next 4 ingredients in a small bowl; add the olive oil in a slow, steady stream, whisking constantly until smooth. Makes 1 cup

---

# Fried Green Tomatoes

———— ◇ ————

Fried green tomatoes were revered in the South long before Fannie Flagg's fictional Whistle Stop Cafe made them famous. In other regions it's a dish that signals summer's end, but here tomato season comes early and farmers stagger plantings to ensure a plentiful harvest until November's frost. The best fried green tomatoes are seasoned with salt and pepper, dredged in cornmeal, and pan-fried to a soulful crisp in a hot cast-iron skillet. Cream gravy optional.

Serves 4   Hands-on 30 minutes   Total 30 minutes

Vegetable oil
3 large, firm green tomatoes
   (about 2 pounds)
1 cup buttermilk

1 large egg, lightly beaten
1 cup plain yellow cornmeal
½ teaspoon table salt
½ teaspoon ground black pepper

1. Pour oil to a depth of 3 inches in a large Dutch oven; heat over medium-high to 360°F.

2. Meanwhile, cut the tomatoes into ¼-inch-thick slices.

3. Whisk together the buttermilk and egg until blended in a bowl. Stir together the cornmeal, salt, and pepper in a second bowl. Dip the tomatoes in the buttermilk mixture, shaking off excess, and dredge in cornmeal mixture.

4. Fry the tomatoes, in batches, in hot oil 3 to 4 minutes or until golden brown. Season with salt and pepper to taste. Serve immediately.

1970s

Green tomatoes go from the frying pan into the fire with this chargrilled twist on the classic caprese.

**Grilled Green Tomatoes Caprese:** Combine ½ cup olive oil; ¼ cup white balsamic vinegar; 2 garlic cloves, minced; 1 Tbsp. brown sugar; and ⅛ tsp. salt in a zip-top plastic freezer bag; add 4 medium-size green tomatoes, cut into ¼-inch-thick slices. Seal and shake gently to coat. Chill 1 hour. Preheat the grill to 350° to 400°F (medium-high). Remove tomatoes from the marinade, reserving the marinade. Grill, covered with grill lid, 3 to 4 minutes on each side or until tender. Arrange alternating slices of warm grilled tomatoes and 1 lb. sliced fresh mozzarella cheese on a platter. Drizzle with reserved marinade; season with kosher salt and freshly ground black pepper to taste. Sprinkle with ⅓ cup sliced fresh basil. Serves 8 to 10

# FRIED GREEN TOMATOES

Easy changes in method and ingredients lighten the classic. Four decidedly different dipping sauces mean something for everyone.

Makes about 20 slices   Hands-on 1 hour
Total 1 hour 25 minutes, including sauces

4 medium-size green tomatoes (about 1 ⅓ pounds)
½ teaspoon salt
½ teaspoon pepper
1 cup self-rising cornmeal mix

½ cup panko (Japanese breadcrumbs)
½ cup all-purpose flour
4 large egg whites
3 tablespoons olive oil

1. Cut the tomatoes into ½-inch-thick slices; sprinkle with the salt and pepper. Let stand 10 minutes.

2. Combine the cornmeal mix and panko in a shallow dish. Place the flour in a second shallow dish. Whisk the egg whites in a medium bowl until foamy. Dredge the tomato slices in the flour, shaking off excess. Dip in the egg whites, and dredge in the cornmeal mixture.

3. Cook half of the tomato slices in 1½ tablespoons of the hot oil in a nonstick skillet over medium 4 to 5 minutes on each side or until golden brown. Season with additional salt to taste. Place on a wire rack in a jelly-roll pan, and keep warm in a 225°F oven. Repeat procedure with the remaining tomato slices and oil.

## PEPPER JELLY SAUCE

⅔ cup red pepper jelly
2 tablespoons brown mustard
1 teaspoon orange zest

1 teaspoon prepared horseradish
Garnish: chopped fresh parsley

Stir together first 4 ingredients. Makes ¾ cup

## CITRUS-GINGER AIOLI

1 cup mayonnaise
1 teaspoon lime zest
1 teaspoon orange zest
4 teaspoons fresh lime juice
1 tablespoon fresh orange juice
2 teaspoons finely grated fresh ginger

1 garlic clove, minced
¼ teaspoon table salt
⅛ teaspoon ground black pepper

Stir together all the ingredients. Makes 1¼ cups

## BLUE CHEESE-DILL SAUCE

½ cup sour cream
½ cup 2% low-fat plain
   yogurt
2 teaspoons chopped
   fresh dill

2 ounces crumbled blue
   cheese
1 teaspoon fresh lemon juice
¼ teaspoon table salt

Stir together all the ingredients. Makes 1⅓ cups

## SRIRACHA RÉMOULADE

1½ cups mayonnaise
4 green onions, sliced
2 tablespoons chopped
   fresh parsley

2 to 3 tablespoons Asian
   hot chili sauce (such as
   Sriracha)
1 garlic clove, pressed

Stir together all the ingredients. Makes 2 cups

# Classic
# Okra and Tomatoes

◆

Okra and tomatoes are a centuries-old pairing. It's a remarkable union of late-summer flavors that comes from using peak-season produce—tiny fresh-picked okra and plump ripe tomatoes still firm enough to hold their shape when simmered. To minimize okra's infamous textural issues, take care not to cut the stem end so closely that the pod is severed.

Serves 4   Hands-on 35 minutes   Total 1 hour 15 minutes

1 pound fresh okra
¼ cup bacon drippings
1 onion, chopped
1 green bell pepper, chopped
1 (28-ounce) can whole tomatoes
1 teaspoon sugar

1 teaspoon table salt
½ teaspoon ground black pepper
1 lemon, cut in wedges
1 tablespoon all-purpose flour
1 tablespoon water

1. Cook the okra in boiling water to cover in a saucepan 10 minutes or until tender; drain. Cool completely (about 30 minutes).

2. Cut the okra into ¼-inch-thick slices, discarding the stems.

3. Heat the bacon drippings in a saucepan over medium-high; add the onion and bell pepper, and sauté 6 minutes or until tender. Add the tomatoes, sugar, salt, pepper, lemon, and okra. Reduce heat to medium; cover and simmer 10 minutes.

4. Stir together the flour and 1 tablespoon water until smooth; add to the okra mixture. Cook, stirring constantly, 2 to 3 minutes or until thickened.

1970s

# OKRA AND TOMATOES

It's a garden-fresh flash in the pan. Thin-sliced okra and shallots cook fast and crisp before merging with the sweet, garlic-infused grape tomatoes and herbs. We love it dished out over fried catfish fillets for an all-in-one summer supper.

Serves 4   Hands-on 25 minutes   Total 25 minutes

2 tablespoons olive oil
8 ounces fresh okra, thinly sliced
1 large shallot, thinly sliced
1 large green tomato, chopped
1 pint grape tomatoes, halved
2 garlic cloves, minced

⅓ cup torn fresh basil
¼ cup fresh flat-leaf parsley leaves
½ teaspoon table salt
½ teaspoon freshly ground black pepper

1. Heat 1 tablespoon of the oil in a skillet over medium-high. Add the okra and shallot; sauté 5 minutes or until the okra is golden brown; transfer to a bowl.

2. Heat the remaining olive oil. Add the green and grape tomatoes and garlic. Cook, stirring often, 2 minutes. Combine the tomatoes and okra. Stir in the basil, parsley leaves, salt, and pepper.

## FRESH TAKE

### Two More Favorites to Try

The tastiest okra-and-tomato pairings don't always happen in a skillet—or in a gumbo. Case in point: hot crispy bites of fried okra and cool tomato salads. For a Deep-South twist on Italian Panzanella, toss together coarsely chopped tomatoes, diced red onion, and chopped fresh basil with your favorite red wine vinaigrette. Then put a hold on the toasted bread cubes and toss with classic fried okra just before serving. Or, head south-of-the-border for a fried okra taco. (Yes, you read that right.) Fill warm corn tortillas with shredded lettuce, hot fried okra, and a chunky fresh tomato salsa. Then top that with some sour cream and shredded pepper Jack cheese. We guarantee you won't be disappointed.

# Sweet Potato Casserole

Old-school sweet potato casseroles are one of those deliciously indulgent sugar-laden Southern sides capable of dancing merrily between a Pyrex baking dish and a pâte sucrée pie shell without the first thought of altering the ingredient list. This is exactly what we love about the recipe—well that and the eye-catching pecan streusel.

Serves 8  Hands-on 20 minutes  Total 55 minutes

3½ cups mashed cooked sweet potatoes
   (about 3 medium-size sweet potatoes)
½ cup granulated sugar
½ cup milk
¼ cup plus 3 tablespoons butter, melted
2 large eggs, beaten

1½ teaspoons vanilla extract
½ teaspoon table salt
1 cup chopped pecans
½ cup firmly packed brown sugar
⅓ cup all-purpose flour

1. Preheat the oven to 350°F. Stir together the first 3 ingredients, ¼ cup of the butter, eggs, vanilla, and salt in a bowl. Spoon into an 8-inch-square baking dish.

2. Combine the pecans, brown sugar, flour, and remaining 3 tablespoons butter. Spread over sweet potato mixture.

3. Bake at 350°F for 35 minutes.

1970s

# SWEET POTATO-CARROT CASSEROLE

The pecan-and-miniature marshmallow topping pays homage to the past, but the heart of this dish relies on the natural sweetness of the pureed potatoes and carrots rather than a jolt of added sugar.

Serves 8 to 10   Hands-on 1 hour 20 minutes
Total 4 hours 30 minutes, including pecans and carrot curls

6 large sweet potatoes (about 5 pounds)
1½ pounds carrots, sliced
¼ cup butter
1 cup sour cream
2 tablespoons sugar
1 teaspoon lemon zest

½ teaspoon table salt
½ teaspoon ground nutmeg
½ teaspoon freshly ground black pepper
1½ cups miniature marshmallows
1 cup Sugar-and-Spice Pecans (see below)

1. Preheat the oven to 400°F. Bake the sweet potatoes on an aluminum foil-lined 15- x 10-inch jelly-roll pan 1 hour or until tender. Reduce the oven temperature to 350°F. Cool the potatoes 30 minutes.

2. Meanwhile, cook the carrots in boiling water to cover 20 to 25 minutes or until very tender; drain.

3. Process the carrots and butter in a food processor until smooth, stopping to scrape down sides as needed. Transfer the carrot mixture to a large bowl.

4. Peel and cube the sweet potatoes. Process, in batches, in a food processor until smooth, stopping to scrape down sides as needed. Add the sweet potatoes to the carrot mixture. Stir in the sour cream and next 5 ingredients, stirring until blended. Spoon mixture into a lightly greased 13- x 9-inch baking dish.

5. Bake at 350°F for 30 minutes or until thoroughly heated. Remove from the oven. Sprinkle with the marshmallows. Bake at 350°F for 10 more minutes or until marshmallows are golden brown. Remove from the oven, and sprinkle with Sugar-and-Spice Pecans.

## SUGAR-AND-SPICE PECANS

1 large egg white
4 cups pecan halves and pieces
½ cup sugar

1 tablespoon orange zest
1 teaspoon ground cinnamon
1 teaspoon ground ginger

1. Preheat the oven to 350°F. Whisk the egg white in a large bowl until foamy. Add the pecans, and stir to coat.

2. Stir together the sugar and next 3 ingredients in a bowl. Sprinkle the sugar mixture over the pecans, and stir until evenly coated. Spread the pecans in a single layer in a lightly greased 15- x 10-inch jelly-roll pan.

3. Bake at 350°F for 25 minutes, stirring once after 10 minutes. Remove from the oven; cool completely. Makes 4 cups

# CANDIED CARROT CURLS

Parchment paper
Vegetable cooking spray
1 or 2 large peeled carrots

1 cup water
1 cup sugar
Sugar (optional)

1. Preheat the oven to 225°F. Line a baking sheet with the parchment paper; grease with the cooking spray. Remove 15 to 20 long strips from the carrots with a vegetable peeler.

2. Bring 1 cup water and 1 cup sugar to a boil in a large heavy-duty saucepan over medium-high. Add the strips, reduce heat to medium-low, and simmer 15 minutes. Drain; cool 5 minutes.

3. Spread the cooked carrot strips 1 inch apart in a single layer on the prepared baking sheet. Bake at 225°F for 30 minutes. As the carrot strips bake, they will become translucent. Remove from the oven.

4. Working quickly, wrap each warm carrot strip around the handle of a wooden spoon, forming curls. Gently slide off the spoon. Sprinkle with the sugar, if desired. Let the curls stand at room temperature until completely dry. Makes 15 to 20 curls

# Easy Succotash

◈

Succotash is a summer delicacy, at its finest when butter beans are just in and fresh corn is at its sweetest. It's a quick dish, not meant to be long simmered or highly seasoned so that the harvest flavors shine. When perfectly cooked, a butter bean becomes creamy with a rich, buttery texture—an inspired match for the crispness of just-picked corn. Taste of the South Trivia: In *A Tramp Abroad*, Mark Twain listed succotash among the foods from home that he missed most while traveling in Europe.

Serves 6   Hands-on 35 minutes   Total 35 minutes

2 cups fresh shelled lima beans
   (about 1 pound)
4 cups fresh corn kernels
   (about 6 ears)

½ cup whipping cream
3 tablespoons butter
½ teaspoon table salt
⅛ teaspoon ground black pepper

1. Cook the beans in boiling salted water to cover in a saucepan 15 minutes or until almost tender; drain and return to pan.

2. Stir in the corn, whipping cream, butter, salt, and pepper. Cook over low, stirring often, 7 to 10 minutes or until corn is done.

1980s

# EDAMAME SUCCOTASH

Known for his twists on traditional Southern dishes, Atlanta chef Marvin Woods brings a rainbow of flavors and textures to weeknight succotash. Originally featured as a recipe in a family-friendly dinners story that highlighted popular convenience products from the pantry and freezer, this dish is even better with fresh corn. Edamame, a once-trendy but still delicious little soybean, stands in for the butter beans.

Serves 8   Hands-on 20 minutes   Total 35 minutes

1 medium onion, chopped
2 tablespoons canola oil
1 medium-size orange bell pepper, seeded and diced
1 medium-size red bell pepper, seeded and diced
1 medium-size yellow bell pepper, seeded and diced

2½ cups frozen whole kernel corn
½ cup chicken broth
1 (16-ounce) package frozen edamame, thawed
1 tablespoon butter
1 tablespoon chopped fresh mint
Salt and pepper

1. Sauté the onion in hot oil in a large skillet over medium 3 minutes or until tender. Add the bell peppers and corn, and cook 5 more minutes or until tender.

2. Stir in the chicken broth, and bring to a boil over medium-high; reduce heat to low. Stir in the edamame; cook 3 minutes. Stir in the butter until melted. Remove from the heat, and stir in the mint and table salt and black pepper to taste. Serve immediately.

# Southern-Style Green Beans

As much as we love all the new crunchy, barely blanched, paired-with-walnuts-and-feta green bean creations (and we truly do), there's still something wonderful about the way a hambone broth infuses old-fashioned Southern-style green beans with a salty, meaty smokiness.

Serves 10 to 12   Hands-on 10 minutes   Total 1 hour 40 minutes

3 pounds fresh green beans, trimmed
1 (½-pound) ham hock
5 cups water

2 teaspoons table salt
¼ teaspoon freshly ground black pepper

1. Remove the strings from the beans, and cut the beans into 2-inch pieces. Wash the beans thoroughly.

2. Place the ham hock and 5 cups water in a Dutch oven; bring to a boil. Reduce heat, and simmer 1 hour. Add the beans, salt, and pepper; cook, stirring occasionally, 30 minutes or until tender.

1970s

# SKILLET GREEN BEANS

Pencil-thin green beans laced with crispy bits of bacon and the fiery-sweet crunch of Candied Jalapeños turn up the heat on traditional. No special jars or canning required.

Serves 8 to 10   Hands-on 1 hour 25 minutes
Total 1 hour 25 minutes, including Candied Jalapeños

2 pounds haricots verts (French green beans), trimmed

4 thick hickory-smoked bacon slices, cut crosswise into ¼-inch-thick pieces

6 large shallots, quartered

1 tablespoon olive oil

¼ cup syrup from Candied Jalapeños

2 tablespoons red wine vinegar

Candied Jalapeños (optional, see below)

1. Cook the green beans in boiling salted water to cover 3 to 4 minutes or until crisp-tender; drain. Plunge the beans into ice water to stop the cooking process; drain.

2. Cook the bacon in a large skillet over medium 5 to 6 minutes or until crisp. Remove with a slotted spoon, and drain on paper towels, reserving 2 tablespoons drippings in skillet.

3. Sauté the shallots in hot olive oil and reserved hot drippings over medium 8 to 10 minutes or until golden brown and tender. Stir in the jalapeño syrup and vinegar. Increase heat to medium-high; add the green beans. Sauté 5 minutes or until hot. Add salt and pepper to taste. Toss with the bacon. Serve with the Candied Jalapeños, if desired.

## CANDIED JALAPEÑOS

1 (12-ounce) jar pickled jalapeño pepper slices

4 red chile peppers, sliced

¾ cup sugar

1 teaspoon lime zest

Drain the jalapeño slices. Discard the liquid, and reserve the jar and lid. Toss together the jalapeño slices and next 3 ingredients. Let stand 5 minutes, stirring occasionally. Spoon into the reserved jar, scraping any remaining sugar mixture from the bowl into the jar. Seal and chill 48 hours to 1 week, shaking the jar several times a day to dissolve any sugar that settles. Makes 1⅓ cups

# Hash Brown Potato Casserole

Southerners are unapologetic about their fondness for hash brown casseroles. Also known as "The Funeral Casserole," its creamy goodness has comforted the bereaved for decades. And let's face it, no other dish on earth can transition so seamlessly from a country club breakfast buffet to a potluck church supper. For what it's worth, casserole connoisseurs caution against using off-brand generic cornflakes for the topping. Best to leave them off all together—like they do at Nashville's Loveless Cafe and at Cracker Barrel.

Serves 10 to 12   Hands-on 20 minutes   Total 1 hour 10 minutes

1 (32-ounce) package frozen diced hash brown potatoes, thawed
1 (10 ¾-ounce) can cream of chicken soup
1 (8-ounce) container sour cream
1 cup (4 ounces) shredded mild Cheddar cheese
½ cup chopped onion
¾ cup butter, melted
2 cups cornflakes cereal
Garnishes: fresh curly-leaf parsley sprigs

1. Preheat the oven to 350°F. Stir together the first 5 ingredients and ½ cup of the butter until well blended. Spoon into a greased 2- to 3-quart baking dish.

2. Crush the cereal, and stir in the remaining ¼ cup butter. Sprinkle over the potato mixture.

3. Bake at 350°F for 50 minutes.

1980s

# FENNEL-AND-POTATO GRATIN

Mandoline slicers have gone mainstream, making fancy creamy gratins layered with thinly sliced potatoes and aromatic fennel as easy to assemble as a frozen hash brown casserole. Of course, there is the added step of stirring together a stove top béchamel. But all bake times being equal, the results are definitely worth it.

Serves 8   Hands-on 30 minutes   Total 1 hour 22 minutes

3 tablespoons butter
1 shallot, sliced
1 garlic clove, minced
2 tablespoons all-purpose flour
1¼ cups half-and-half
½ (10 ounces) block sharp white Cheddar cheese, shredded
½ teaspoon table salt

¼ teaspoon freshly ground black pepper
⅛ teaspoon ground nutmeg
2 large baking potatoes (about 2 pounds), peeled and thinly sliced
1 small fennel bulb, thinly sliced
Garnish: fresh rosemary leaves

1. Preheat the oven to 400°F. Melt the butter in a heavy saucepan over medium. Add the shallot; sauté 2 to 3 minutes or until tender. Add the garlic, and sauté 1 minute.

2. Whisk in the flour; cook, whisking constantly, 1 minute. Gradually whisk in the half-and-half; cook, whisking constantly, 3 to 4 minutes or until thickened and bubbly. Remove from the heat. Whisk in the Cheddar cheese until melted and smooth. Stir in the salt and next 2 ingredients.

3. Layer the potato and fennel slices alternately in a lightly greased, broiler-safe ceramic 2-quart casserole dish. Spread the cheese sauce over the layers. Cover with the aluminum foil.

4. Bake at 400°F for 50 minutes or until the potatoes are tender. Remove from the oven. Increase the oven temperature to broil with oven rack 5 inches from the heat. Uncover the dish, and broil 2 to 4 minutes or until golden brown.

## FLASHBACK
### Going Green

Fresh asparagus are the perfect foil for the creamy richness of potato gratins. Atlanta's well-known food writer and culinary sleuth Shirley Corriher shared her technique for roasting asparagus with us years ago and we've been using it ever since. The simplicity of the recipe belies its sweet succulent flavor.

**Simple Roasted Asparagus:** Preheat the oven to broil. Snap off and discard tough ends of 2 lb. asparagus. Arrange in a single layer in 2 (15- x 10-inch) jelly-roll pans. Drizzle with ¼ cup olive oil. Broil, in 2 batches, 5 ½ inches from heat 4 minutes or until tender. Sprinkle with 1 tsp. sugar and ½ tsp. each of table salt and freshly ground black pepper.

# Black Bing Cherry Salad

Jewel-tone congealed salads were a craze for decades, dominating spiral-bound cookbooks with a dazzling array of sweet and savory options. Fifty years ago, this simple black cherry salad inspired dozens of improvs. Cooks with a creative flair replaced the water with bubbly colas or port wine, added pineapple tidbits and nuts, or "iced" the salad with a sweetened cream cheese frosting.

Serves 6 to 8   Hands-on 10 minutes
Total 5 hours 20 minutes, including chill time

1 (15-ounce) can pitted Bing cherries
¼ teaspoon unflavored gelatin
2 cups boiling water

1 (3-ounce) package black-cherry-flavored gelatin
Salad greens (optional)

1. Drain the cherries, reserving ½ cup liquid.

2. Sprinkle the unflavored gelatin over the reserved cherry liquid in a large bowl, and stir until dissolved. Gradually stir in the boiling water; add the flavored gelatin, and stir until the gelatin is melted. Let stand 10 minutes. Cover and chill until slightly thickened (about 1 hour).

3. Stir in the drained cherries. Spoon the mixture into a 4- to 4½-cup mold, and chill 4 hours or until firm. Serve over the salad greens, if desired.

1970s

# ORANGE AND BASIL MACERATED CHERRIES

A splash of citrus and a sprinkling of sugar bring out natural juices while fragrant basil makes it all pop. We like to pair crimson Bing cherries and rosy Rainiers. If you're feeling a bit nostalgic, you could always swap the fresh cherries for canned.

Serves 6 to 8   Hands-on 20 minutes   Total 1 hour 30 minutes

1 pound fresh cherries, pitted
1 tablespoon firmly packed orange zest
2 tablespoons fresh orange juice
2 tablespoons dark brown sugar
1 tablespoon chopped fresh basil
⅛ teaspoon kosher salt
Ricotta cheese
Garnish: fresh basil

1. Cut half of the cherries in half crosswise. Place the whole cherries and cherry halves in a large bowl; add the zest and next 4 ingredients, tossing to coat. Cover and chill 1 hour.

2. Remove the cherries from the refrigerator, and let stand 10 minutes. Spoon over the ricotta cheese, and serve immediately.

# Watermelon Rind Pickles

Sweetly spiced watermelon rind pickles are the thrifty vegan version of nose-to-tail cooking. They're divine straight from the jar or served alongside anything that's smoked, grilled, or barbecued. Heirloom watermelons with thick, crisp rinds are best for pickling—many seedless varieties have thin rinds that tend to soften when pickled. The rind is easier to peel if you first cut it into long strips. And keep in mind, you can always make extra fancy pickles with a fluted chopper.

Makes 5 pints   Hands-on 1 hour   Total 14 hours, including stand time

3 quarts watermelon rinds
3/4 cup kosher salt
3 quarts cold water
2 quarts ice cubes
9 cups sugar
3 cups white vinegar

3 cups water
6 (1-inch) cinnamon sticks
1 tablespoon whole cloves
Cheesecloth
Kitchen string
1 lemon, thinly sliced (optional)

1. Remove the green rind and pink edges from the rinds; cut into 1-inch pieces. Place in a large pot. Stir together the salt and cold water; pour over the rind. Add the ice; let stand 5 hours.

2. Drain; rinse the rinds under cold water. Return to the pot, and add water to cover. Bring to a boil; cook 10 minutes or until fork-tender (do not overcook). Drain and return to the pot.

3. Combine the sugar, vinegar, and 3 cups water in a saucepan. Tie the cinnamon sticks and cloves in a square of cheesecloth with the kitchen string. Add the spice bundle to the pot. Bring to a boil; boil 5 minutes. Pour the boiling liquid over the rind; reserve the spice bundle. Add the lemon to the pot, if desired. Let stand 8 to 24 hours.

4. Bring to a boil, and cook 10 minutes or until translucent.

5. Place hot rind in 5 (1-pint) jars. Add 1 cinnamon stick from the spice bag to each jar; pour boiling liquid to 1/2 inch from the top. Wipe the jar rims. Cover at once with metal lids and bands.

6. Process the jars in a water bath 5 minutes. Remove the jars; set on a wire rack to cool. Store in a cool, dry place.

1970s

# SOUTHWEST WATERMELON SALAD

We enjoyed a Texas Hill Country supper hosted by Parkside Chef Shawn Cirkiel in 2011. Grilled steak was paired with a summer-perfect watermelon salad. Sweet watermelon rind pickles added a tangy surprise.

Serves 8 to 10   Hands-on 1 hour 35 minutes
Total 2 hours 35 minutes, plus chill time for
Pickled Watermelon Rind

4 cups seeded and cubed red watermelon
4 cups seeded and cubed yellow watermelon
2 tablespoons sugar
1 tablespoon lime zest
2 tablespoons fresh lime juice
½ cup Pickled Watermelon Rind (see below)
¼ cup coarsely chopped fresh cilantro
¼ cup coarsely chopped fresh basil

1 tablespoon chopped fresh chives
1 tablespoon seeded and thinly sliced jalapeño pepper
1 tablespoon thinly sliced shallots
1 teaspoon minced garlic
2 tablespoons olive oil
½ cup crumbled Cotija or feta cheese

Combine the first 5 ingredients in a large glass bowl. Stir in the Pickled Watermelon Rind and next 6 ingredients. Drizzle with the oil; sprinkle with the Cotija cheese. Serve immediately, or cover and chill up to 2 hours.

# PICKLED WATERMELON RIND

½ small watermelon (about 5 pounds)
3 tablespoons table salt
3¾ cups water

¾ cup sugar
¾ cup vinegar
2 star anise

1. Remove the rind from the melon, leaving a bit of red flesh attached. Reserve the flesh for another use. Peel and cut the rind into 1-inch cubes (about 5 cups cubed). Place in a large bowl.

2. Stir together the salt and 3 cups water. Pour over the rind. Cover and chill 24 hours. Drain; rinse well.

3. Combine the rind, sugar, next 2 ingredients, and remaining ¾ cup water in a large Dutch oven. Bring to a boil; remove from the heat. Cool completely (about 1 hour). Cover and chill 24 hours before serving. Store in the refrigerator up to 1 week. Makes 1 quart

# 6

# DESSERTS

Sweet dreams, baby! We've got layer upon layer of delectable cakes, cookies, and mile-high homemade pies designed to dazzle. Who could possibly say no?

# THE WAY WE DINE

## Today's Dessert Party

The latest trend on the party circuit?
The dessert bar. A fun and flirty
parade of make-ahead sweets and
sparkling Prosecco set the stage
for the sweetest happy hour in town.

# White Cake with Caramel Icing

---◇---

Caramel layer cakes, for all their fame and glory, have a reputation for being big trouble, which is why so many people steer clear of the kitchen and simply wait for a sudden windfall on a bereavement buffet. True, there's definitely an art to spinning caramelized sugar into a flawless frosting, but with this classic recipe (and a little practice) you'll be able to turn out a grand cake every time.

Serves 12   Hands-on 30 minutes   Total 2 hours 35 minutes, including icing

1 cup butter, softened
2 cups sugar
1 teaspoon vanilla extract
3 cups all-purpose flour
1 tablespoon baking powder

¼ teaspoon table salt
1 cup milk
6 large egg whites
Caramel Icing (see below)

1. Preheat the oven to 350°F. Beat the butter and sugar at medium speed with an electric mixer until light and fluffy. Beat in the vanilla. Sift together the flour, baking powder, and salt; add to the butter mixture alternately with the milk, beginning and ending with the flour mixture. Beat at low speed after each addition.

2. Beat the egg whites at high speed until stiff peaks form; fold into the batter. Divide the batter between 2 greased and floured 9-inch round cake pans.

3. Bake at 350°F for 28 to 32 minutes or until a wooden pick inserted in the center comes out clean. Cool in the pans 10 minutes; remove from the pans to a wire rack, and cool completely (about 1 hour). Spread Caramel Icing between the layers and on the top and the sides of the cake.

# Caramel Icing

4 cups sugar
1 cup milk

1 cup butter

1. Bring 3 cups of the sugar, milk, and butter to a boil in a heavy 4-quart saucepan over medium heat, stirring occasionally. Reduce heat to low, and maintain at a simmer, stirring occasionally.

2. Meanwhile, spread remaining 1 cup sugar in an even layer in a large stainless steel skillet. Cook over medium heat, without stirring, 6 minutes or until amber-colored. (Shake the pan occasionally so that the sugar caramelizes evenly.)

3. Carefully whisk the caramelized sugar into the simmering milk mixture, whisking constantly (mixture will bubble vigorously). Increase the heat to medium, and cook, stirring often, 8 minutes or until a candy thermometer registers 235°F (soft ball stage).

4. Remove from the heat, and transfer to a bowl. Beat with an electric mixer at medium speed 5 to 7 minutes or until the mixture is lukewarm, loses its gloss, and thickens. Makes about 4 cups

1970s

# CARAMEL ITALIAN CREAM CAKE

A quest for the end-all, be-all holiday cake led us to a decadent fusion—a can't-miss combination of ultra-moist Italian cream cake layers sandwiched with caramel fudge frosting. Brown sugar delivers a foolproof shortcut for the novice baker. And yes, we know that brown sugar technically makes it butterscotch, but the cake's rich caramel flavor is undeniably divine.

Serves 12   Hands-on 50 minutes
Total 2 hours 25 minutes, including frostings

3 cups shaved coconut
1 cup finely chopped pecans
½ cup butter, softened
½ cup shortening
1½ cups granulated sugar
½ cup firmly packed dark
   brown sugar
5 large eggs, separated
1 tablespoon vanilla extract

2 cups all-purpose flour
1 teaspoon baking soda
1 cup buttermilk
1 cup sweetened flaked
   coconut
Quick Caramel Frosting
   (at right)
Cream Cheese Frosting
   (at right)

1. Preheat the oven to 350°F. Place the shaved coconut in a single layer in a shallow pan. Place the pecans in a second shallow pan. Bake the coconut and pecans at the same time at 350°F for 5 minutes or until the coconut and pecans are toasted and fragrant, stirring both halfway through.

2. Beat the butter and shortening at medium speed with an electric mixer until fluffy; gradually add the granulated and brown sugars, beating well. Add the egg yolks, 1 at a time, beating until blended after each addition. Add the vanilla, beating until blended.

3. Combine the flour and baking soda; add to butter mixture alternately with buttermilk, beginning and ending with flour mixture. Beat at low speed just until blended after each addition. Stir in the pecans and 1 cup sweetened flaked coconut.

4. Beat the egg whites to stiff peaks at high speed and fold into batter. Pour the batter into 3 greased and floured 9-inch round cake pans.

5. Bake at 350°F for 25 minutes or until a wooden pick inserted in center comes out clean. Cool in pans on wire racks 10 minutes; remove to wire racks, and cool completely (about 1 hour).

6. Make Quick Caramel Frosting. Immediately spread the frosting between the layers and on top of the cake. Spread Cream Cheese Frosting over the sides of the cake; press the 3 cups toasted shaved coconut onto the sides of the cake.

## FLASHBACK
### The Midas Touch

Caramelizing sugar may seem like tricky business, but the age-old secret is all in the timing. Once sugar begins to caramelize, the color changes rapidly from pale yellow to gold to amber to dark brown. Pull it off the fire just before it reaches the desired color—residual heat continues to darken the caramel. Stop the cooking process by placing the bottom of the pan in ice water. First time making caramel frosting? Be fearless: Adding cold butter or liquids such as cream causes hot caramel to bubble up and spatter and often creates lumps. Just step back and keep stirring. Once the icing begins to cool, start spreading it over the cake layers before it loses its gloss.

# QUICK CARAMEL FROSTING

1 cup butter

1 cup firmly packed light brown
  sugar

1 cup firmly packed dark brown
  sugar

½ cup heavy cream

4 cups powdered sugar, sifted

2 teaspoons vanilla extract

1. Bring the first 3 ingredients to a rolling boil in a 3½-quart saucepan over medium, whisking constantly, 7 minutes.

2. Stir in the cream, bring to a boil, and remove from heat. Pour into the bowl of a heavy-duty electric stand mixer. Gradually beat in the powdered sugar and vanilla at medium speed, using whisk attachment; beat 10 minutes until thickened. Use immediately. Makes 5 cups

# CREAM CHEESE FROSTING

¼ cup butter, softened

½ (8-ounce) package cream
  cheese, softened

2 cups powdered sugar

1 teaspoon vanilla extract

Beat the butter and cream cheese at medium speed with an electric mixer until creamy. Gradually add the powdered sugar, and beat at low speed until blended; stir in the vanilla. Makes 1¾ cups

# Lemon Bars

Pastel layers strike the perfect balance between buttery shortbread and tartly sweet lemon custard. Recipes date back to the early 60s—in the *Chicago Tribune* and a Betty Crocker cookbook—but lemon bars soon migrated South to become a standard in the ladies luncheon repertoire.

Makes 24 bars   Hands-on 15 minutes   Total 2 hours 25 minutes

2½ cups all-purpose flour
¾ cup powdered sugar
1 cup cold butter, cut into pieces
2 cups granulated sugar

½ teaspoon baking powder
4 large eggs, lightly beaten
⅓ cup fresh lemon juice
Garnishes: fresh mint leaves

1. Lightly grease an aluminum foil-lined 13- x 9-inch pan. Preheat the oven to 350°F. Combine 2 cups of the flour and ½ cup of the powdered sugar. Cut the butter pieces into the flour mixture with a pastry blender until the mixture is crumbly. Press the mixture into prepared pan.

2. Bake at 350°F for 20 minutes or until lightly browned. Cool 30 minutes.

3. Combine the granulated sugar, baking powder, and remaining ½ cup flour; whisk in the eggs and lemon juice. Pour over the cooled crust.

4. Bake at 350°F for 20 to 25 minutes or until set and edges are lightly browned. Cool completely on a wire rack (about 1 hour). Sprinkle with the remaining ¼ cup powdered sugar, and cut into bars.

1970s

# LEMON BAR CHEESECAKE

Looking for a way to elevate those luscious lemon bars to dinner-party heights? Consider it found. A velvety golden-crusted cheesecake topped with lemon curd captures everything we love about the classic.

Serves 10   Hands-on 40 minutes   Total 4 hours 15 minutes, plus chill time, including lemon curd and Candied Lemon Slices

2 cups all-purpose flour
½ cup powdered sugar
¼ teaspoon table salt
½ cup cold butter, cubed
2 large egg yolks
1 to 2 tablespoons ice water
4 (8-ounce) packages cream cheese, softened

1 cup granulated sugar
4 large eggs
2 teaspoons vanilla extract
2 cups Quick and Easy Lemon Curd (at right)
Candied Lemon Slices (optional, at right)

1. Pulse first 3 ingredients in a food processor 3 or 4 times or just until blended. Add the butter, and pulse 5 or 6 times or until crumbly. Whisk together the egg yolks and 1 tablespoon ice-cold water in a small bowl; add to the butter mixture, and process until the dough forms a ball and pulls away from sides of the bowl, adding up to 1 tablespoon remaining ice-cold water, 1 teaspoon at a time, if necessary. Shape the dough into a disk; wrap in plastic wrap. Chill 4 to 24 hours.

2. Roll the dough into a 14-inch circle on a lightly floured surface. Fit the dough into a lightly greased 9-inch dark springform pan, gently pressing on the bottom and up sides of pan; trim and discard excess dough. Chill 30 minutes.

3. Meanwhile, preheat the oven to 325°F. Beat the cream cheese at medium speed with an electric mixer 3 minutes or until smooth. Gradually add the granulated sugar, beating until blended. Add the eggs, 1 at a time, beating just until yellow disappears after each addition. Beat in the vanilla.

4. Pour two-thirds of the cheesecake batter (about 4 cups) into the prepared crust; dollop 1 cup of the lemon curd over the batter in the pan, and gently swirl with a knife. Spoon remaining batter into pan.

5. Bake at 325°F for 1 hour to 1 hour and 10 minutes or just until the center is set. Turn the oven off. Let the cheesecake stand in the oven, with door closed, 15 minutes. Remove the cheesecake from the oven, and gently run a knife around the outer edge of the cheesecake to loosen from the sides of the pan. (Do not remove the sides of the pan.) Cool completely in the pan on a wire rack (about 1 hour). Cover and chill 8 to 24 hours.

6. Remove the sides of the pan, and transfer the cheesecake to a serving platter. Spoon remaining 1 cup lemon curd over the cheesecake, and, if desired, top with Candied Lemon Slices.

# QUICK AND EASY LEMON CURD

6 lemons

1/2 cup butter, softened

2 cups sugar

4 large eggs

1. Grate 2 tablespoons zest from the lemons. Cut the lemons in half; squeeze the juice to equal 1 cup. Beat together the butter and sugar at medium speed with an electric mixer. Add the eggs, 1 at a time; beat just until blended. Add the lemon juice to the butter mixture, beating at low speed until blended; stir in the zest. (Mixture will look curdled.) Transfer to a 3-quart microwave-safe bowl.

2. Microwave at HIGH 5 minutes, stirring at 1-minute intervals. Microwave, stirring at 30-second intervals, 1 to 2 more minutes until the mixture thickens and starts to mound slightly when stirred.

3. Place plastic wrap directly on the warm curd; chill 4 hours or until firm. Chill in an airtight container up to 2 weeks. Makes 2 cups

# CANDIED LEMON SLICES

1 cup sugar

2 tablespoons fresh lemon juice

3/4 cup water

2 small lemons, thinly sliced

Line a jelly-roll pan with wax paper. Stir together first 3 ingredients in a large skillet over medium until the sugar dissolves. Add the lemon slices; simmer gently, in a single layer and turning occasionally, 15 minutes until slightly translucent and rinds are soft. Remove from the heat. Place in a single layer in the pan. Cool completely. Cover and chill 2 hours to 2 days. Reserve the syrup for another use. Makes 8 to 10 slices

# Brown Sugar Cocoa Fudge

◆

This is a simple old-fashioned fudge with impressive dividends—the only trick is in the timing. Eliminate the guesswork with a candy thermometer. Undercooking by just 2 to 3 degrees prevents the fudge from setting. Worst case scenario? A stellar batch of hot fudge sauce.

Makes 36 pieces   Hands-on 20 minutes   Total 1 hour 20 minutes

Parchment paper
2 cups firmly packed light brown sugar
2 cups granulated sugar
1 cup milk
6 tablespoons unsweetened cocoa

3 tablespoons light corn syrup
¼ teaspoon cream of tartar
⅛ teaspoon table salt
3 tablespoons butter
2 teaspoons vanilla extract

1. Line the bottom and sides of a 9-inch square pan with parchment paper, allowing 2 to 3 inches to extend over sides.

2. Combine the brown sugar and next 6 ingredients in a heavy 4-quart saucepan. Bring to a boil over medium-high; cook, stirring constantly, 4 minutes or until a candy thermometer registers 234°F (soft ball stage). Remove from heat; stir in the butter and vanilla.

3. Beat 3 to 4 minutes with a wooden spoon or until the mixture begins to thicken. Pour into the prepared pan, and spread into an even layer. Cool completely (about 1 hour). Remove from pan, using parchment paper sides as handles; cut into 1½-inch squares.

1960s

# PUMPKIN FUDGE

Come fall, pumpkin-spiced lattes, cupcakes, and cream-filled cookies abound, so it was only fitting we added our favorite pumpkin-spiced fudge to the mix. The recipe starts with an old-school technique and ends with an addictive white chocolate-marshmallow finish.

Makes 3 pounds   Hands-on 10 minutes
Total 2 hours 25 minutes

3 cups sugar
¾ cup melted butter
⅔ cup evaporated milk
½ cup canned pumpkin
2 tablespoons corn syrup
1 teaspoon pumpkin pie spice

1 (12-ounce) package white chocolate morsels
1 (7-ounce) jar marshmallow crème
1 cup chopped pecans, toasted
1 teaspoon vanilla extract

1. Grease a foil-lined 9-inch pan. Stir together the first 6 ingredients in a 3½-quart saucepan over medium-high; cook, stirring constantly, until mixture comes to a boil. Continue until a candy thermometer registers 234°F (soft ball stage) or for 12 minutes.

2. Remove the pan from the heat; stir in the remaining ingredients. Pour into the prepared pan. Let stand 2 hours until cool; cut into even squares.

## FLASHBACK
### Be Your Own Candy Maker

In 1981, we wrote: "Each year about this time, candy makers crowd Southern kitchens to stir up batches of homemade candy—a ritual as much a part of the season as a decorated tree." Southern cooks are famous for their candy-making skills—in spite of candy-making rule number one: Don't even think about making candy on a humid day, which pretty much lets out rainy days and the near six months of summer we have here in the Deep South. That's why so many of our candy-making features fall in the month of December— well that and the fact that homemade candy is still highly prized as a holiday gift. If you do risk turning out a batch of candy when the humidity is high, take the temp up a degree or two—say from 238° to 240°F.

# Glazed Strawberry Pie

———◆———

This is pie at its simplest and best: fresh-picked, ripe berries piled high in a flaky crust. Strawberry season begins in February in southern Florida and slowly makes its way north, reaching the Midsouth just as May gives way to early summer. Don't let it pass you by. Oh, and that shimmering glaze? Divine—and definitely not off a supermarket shelf.

Makes one 9-inch pie    Hands-on 25 minutes    Total 3 hours 20 minutes

½ (14.1-ounce) package refrigerated
    piecrusts
6 cups fresh strawberries, hulled
½ cup water
1 cup granulated sugar

⅓ cup cornstarch
1 tablespoon butter
Red liquid food coloring (optional)
1½ cups heavy cream
2 tablespoons powdered sugar

1. Fit the piecrust into a 9-inch pie plate according to package directions; fold the edges under, and crimp. (Do not prick the crust.) Bake according to the package directions. Cool completely.

2. Place 4 cups of the strawberries, cut sides down, in cooled, baked piecrust. Crush the remaining 2 cups strawberries in a medium saucepan; add ½ cup water. Bring to a boil over medium; reduce heat to medium-low, and simmer 3 minutes.

3. Pour the mixture through a fine wire-mesh strainer into a bowl. Discard the solids. Return ¾ cup strawberry liquid to the pan; discard any remaining strawberry liquid.

4. Whisk together the granulated sugar and cornstarch; whisk into the strawberry liquid in the pan. Boil over medium 2 to 3 minutes or until the mixture is translucent. Remove from heat; stir in the butter and, if desired, 6 drops food coloring. Cool 10 minutes.

5. Spoon the strawberry glaze over the berries, making sure to cover all berries. Chill 2 hours.

6. Beat the cream and powdered sugar at medium-high speed with an electric mixer until stiff peaks form. Spread over or pipe around the strawberry mixture in the crust.

1960s

# STRAWBERRY CREAM PIE

A down-home pie with uptown flair. Nestled in a chocolate cookie-crumb crust, French pastry cream and jewel-bright berries update the classic in all the right ways. Red currant jelly spiked with orange liqueur adds a sophisticated finish. Yes, it looks too good to eat, but don't let that stop you.

Serves 8   Hands-on 35 minutes   Total 5 hours 45 minutes

3 tablespoons cornstarch
2 tablespoons all-purpose flour
1/4 teaspoon table salt
1 cup sugar
3 cups half-and-half
6 large egg yolks
2 teaspoons vanilla extract
1 (9-ounce) package chocolate wafer cookies

1/2 (4-ounce) semisweet chocolate baking bar, chopped
1/2 cup butter, melted
1 quart fresh strawberries
1/4 cup red currant jelly
1 tablespoon orange liqueur

1. Lightly grease a 9-inch pie plate. Whisk together the first 3 ingredients and 2/3 cup of the sugar in a medium-size heavy saucepan. Whisk together the half-and-half and the next 2 ingredients in a small bowl; gradually add to the cornstarch mixture, whisking constantly.

2. Bring to a boil over medium, whisking constantly, and cook, whisking constantly, 1 minute. Remove from the heat, and transfer to a bowl; cover and chill 4 to 24 hours.

3. Preheat the oven to 350°F. Pulse the wafer cookies and chopped chocolate in a food processor 8 to 10 times or until finely crushed. Stir together the cookie crumb mixture, melted butter, and remaining 1/3 cup sugar; firmly press the mixture on the bottom, up sides, and onto lip of the prepared pie plate.

4. Bake at 350°F for 10 minutes. Transfer to a wire rack, and cool completely (about 30 minutes).

5. Spoon the chilled half-and-half mixture into the prepared crust. Cut 8 to 10 strawberries in half, and arrange around the outer edge of the pie (leaving the tops on, if desired); hull and slice the remaining strawberries, and arrange in the center of the pie.

6. Cook the jelly in a small saucepan over medium 2 to 3 minutes or until melted. Remove from the heat, and stir in the liqueur. Brush the jelly mixture gently over the strawberries. Chill, uncovered, 30 minutes.

## FRESH TAKE

### The Big Chill

That double-chocolate crumb crust we used for Strawberry Cream Pie? It just happens to be the perfect fill-and-freeze vehicle for our favorite frozen yogurt.

**Strawberry-Basil Frozen Yogurt:** Stir together 2 cups sliced fresh strawberries and 1 cup sugar in a medium bowl. Let stand 30 minutes, stirring occasionally. Pulse the strawberry mixture, 2 Tbsp. chopped fresh basil, and 1 tsp. lime zest in a food processor 9 or 10 times or until berries are finely chopped (almost pureed), stopping to scrape down the sides as needed. Whisk together 1 cup plain Greek yogurt and 1 cup whipping cream in a medium bowl until smooth; stir the strawberry mixture into the yogurt mixture until well blended. Cover and chill 1 hour. Pour the strawberry mixture into the freezer container of a 1 1/2-qt. electric ice-cream maker, and freeze according to manufacturer's instructions. Makes about 1 quart

# Delicious Banana Pudding

Just over 100 years ago, the first commercial shipment of tropical bananas arrived in the port of New Orleans. Celebratory dishes of banana pudding soon followed. Early recipes resembled trifles and called for sponge cake or ladyfingers, but by 1921, the *Atlanta Woman's Club Cookbook* had made the switch to vanilla wafers. Time-pressed cooks created shortcut versions using sweetened condensed milk and instant pudding, but it's hard to beat a homemade custard—especially when it's butterscotch.

Serves 8   Hands-on 25 minutes   Total 35 minutes

1¼ cups firmly packed brown sugar
¼ cup all-purpose flour
⅛ teaspoon table salt
1 (12-ounce) can evaporated milk
¾ cup water
3 large eggs, separated and at room temperature

¼ cup butter
1 teaspoon vanilla extract
1 (11-ounce) box vanilla wafers
3 large bananas
2 tablespoons granulated sugar

1. Whisk together the brown sugar, flour, and salt in a medium saucepan. Whisk in the evaporated milk and ¾ cup water. Cook over medium, whisking constantly, 7 minutes or until mixture boils and thickens.

2. Whisk the egg yolks in a medium bowl until thick and pale; gradually whisk half of the hot pudding mixture into the yolks. Whisk the egg yolk mixture into the remaining pudding mixture in the pan, whisking constantly. Cook over medium 2 minutes or until mixture thickens, stirring constantly. Pour through a fine wire-mesh strainer into a bowl; discard solids. Stir in the butter and vanilla until blended.

3. Preheat the oven to 375°F. Line the bottom and sides of a 2-quart baking dish with the vanilla wafers. Slice enough of the bananas to cover the bottom of the dish; top with half of the pudding. Layer with the vanilla wafers, banana slices, and remaining pudding.

4. Beat the egg whites at high speed with an electric mixer until soft peaks form; gradually add 2 tablespoons sugar, and beat until stiff peaks form. Spread over the pudding.

5. Bake at 375°F for 10 minutes or until golden brown. Serve warm or chilled.

1980s

# BANANA PUDDING CHEESECAKE

We've featured countless riffs on banana pudding, but the most spectacular by far was a meringue-topped cheesecake from Rhonda Harms of Clearwater, Florida. Equally wonderful? This festive twist, crowned with sweetened whipped cream and extra vanilla wafers.

Serves 10 to 12   Hands-on 45 minutes
Total 11 hours 10 minutes

1½ cups finely crushed vanilla wafers
½ cup chopped pecans
¼ cup butter, melted
17 vanilla wafers
2 large ripe bananas, diced
1 tablespoon lemon juice
2 tablespoons light brown sugar
3 (8-ounce) packages cream cheese, softened

1 cup granulated sugar
3 large eggs
2 teaspoons vanilla extract
½ cup coarsely crushed vanilla wafers
Garnishes: sweetened whipped cream, vanilla wafers, sliced bananas tossed in lemon juice

1. Preheat the oven to 350°F. Stir together the first 3 ingredients in a small bowl until well blended. Press the mixture onto the bottom of a greased and floured 9-inch springform pan. Stand 17 vanilla wafers around the edge of the pan (rounded sides against pan), pressing gently into the crust to secure. Bake at 350°F for 10 minutes. Cool completely on a wire rack (about 30 minutes).

2. Combine the bananas and lemon juice in a small saucepan. Stir in the brown sugar. Cook over medium-high, stirring constantly, 1 minute or just until the sugar has dissolved.

3. Beat the cream cheese at medium speed with an electric mixer 3 minutes or until smooth. Gradually add the granulated sugar, beating until blended. Add the eggs, 1 at a time, beating just until yellow disappears after each addition. Beat in the vanilla. Gently stir the banana mixture into the cream cheese mixture. Pour the batter into the prepared crust.

4. Bake at 350°F for 45 to 55 minutes or until the center is almost set. Remove the cheesecake from the oven; gently run a knife around the edge of the cheesecake to loosen. Sprinkle the top of the cheesecake with the coarsely crushed wafers. Cool completely on a wire rack (about 1 hour). Cover and chill 8 hours.

# Warm Blueberry-Nectarine Shortcake

Cobbler-sweet fruits and sour cream shortcake (split and buttered while still warm from the oven) collide in this colorful salute to summer. Early versions of shortcake were little more than crisp flaky rounds of piecrust topped with sugared berries and cream. All well and good, but not as good as this.

Serves 9   Hands-on 25 minutes   Total 40 minutes

Parchment paper
2 pounds ripe nectarines, cut into wedges (about 5 cups)
1/4 teaspoon freshly grated nutmeg
1/4 teaspoon almond extract
3/4 cup plus 3 tablespoons sugar
2 cups heavy cream
2 1/2 cups all-purpose flour

4 teaspoons baking powder
3/4 cup cold butter, cut into pieces
2 large eggs
1 cup sour cream
1 teaspoon vanilla extract
1 cup fresh blueberries
Garnish: freshly grated nutmeg

1. Line a baking sheet with parchment paper. Cook the nectarines, nutmeg, almond extract, and 1/2 cup of the sugar in a medium saucepan over medium, stirring often, 3 to 4 minutes or until the sugar dissolves. Remove from the heat; cover and keep warm.

2. Beat the heavy cream at medium speed with an electric mixer until foamy; gradually beat in 3 tablespoons sugar at high speed until stiff peaks form. Cover and chill.

3. Preheat the oven to 450°F. Combine the flour, baking powder, and remaining 1/4 cup sugar in a large bowl; cut in the butter with a pastry blender or fork until the mixture is crumbly.

4. Whisk together the eggs, sour cream, and vanilla until blended; add to the flour mixture, stirring just until dry ingredients are moistened. Turn the dough out onto a lightly floured surface, and knead 10 times. Pat dough into a 9-inch square; cut into 9 (3-inch) squares, and place on the prepared baking sheet.

5. Bake at 450°F for 12 to 14 minutes or until golden brown. Cool 5 minutes.

6. Split the shortcakes in half horizontally. Stir the blueberries into the nectarine mixture. Spoon the fruit mixture onto the bottom halves of the shortcakes; cover with the shortcake tops. Serve with sweetened whipped cream.

1990s

# PEACH MELBA SHORTCAKES

Chef Shae Rehmel, formerly of Georgia's Five & Ten in Athens, set our hearts aflutter with this peach-filled shortcake in raspberry sauce with a satiny sorghum-sweetened cream.

*Serves 8   Hands-on 55 minutes   Total 1 hour 15 minutes*

Parchment paper
2½ cups all-purpose flour
1 tablespoon plus 1 teaspoon baking powder
1 teaspoon table salt
7 tablespoons sugar
¼ cup cold butter, cut into small cubes
1 large egg
½ teaspoon vanilla extract

¾ cup plus 1 tablespoon half-and-half
6 large fresh, ripe peaches, peeled and sliced
1 tablespoon fresh lemon juice
1½ teaspoons vanilla bean paste
2 pints fresh raspberries
¼ cup honey
Sorghum Whipped Cream

1. Line a baking sheet with parchment paper. Preheat the oven to 425°F. Combine the flour, next 2 ingredients, and 1 tablespoon of the sugar in a bowl; cut in the butter with a pastry blender or fork until crumbly. Whisk together the egg, vanilla, and ¾ cup of the half-and-half; add to the dry ingredients, stirring just until the dough comes together.

2. Turn the dough out onto a floured surface; roll into a 7-inch circle (1 inch thick). Cut into 8 wedges; place on the baking sheet. Brush with remaining 1 tablespoon half-and-half; sprinkle with 2 tablespoons of the sugar. Bake at 425°F for 15 to 20 minutes or until golden.

3. Stir together the peaches, next 2 ingredients, and remaining sugar.

4. Cook the raspberries and honey in a medium saucepan over medium-low 3 minutes, stirring with a fork to lightly crush berries. Spoon raspberry mixture onto 8 individual serving plates.

5. Split warm shortcakes in half horizontally. Place shortcake bottoms on top of raspberry mixture, and top with peaches and shortcake tops. Serve immediately with Sorghum Whipped Cream.

## SORGHUM WHIPPED CREAM

1 cup whipping cream                    2 tablespoons sorghum syrup

Beat the whipping cream at high speed with an electric mixer until foamy; add the sorghum syrup, and beat until soft peaks form. Makes 2 cups

# Blackberry Cobbler

There's nothing the least bit fussy about an old-fashioned blackberry cobbler, just a deep dish of summer-fresh flavor bubbling beneath a crisp golden crust. You'll find cultivated berries by the basketful at local farmers' markets, but the real treasure? Those tiny jewel-like gems, no bigger than a jellybean, that grow wild in tangled thickets alongside sunny country roads. When foraging, keep in mind that color isn't the only indicator of ripeness. Blackberries are sweetest when their glossy sheen changes to matte and they slip from the stem with a light touch.

Serves 6   Hands-on 15 minutes   Total 1 hour

4 cups fresh blackberries*
¾ cup sugar
1¼ cups all-purpose flour
2 tablespoons butter, cut into pieces

½ teaspoon table salt
⅓ cup shortening, cut into pieces
2½ tablespoons ice-cold water

1. Preheat the oven to 375°F. Lightly grease an 8-inch square baking dish. Stir together the blackberries, sugar, and ¼ cup of the flour. Spoon into the prepared baking dish; dot with the butter.

2. Combine the remaining 1 cup flour and salt; cut in the shortening with a pastry blender until the mixture is crumbly. Sprinkle the ice-cold water over the flour mixture, and stir with a fork until the dry ingredients are moistened. Shape the dough into a ball.

3. Roll the pastry into an 8-inch square on a lightly floured surface. Place the pastry over the baking dish, sealing the edges to the sides of the dish. Cut slits in the pastry.

4. Bake at 375°F for 45 to 50 minutes or until golden brown. Serve warm.

*2 (16-ounce) packages frozen blackberries, thawed, may be substituted.

1980s

# TENNTUCKY BLACKBERRY COBBLER SUNDAES

The cobbler? It's a longtime favorite with a buttery, cake-like crust and deliciously crisp caramelized edges. At first glance, the update may seem all about the clever soda fountain presentation, but then you spoon into the creamy richness of warm caramel sauce and the salty crunch of roasted pecans and experience a whole new revelation of texture and flavor.

Serves 6 to 8   Hands-on 20 minutes   Total 1 hour 25 minutes

3 tablespoons cornstarch
1½ cups sugar
6 cups fresh blackberries
½ cup butter, softened
2 large eggs
1½ cups all-purpose flour
1½ teaspoons baking powder

1 (8-ounce) container sour cream
½ teaspoon baking soda
Vanilla ice cream
Caramel sauce, warmed
Toasted salted pecans

1. Preheat the oven to 350°F. Lightly grease an 11- x 7-inch baking dish. Stir together the cornstarch and ½ cup of the sugar. Toss the berries with the cornstarch mixture, and spoon into the prepared baking dish.

2. Beat the butter at medium speed with an electric mixer until fluffy; gradually add the remaining 1 cup sugar, beating well. Add the eggs, 1 at a time, beating just until blended after each addition.

3. Combine the flour and baking powder. Stir together the sour cream and baking soda. Add the flour mixture to the butter mixture alternately with the sour cream mixture, beginning and ending with flour mixture. Beat at low speed just until blended after each addition. Spoon the batter over the berry mixture.

4. Bake at 350°F for 45 minutes; shield loosely with aluminum foil to prevent excessive browning, and bake at 350°F for 20 to 25 more minutes or until a wooden pick inserted in center of the cake topping comes out clean.

5. Layer the cobbler in parfait glasses with the vanilla ice cream, caramel sauce, and the salted pecans.

## FRESH TAKE

### Berried Treasure

Cobbler holds the power to conjure up deep cravings long after summer is over, but you won't find that fresh-picked Southern flavor in out-of-season imports. The solution? Freeze local berries at their peak to lock in the flavor. Just before freezing, gently wash the berries in cool water, and pat dry with paper towels. Remove and discard the stems, leaves, and any underripe or damaged fruit. Place the berries in a single layer on a jelly-roll pan, and freeze until firm. Transfer berries to zip-top plastic freezer bags, leaving 1-inch of headspace. Squeeze out the excess air; seal and freeze up to eight months. Add the frozen berries to muffins, cobblers, or anything else your winter dreams inspire.

# German Chocolate Cake

With a coconut-pecan frosting only a Southerner could have conjured up, German Chocolate Cake first appeared as Recipe of the Day in a Dallas, Texas, newspaper. Sent in by a local homemaker, it was an instant hit. The name? It came from the bar of Baker's German's Chocolate (created a century earlier by Samuel German) that gave the tender cake layers their distinctive flavor.

Serves 10 to 12   Hands-on 20 minutes   Total 3 hours 15 minutes, including frosting

1 (4-ounce) package sweet baking chocolate
½ cup water
1 teaspoon vanilla extract
1 cup butter, softened
2 cups sugar
4 large eggs, separated

3 cups cake flour
1 teaspoon baking soda
½ teaspoon table salt
1 cup buttermilk
Coconut-Pecan Frosting (see below)

1. Preheat the oven to 350°F. Grease and flour 3 (9-inch) round cake pans. Cook the chocolate and ½ cup water in a small saucepan over medium-low, stirring constantly, 2 minutes or until chocolate melts. Cool 5 minutes; stir in the vanilla.

2. Beat the butter and sugar at medium speed with an electric mixer until light and fluffy. Add the egg yolks, 1 at a time, beating well after each addition. Add the chocolate mixture; beat until blended.

3. Combine the flour, baking soda, and salt; add to the butter mixture alternately with the buttermilk, beginning and ending with the flour mixture.

4. Beat the egg whites at high speed with an electric mixer until stiff peaks form; fold into batter. Pour into the prepared pans.

5. Bake at 350°F for 25 to 30 minutes or until a wooden pick inserted in the center comes out clean. Cool in the pans on wire racks 10 minutes; remove from the pans to wire racks, and cool completely (about 1 hour). Spread Coconut-Pecan Frosting between the layers and on the top of the cake.

## Coconut-Pecan Frosting

1⅓ cups sugar
1⅓ cups evaporated milk
4 large egg yolks
⅔ cup butter

1⅓ cups sweetened flaked coconut
1⅓ cups chopped toasted pecans
1½ teaspoons vanilla extract

1. Bring the sugar, milk, egg yolks, and butter to a boil in a medium-size heavy saucepan over medium, stirring constantly. Reduce to medium-low. Cook, stirring constantly, 10 minutes.

2. Stir in the coconut, pecans, and vanilla. Cool 1 hour or until the mixture is spreading consistency, stirring occasionally. Makes 3¾ cups

1980s

# GERMAN CHOCOLATE PECAN PIE BARS

The very things that make a German chocolate layer cake so delicious also make it extremely difficult to tote to a tailgate. One sunny fall weekend, we took all that luscious coconut-caramel-pecan flavor and poured it over a crisp cocoa-rich shortbread crust with totally portable results guaranteed to score big on game day.

Makes 2 dozen   Hands-on 20 minutes
Total 3 hours 20 minutes

1 3/4 cups all-purpose flour
3/4 cup powdered sugar
3/4 cup cold butter, cubed
1/4 cup unsweetened cocoa
1 1/2 cups semisweet chocolate morsels
3/4 cup firmly packed brown sugar
3/4 cup light corn syrup
1/4 cup butter, melted
3 large eggs, lightly beaten
1 cup sweetened flaked coconut
3 cups toasted pecan halves and pieces

1. Preheat the oven to 350°F.

2. Line the bottom and sides of a 13- x 9-inch pan with heavy-duty aluminum foil, allowing 2 to 3 inches to extend over the sides. Lightly grease the foil.

3. Pulse the flour and next 3 ingredients in a food processor 5 or 6 times or until the mixture is crumbly. Press the mixture on the bottom and 3/4 inch up the sides of the prepared pan.

4. Bake the crust at 350°F for 15 minutes. Remove from the oven, and sprinkle the chocolate morsels over the crust. Cool completely on a wire rack (about 30 minutes).

5. Whisk together the brown sugar and next 3 ingredients until smooth. Stir in the coconut and toasted pecans, and spoon into the prepared crust.

6. Bake at 350°F for 25 to 30 minutes or until golden and set. Cool completely on a wire rack (about 1 hour). Chill 1 hour. Lift from the pan, using foil sides as handles. Transfer to a cutting board; cut into bars.

# Red Velvet Cake

Red velvet takes the cake for the most urban legends. Tales date back to the Great Depression and hopscotch from Texas to a Canadian department store. The beguiling Mystery Icing is actually a French-style butter roux frosting known as Ermine Icing. The chocolate-flavored drink mix? We have no explanation, but feel free to sub in unsweetened cocoa.

Serves 10 to 12   Hands-on 10 minutes   Total 2 hours 15 minutes, including icing

2½ cups cake flour
½ teaspoon table salt
3 tablespoons chocolate-flavored drink mix
⅔ cup butter, softened
1½ cups granulated sugar
2 large eggs

2 (1-ounce) bottles red food coloring
1 teaspoon vanilla extract
1 cup buttermilk
1 tablespoon white vinegar
1 teaspoon baking soda
Mystery Icing (see below)

1. Preheat the oven to 350°F. Grease and flour 2 (9-inch) round cake pans. Sift together the flour, salt, and chocolate-flavored mix. Beat the butter and sugar at medium speed with an electric mixer until light and fluffy. Beat in the eggs, 1 at a time. Beat in the food coloring and vanilla.

2. Stir together the buttermilk, vinegar, and baking soda in a 2-cup glass measuring cup (mixture will be foamy). Add the buttermilk mixture to the butter mixture alternately with the flour mixture, beginning and ending with the flour mixture; beat at low speed after each addition. Divide the batter between the prepared cake pans.

3. Bake at 350°F for 30 minutes or until a wooden pick inserted in the center comes out clean. Cool in pans on a wire rack 10 minutes; remove to wire rack; cool completely (about 1 hour).

4. Spread the Mystery Icing between the layers and on the top and the sides of the cake.

# Mystery Icing

¼ cup all-purpose flour
1 cup milk
1 cup sugar

1 cup butter, softened
1 teaspoon vanilla extract

1. Place the flour in a saucepan; gradually whisk in milk. Cook over medium, whisking constantly, until the mixture thickens, 4 minutes. Transfer to a bowl, and cool 15 to 20 minutes.

2. Beat the sugar, butter, and vanilla at medium speed with an electric mixer 5 minutes until fluffy. Gradually beat in the cooled milk mixture, beating 3 minutes until the icing is smooth and fluffy and the sugar is dissolved. Makes 3¼ cups

1970s

# RED VELVET– WHITE CHOCOLATE CHEESECAKE

The red velvet craze continues into the new millennium, which is one reason we chose this delectable creation for our December 2013 cover.

Serves 12   Hands-on 45 minutes   Total 13 hours 45 minutes

## CHEESECAKE LAYERS:

2 (8-inch) round disposable aluminum foil cake pans
1 (12-ounce) package white chocolate morsels
5 (8-ounce) packages cream cheese, softened
1 cup granulated sugar
2 large eggs
1 tablespoon vanilla extract

## RED VELVET LAYERS:

1 cup butter, softened
2½ cups granulated sugar
6 large eggs
3 cups all-purpose flour
3 tablespoons unsweetened cocoa
¼ teaspoon baking soda
1 (8-ounce) container sour cream
2 teaspoons vanilla extract
2 (1-ounce) bottles red liquid food coloring
3 (8-inch) round disposable aluminum foil cake pans

## WHITE CHOCOLATE FROSTING:

2 (4-ounce) white chocolate baking bars, chopped
½ cup boiling water
1 cup butter, softened
1 (32-ounce) package powdered sugar, sifted
⅛ teaspoon table salt
Garnishes: store-bought coconut candies, white candy leaves

1. Make the Cheesecake Layers: Preheat the oven to 300°F. Line the bottom and sides of 2 disposable cake pans with aluminum foil, allowing 2 to 3 inches to extend over the sides; lightly grease the foil.

2. Microwave the white chocolate morsels in a microwave-safe bowl according to package directions; cool 10 minutes.

3. Beat the cream cheese and melted chocolate at medium speed with an electric mixer until creamy; add 1 cup sugar, beating well. Add 2 eggs, 1 at a time, beating just until yellow disappears after each addition. Stir in the vanilla. Pour into prepared pans.

4. Bake at 300°F for 30 to 35 minutes or until almost set. Turn oven off. Let the cheesecakes stand in the oven, with the door closed, 30 minutes. Remove from the oven to wire racks; cool completely (about 1½ hours). Cover and chill 8 hours, or freeze 24 hours to 2 days.

5. Make the Red Velvet Layers: Preheat the oven to 350°F. Beat 1 cup butter at medium speed with a heavy-duty electric stand mixer until creamy. Gradually add the 2½ cups sugar, beating until light and fluffy. Add the 6 eggs, 1 at a time, beating just until blended after each addition.

6. Stir together the flour and next 2 ingredients; add to the butter mixture alternately with the sour cream, beginning and ending with the flour mixture. Beat at low speed just until blended after each addition. Stir in 2 teaspoons vanilla; stir in the food coloring. Spoon the batter into 3 greased and floured 8-inch disposable cake pans.

7. Bake at 350°F for 20 to 24 minutes or until a wooden pick inserted in the center comes out clean. Cool in the pans on wire racks 10 minutes. Remove from the pans to wire racks; cool completely (about 1 hour).

8. Make the Frosting: Whisk together the chocolate and ½ cup boiling water until the chocolate melts. Cool 20 minutes; chill 30 minutes.

9. Beat 1 cup butter and chilled chocolate mixture at low speed until blended. Beat at medium speed 1 minute. Increase the speed to high; beat 2 to 3 minutes or until fluffy. Gradually add the powdered sugar and salt, beating at low speed until blended. Increase the speed to high; beat 1 to 2 minutes or until smooth and fluffy.

10. Assemble the cake: Place 1 Red Velvet layer on a serving platter. Top with 1 Cheesecake layer. Repeat with remaining layers of Red Velvet and Cheesecake, alternating and ending with Red Velvet on top. Spread the top and sides of the cake with White Chocolate Frosting. Store in the refrigerator.

## FLASHBACK
### What's in a Name?

Sometime long ago, a basic chocolate cake baked up North blushed red due to the serendipitous result of natural cocoa reacting with acids like vinegar or buttermilk in the batter, which revealed the red anthocyanin in the chocolate. Somehow, the reddish-brown cake with its moist, velvety texture yielded a recipe name that over the decades has become synonymous with the South: Red Velvet. The Dutch process cocoa of recent times is treated with an alkalizing agent that inhibits this chemical reaction, making the addition of red food dye or even grated red beets (which also lends moistness to the crumb) necessary to give the cake its namesake color.

# Lemon-Orange Pound Cake

◇

It was the decade of the five-flavor pound cake (that glorious extract extravaganza—spiked with vanilla, coconut, rum, lemon, and artificial butter flavoring). This citrus-glazed showstopper used just two extracts, allowing the rich tang of the buttermilk to shine through. Purists frown on leavening agents in pound cake, but trust us, the velvety texture of this cake is nothing short of perfection.

Serves 12 to 16   Hands-on 15 minutes   Total 3 hours 25 minutes, including glaze

½ cup shortening
½ cup butter, softened
2 cups sugar
6 large eggs
3 cups all-purpose flour
1 teaspoon baking powder
½ teaspoon table salt

½ teaspoon baking soda
1 cup buttermilk
1 teaspoon vanilla extract
1 teaspoon lemon extract
Citrus Glaze (see below)
Garnishes: fresh mint sprigs, orange and
    lemon slices

1. Preheat the oven to 350°F. Grease and flour a 10-inch (16-cup) tube pan or 14-cup Bundt pan. Beat the shortening, butter, and sugar at medium speed with a heavy-duty electric stand mixer until light and fluffy. Add the eggs, 1 at a time, beating well after each addition.

2. Combine the flour, baking powder, salt, and baking soda; add to the butter mixture alternately with the buttermilk, beginning and ending with the flour mixture. Beat in the vanilla and lemon extracts. Pour the batter into the prepared pan.

3. Bake at 350°F for 55 minutes to 1 hour or until a long wooden pick inserted in the center comes out clean. Cool in the pan 10 minutes; remove from the pan to a wire rack.

4. Pierce the top of warm cake all over using a wooden pick; gradually spoon the glaze over the cake, allowing it to soak into the cake after each addition. Cool completely (about 2 hours).

# Citrus Glaze

1½ cups powdered sugar
1½ teaspoons lemon zest
1½ teaspoons orange zest

3 tablespoons fresh orange juice
3 tablespoons fresh lemon juice

Whisk together all the ingredients until well blended. Makes about ⅔ cup

1970s

# BUTTERMILK POUND CAKE

The new millennium marked a return to the comforts of delicious simplicity. This old-fashioned favorite gets its lift the traditional way—from well-creamed butter and sugar and a half dozen eggs. It stays moist for days. There's no wrong way to serve this duo, but may we suggest starting with warm cake and cold custard?

Serves 12   Hands-on 35 minutes
Total 2 hours 45 minutes, including sauce

1⅓ cups butter, softened
2½ cups sugar
6 large eggs
3 cups all-purpose flour

½ cup buttermilk
1 teaspoon vanilla extract
Buttermilk Custard Sauce
   (see below)

1. Preheat the oven to 325°F. Grease and flour a 10-inch (12-cup) tube pan. Beat the butter at medium speed with a heavy-duty electric stand mixer until creamy. Gradually add the sugar, beating at medium speed until light and fluffy. Add the eggs, 1 at a time, beating just until blended after each addition.

2. Add the flour to the butter mixture alternately with the buttermilk, beginning and ending with the flour. Beat at low speed just until blended after each addition. Stir in the vanilla. Pour the batter into the prepared pan.

3. Bake at 325°F for 1 hour and 5 minutes to 1 hour and 10 minutes or until a long wooden pick inserted in the center comes out clean. Cool in the pan on a wire rack 10 to 15 minutes; remove from the pan to wire rack, and cool completely (about 1 hour). Serve with Buttermilk Custard Sauce.

# BUTTERMILK CUSTARD SAUCE

2 cups buttermilk
½ cup sugar
1 tablespoon cornstarch

3 large egg yolks
1 teaspoon vanilla extract

Whisk together the buttermilk, sugar, cornstarch, and egg yolks in a heavy 3-quart saucepan. Bring to a boil over medium heat, whisking constantly, and boil 1 minute. Remove from heat, and stir in the vanilla. Serve warm or cold. Store leftovers in an airtight container in refrigerator up to 1 week. Makes about 2⅓ cups

# Manny and Isa's Key Lime Pie

For four decades, Manny and Isa Ortiz owned the eponymous landmark restaurant in Islamorado, Florida. Although we offered a shortcut with refrigerated piecrust (a 90s novelty), the flaky pastry of their legendary pie was made from scratch, and the Key limes came from their own backyard. The topping? Glossy, golden peaks of featherlight meringue.

Serves 8   Hands-on 15 minutes   Total 4 hours 25 minutes

½ (14.1-ounce) package refrigerated piecrusts
5 large eggs, separated
1 (14-ounce) can sweetened condensed milk

½ cup fresh or bottled Key lime juice
¼ teaspoon cream of tartar
⅓ cup sugar

1. Preheat the oven to 425°F. Unroll the piecrust, and place in a 9-inch pie plate; fold the edges under, and crimp. Line the piecrust with aluminum foil; fill with pie weights or dried beans.

2. Bake at 425°F for 15 minutes or until the crust is set and the edges are golden brown. Remove the pie weights and foil; bake at 425°F for 5 to 7 more minutes or until golden brown. Cool completely on a wire rack (about 30 minutes).

3. Reduce oven temperature to 325°F. Combine the egg yolks, condensed milk, and lime juice in a heavy nonaluminum saucepan. Cook over medium, whisking constantly, 6 minutes or until the mixture boils and thickens. Pour into the piecrust.

4. Beat the egg whites and cream of tartar at high speed with an electric mixer until foamy. Gradually add the sugar, 1 tablespoon at a time, beating until stiff peaks form and sugar dissolves (about 2 to 4 minutes). Spread the meringue over the warm filling, sealing to the edge of the crust.

5. Bake at 325°F for 20 minutes or until golden brown. Cool completely on a wire rack (about 1 hour). Chill 2 hours before serving.

1990s

# PRALINE KEY LIME PIE

The inspiration for this delectable update? A summer cover shoot. Photographer Beth Dreiling Hontzas brought lunch in for the crew: fresh vegetable plates and a Key lime pie from her husband, Tim's, restaurant, Johnny's, in Homewood, Alabama. Not just any Key lime pie but one with an irresistible layer of caramel and pecans baked between the filling and crust. One extravagant forkful and we knew we absolutely had to re-create it for our readers.

Serves 8   Hands-on 30 minutes   Total 7 hours

2 cups graham cracker crumbs
½ cup butter, melted
¼ cup firmly packed light brown sugar
1¼ cups chopped toasted pecans
½ cup plus 2 tablespoons jarred caramel topping
2 (14-ounce) cans sweetened condensed milk
6 large egg yolks
2 teaspoons Key lime or lime zest
1 cup fresh Key lime or lime juice
1½ cups whipping cream
¼ cup plus 2 tablespoons powdered sugar
Garnishes: lime slices, caramel topping, chopped toasted pecans

1. Preheat the oven to 350°F. Lightly grease a 10-inch deep-dish pie plate.

2. Stir together the graham cracker crumbs, next 2 ingredients, and ½ cup of the toasted pecans until blended. Press the crumb mixture on the bottom, up the sides, and onto the lip of a lightly greased 10-inch deep-dish pie plate.

3. Bake at 350°F for 10 to 12 minutes or until lightly browned. Remove from the oven to a wire rack, and cool completely (about 45 minutes).

4. Sprinkle the remaining ¾ cup toasted pecans over the bottom of the crust; drizzle the caramel topping over the pecans.

5. Whisk together the sweetened condensed milk and the next 3 ingredients. Gently pour into the prepared crust.

6. Bake at 350°F for 20 to 25 minutes or until almost set. (The center will not be firm but will set up as it chills.) Cool completely on a wire rack (about 1 hour). Cover and chill 4 hours.

7. Beat the whipping cream at high speed with an electric mixer until foamy; gradually add the powdered sugar, beating until soft peaks form. Dollop or spread over the pie.

## FLASHBACK
### Key Lime Pie 101

Key lime pies have been around since cans of sweetened condensed milk were first introduced in the late 1800s. The authentic Key lime pie? Well, that depends on who you ask. Rolled and crimped pastry crust or graham cracker crumb crust? A thrifty meringue topping using leftover egg whites or sweetened whipped cream? All matters of opinion. Eggs in the filling? Optional. Some use no eggs, relying on the acid in the lime juice to thicken the condensed milk after a few hours in the refrigerator or freezer. Others add egg yolks and bake the pie just long enough to set the filling. Browning and high-rise souffléing are seriously frowned upon. Food coloring? Strictly forbidden. The filling should echo the pale golden color of ripened Key limes—not the brilliant green of Persian limes that are harvested before turning yellow.

# Captivating Coconut Cream Pie

Electric refrigerators have been humming with icebox pies since the 1930s. Coconut cream pie? It still headlines the dessert list of back-road diners and BBQ joints from West Texas to the Carolinas. And each pie still bears the signature stamp of the cook who makes it—from vodka-spiked pastry crust to mile-high toasted meringue toppings. This favorite boasts a velvety-smooth filling enriched with cream of coconut.

Serves 8 to 10   Hands-on 20 minutes   Total 2 hours 40 minutes

½ (14.1-ounce) package refrigerated piecrusts
½ cup granulated sugar
6 tablespoons cornstarch
½ teaspoon table salt
1½ cups half-and-half
1 cup cream of coconut
4 large egg yolks

6 tablespoons butter
2 teaspoons vanilla extract
1 teaspoon coconut extract
1¾ cups sweetened flaked coconut
1¼ cups whipping cream
¼ cup powdered sugar
Garnish: fresh toasted coconut

1. Preheat the oven to 425°F. Unroll the piecrust, and place in a 9-inch pie plate; fold edges under, and crimp. Line the piecrust with aluminum foil; fill with pie weights or dried beans.

2. Bake at 425°F for 15 minutes or until the crust is set and edges are golden brown. Remove the pie weights and foil; bake at 425°F for 5 to 7 more minutes or until golden brown. Cool completely on a wire rack (about 30 minutes).

3. Combine the granulated sugar, cornstarch, and salt in a large heavy saucepan; gradually stir in the half-and-half and cream of coconut. Cook over medium, whisking constantly, 6 minutes or until the mixture is thickened and bubbly.

4. Whisk the egg yolks in a bowl until well blended. Gradually whisk about one-fourth of the hot sugar mixture into the eggs. Whisk the eggs into the remaining hot sugar mixture, whisking constantly. Cook 1 minute, whisking constantly. Remove from the heat. Whisk in the butter, vanilla, and ½ teaspoon of the coconut extract, whisking until the butter melts. Whisk in 1½ cups of the flaked coconut.

5. Pour the filling into the cooled crust. Cool completely (about 30 minutes); cover and chill at least 2 hours.

6. Meanwhile, preheat the oven to 350°F. Spread the remaining ¼ cup flaked coconut in a single layer on a baking sheet. Bake at 350°F for 6 to 8 minutes or until toasted.

7. Beat the whipping cream at high speed with an electric mixer until foamy. Gradually add the powdered sugar, 1 tablespoon at a time, beating until stiff peaks form. Beat in the remaining ½ teaspoon coconut extract. Spoon the whipped cream onto the chilled pie. Sprinkle with the toasted coconut.

1990s

# PIÑA COLADA ICEBOX PIE

Create this icebox homage to Jimmy Buffett with a double layer of pineapple and coconut-cream cheese custard baked in an over-the-rim crust. Plus, there's no need to wrangle with a rolling pin—but do press the crumb mixture all the way up the sides of the pie plate before baking; otherwise, you'll end up with a thick, uneven crust that's too shallow to hold the filling.

Serves 8   Hands-on 25 minutes   Total 7 hours 10 minutes

2 cups pecan shortbread cookie crumbs (about 16 cookies)
1 cup sweetened flaked coconut
¼ cup butter, melted
⅓ cup sugar
2 tablespoons cornstarch
1 (8-ounce) can crushed pineapple in juice
1 (8-ounce) package cream cheese, softened
1½ cups cream of coconut
2 large eggs
1 cup whipping cream
Garnishes: lightly toasted shaved coconut, pineapple wedges, fresh pineapple mint sprigs

1. Preheat the oven to 350°F. Lightly grease a 9-inch pie plate. Stir together first 3 ingredients; firmly press on the bottom and up sides of prepared pie plate. Bake at 350°F for 12 minutes or until lightly browned. Transfer to a wire rack; cool completely (30 minutes).

2. Stir together the sugar and cornstarch in a small heavy saucepan; stir in the pineapple. While stirring constantly, bring to a boil over medium-high; cook (keep stirring) 1 minute or until thickened. Remove from heat; cool completely (about 20 minutes).

3. Beat the cream cheese at medium speed with a heavy-duty electric stand mixer, using whisk attachment, until smooth. Gradually add 1 cup of the cream of coconut, beating at low speed just until blended. (Chill the remaining ½ cup cream of coconut until ready to use.) Add the eggs, 1 at a time, beating just until blended after each addition.

4. Spread the cooled pineapple mixture over the bottom of the piecrust; spoon the cream cheese mixture over pineapple mixture.

5. Bake at 350°F for 38 to 42 minutes or until set. Cool completely on a wire rack (about 1 hour). Cover and chill 4 hours.

6. Beat the whipping cream at high speed until foamy. Gradually add the remaining ½ cup cream of coconut, beating until soft peaks form; spread over the pie.

# Mississippi Mud Cake

◆

It's one of a trio of cocoa-rich Southern sheet cakes. Texas sheet cake (with toasted pecans added to the boiled chocolate frosting) and Atlanta's Coca-Cola cake (with baby marshmallows stirred into the batter) are noteworthy cousins. An early collection of *Southern Living* cakes extolled Mississippi Mud's curative powers: "It is so dark, so moist, and so rich...Mississippi Mud Cake will cure the most desperate craving for chocolate." We'd say it's lost none of its virtues.

Serves 24   Hands-on 10 minutes   Total 1 hour 40 minutes, including frosting

1 cup butter
½ cup unsweetened cocoa
2 cups sugar
1 teaspoon vanilla extract
4 large eggs, lightly beaten

1½ cups all-purpose flour
⅛ teaspoon table salt
1½ cups chopped toasted pecans
1 (10-ounce) bag miniature marshmallows
Chocolate Frosting (see below)

1. Preheat the oven to 350°F. Grease a 13- x 9-inch pan. Combine the butter and cocoa in a medium saucepan over medium. Cook, stirring often, 2 minutes or until the butter melts and the mixture is smooth.

2. Remove from the heat, and whisk in the sugar and vanilla. Whisk in the eggs. Whisk in the flour and salt; fold in the pecans. Pour the batter into the prepared pan.

3. Bake at 350°F for 20 to 25 minutes or until a wooden pick inserted in center comes out with a few moist crumbs. Sprinkle the marshmallows on the warm cake; bake at 350°F for 5 minutes. Drizzle the warm cake with the Chocolate Frosting. Cool completely on a wire rack (about 1 hour).

# Chocolate Frosting

½ cup butter
⅓ cup unsweetened cocoa

⅓ cup whole milk
1 (1-pound) package powdered sugar

Cook the butter, cocoa, and milk in a medium saucepan over medium, whisking constantly, 2 minutes or until the butter melts and the mixture is smooth. Remove from the heat; whisk in the powdered sugar until smooth. Makes 2 cups

1970s

# MISSISSIPPI MUD CUPCAKES

Rather than turn out mini-me versions of Mississippi Mud Cake, we scaled up the wow factor, reaching new heights with billowy swirls of marshmallow frosting.

Makes 1 dozen   Hands-on 40 minutes
Total 1 hour 20 minutes, including frosting

12 paper baking cups
Vegetable cooking spray
⅓ cup butter, softened
⅔ cup sugar
2 large eggs
1 cup all-purpose flour
⅓ cup unsweetened cocoa
¼ teaspoon table salt
½ cup sour cream
¾ teaspoon baking soda
1 (4-ounce) semisweet chocolate baking bar, finely chopped
Marshmallow Frosting (see below)
⅓ cup roasted glazed pecan pieces

1. Preheat the oven to 350°F. Place paper baking cups in a 12-cup muffin pan, and coat with cooking spray. Beat the butter at medium speed with an electric mixer until fluffy; gradually add sugar, beating well. Add the eggs, 1 at a time, beating just until blended.

2. Combine the flour, cocoa, and salt. Stir together the sour cream and baking soda. Add the flour mixture to butter mixture alternately with sour cream mixture, beginning and ending with flour mixture. Beat at low speed just until blended after each addition. Stir in half of chopped chocolate.

3. Spoon batter into cups, filling two-thirds full.

4. Bake at 350°F for 18 to 20 minutes or until a wooden pick inserted in center comes out clean. Remove from pan to a wire rack, and cool completely (about 30 minutes).

5. Pipe the Marshmallow Frosting onto cupcakes; sprinkle with pecans and remaining chopped chocolate.

## MARSHMALLOW FROSTING

½ (8-ounce) package cream cheese, softened
¼ cup butter, softened
1 (7-ounce) jar marshmallow crème
2 teaspoons vanilla extract
2½ cups powdered sugar

Beat the cream cheese and next 3 ingredients at medium speed with an electric mixer until creamy. Gradually add the powdered sugar, beating at low speed until blended and smooth. Makes 2 cups

## FLASHBACK
### Cocoa Loco

In today's gourmet world of haute chocolate, cooking with cocoa may seem old school, but it still delivers maximum chocolate flavor. Cocoa powder is pure chocolate with most of the cocoa butter removed. There are two basic types of cocoa: natural cocoa and more delicately flavored Dutch process cocoa, which has been treated with an alkali to neutralize the acidity. Both are unsweetened and can be used interchangeably in some recipes but definitely not in baked goods that call for a chemical leaven. While natural cocoa (an acid) reacts with baking soda, Dutch process cocoa must be paired with baking powder unless another acidic ingredient is present in the recipe. Hershey's Special Dark Cocoa? It's a rich blend of natural and Dutch process cocoas.

# Bourbon Chocolate Pecan Tarts

If you're a fan of pecan tassies (and let's face it, who isn't?), move these tarts to the top of your to-do list. Imagine the perfect cream cheese pastry crust paired with a decadent chocolate pecan filling. Then add a splash of bourbon to that thought. And there's more: They pop from the pans perfectly fluted and party-ready.

Makes 5 tarts   Hands-on 15 minutes
Total 3 hours, 20 minutes, including pastry

Vegetable cooking spray
Cream Cheese Pastry (see below)
¾ cup semisweet chocolate morsels
2 large eggs, lightly beaten
½ cup light corn syrup
¼ cup granulated sugar
1 tablespoon all-purpose flour

2 tablespoons firmly packed light brown sugar
3 tablespoons butter, melted
2 tablespoons bourbon
1 teaspoon vanilla extract
1¼ cups pecan halves

1. Preheat the oven to 350°F. Coat a 4½-inch tart pan with cooking spray. Divide Cream Cheese Pastry into 5 equal portions; press each portion into a 4½-inch tart pan coated with cooking spray. Sprinkle chocolate morsels over pastry; chill 30 minutes.

2. Whisk together eggs and next 7 ingredients until blended. Place tart pans on a baking sheet. Pour batter into pans, filling each half full. Arrange pecan halves over filling; drizzle with remaining filling.

3. Bake at 350°F for 30 minutes or until browned and set; cool completely (about 1 hour).

Note: You can bake this in one 9-inch tart pan, if desired. Prepare recipe as directed, increasing bake time to 55 minutes or until filling is set.

## Cream Cheese Pastry

3 ounces cream cheese, softened
½ cup butter, softened

1 cup all-purpose flour

Beat the cream cheese and butter at medium speed with an electric mixer until smooth. Add the flour; beat at low speed until a soft dough forms. Shape dough into a flat disk; wrap in plastic wrap, and chill 1 hour. Makes enough pastry for 5 (4½-inch) tarts or 1 (9-inch) tart

1990s

# CARAMEL PECAN TART

Pure indulgence: honey-rich caramel and crunchy pecans encased in a buttery shortbread crust. How good is it? Let's just say, give it a trial run for your next dinner party and come November, you may rethink your grandmother's heirloom pecan pie. No tart pan? Just use an aluminum foil-lined baking pan and transfer to a serving tray.

Serves 12   Hands-on 20 minutes   Total 1 hour 50 minutes

2 cups all-purpose flour
$^2$/$_3$ cup powdered sugar
$^3$/$_4$ cup butter, cubed
$^1$/$_2$ cup firmly packed brown sugar
$^1$/$_2$ cup honey

$^2$/$_3$ cup butter
3 tablespoons whipping cream
3$^1$/$_2$ cups coarsely chopped toasted pecans

1. Preheat the oven to 350°F. Lightly grease an 11-inch tart pan with a removable bottom.

2. Pulse the flour, powdered sugar, and $^3$/$_4$ cup butter in a food processor 5 or 6 times or until the mixture is crumbly. Pat the mixture evenly on the bottom and up the sides of prepared tart pan.

3. Bake at 350°F for 20 minutes or until edges are lightly browned. Cool on a wire rack 15 minutes or until completely cool.

4. Bring the brown sugar, honey, $^2$/$_3$ cup butter, and whipping cream to a boil in a 3-quart saucepan over medium-high. Stir in the toasted pecans, and spoon the hot filling into the prepared crust.

5. Bake at 350°F for 25 to 30 minutes or until golden and bubbly. Cool on a wire rack 30 minutes or until completely cool.

Caramel-Pecan Bars: Prepare the recipe as directed, pressing the crumb mixture evenly on the bottom and $^3$/$_4$ inch up the sides of a lightly greased heavy-duty aluminum foil-lined 13- x 9-inch pan. When completely cool, using the aluminum foil as handles, carefully lift the tart from the pan, and transfer to a serving tray. Cut into bars. Makes about 2 dozen

## FLASHBACK

### Nuts for Pecan Pie

Early recipes for pecan pie date back to promotions found on Karo syrup bottles in the 30s. We inherited a similar favorite from the mother of former Test Kitchen Pro James Schend. It continues to get rave reviews.

**Mom's Pecan Pie:**
Preheat the oven to 350°F. Stir together 3 large eggs, 1 cup sugar, $^3$/$_4$ cup light or dark corn syrup, 2 tablespoons melted butter, 2 teaspoons vanilla extract, and $^1$/$_2$ teaspoon table salt in a medium bowl; stir in 1$^1$/$_2$ cups toasted pecan pieces. Pour the filling into one 9-inch deep-dish frozen unbaked pie shell. Bake at 350°F for 55 minutes or until set, shielding the pie with aluminum foil after 20 minutes to prevent excessive browning. Serve warm or cold. Serves 8

# Fresh Peach Ice Cream

———◇———

This vintage frozen custard gets its divine richness from evaporated milk and sweetened condensed milk. Both were once popular in the South because they required no refrigeration. Egg safety issues arose in the 80s (after this recipe was originally published) and prompted us to use only cooked custards as an ice-cream base. Today, pasteurized eggs are widely available and eliminate concern.

Makes 9 cups   Hands-on 20 minutes   Total 6 hours 50 minutes, including chill time

5 large egg yolks
½ cup sugar
2 cups whole milk
1 (14-ounce) can sweetened
    condensed milk

1 (12-ounce) can evaporated milk
2 cups mashed peaches
1½ teaspoons vanilla extract

1. Whisk together the egg yolks and sugar in a large heavy saucepan. Whisk in the milks. Cook over medium-low, stirring constantly, 15 minutes or until the mixture coats the back of a spoon. Stir in the peaches and vanilla.

2. Cool completely (about 30 minutes); cover and chill at least 4 hours or up to 8 hours.

3. Pour the custard into the freezer container of a 2½- to 3-quart electric ice-cream maker, and freeze according to manufacturer's instructions. (Instructions and times may vary.) Transfer to a freezer-safe container; freeze 2 hours or until firm.

1970s

# PEACH-AND-TOASTED PECAN ICE CREAM

Double-dessert is the word of the day. It's all about layering in the flavors and merging two Southern favorites into one phenomenal dish (or waffle cone). The ultimate ice cream fusion? Fresh sweet summer peaches and salty butter-roasted pecans made with a cream-rich cooked custard.

Makes about 1 quart    Hands-on 32 minutes
Total 10 hours 32 minutes, not including freezing time

³/₄ cup sugar
2 tablespoons cornstarch
¹/₈ teaspoon table salt
2 cups milk
1 cup heavy whipping cream
1 large egg yolk
1¹/₂ teaspoons vanilla bean paste

1 cup peeled and coarsely chopped peaches
2 tablespoons light corn syrup
1¹/₂ tablespoons butter
1 cup coarsely chopped pecans
¹/₄ teaspoon kosher salt

1. Whisk together the first 3 ingredients in a large heavy saucepan. Gradually whisk in the milk and whipping cream. Cook over medium, stirring constantly, 10 to 12 minutes or until the mixture thickens slightly. Remove from the heat.

2. Whisk the egg yolk until slightly thickened. Gradually whisk about 1 cup hot cream mixture into the yolk. Add the yolk mixture to the remaining hot cream mixture, whisking constantly. Whisk in the vanilla bean paste. Cool 1 hour, stirring occasionally.

3. Meanwhile, cook the peaches and corn syrup in a small saucepan over medium, stirring often, 4 to 5 minutes. Coarsely mash, and let cool 30 minutes. Stir the peach mixture into the cooled cream mixture.

4. Place plastic wrap directly on the cream mixture, and chill 8 to 24 hours.

5. Meanwhile, melt the butter in a small skillet over medium; add the pecans, and cook, stirring constantly, 8 to 9 minutes or until toasted and fragrant. Remove from heat, and sprinkle with ¹/₄ teaspoon kosher salt. Cool completely (about 30 minutes).

6. Pour the chilled cream mixture into the freezer container of a 1¹/₂-quart electric ice-cream maker, and freeze according to manufacturer's instructions. (Instructions and times may vary.) Before transferring the ice cream to an airtight container for further freezing, stir in the pecan mixture.

Memory Book Cookies
1 cup butter, softened        1 cup pecans
2 cups brown sugar            ½ teaspoon salt
2 eggs
1 teaspoon vanilla extract

# Memory Book Cookies

Long before store-bought slice-and-bake cookies, Southern cooks were shaping cookie doughs into cylinders and storing them in the icebox—ready for drop-in company at a moment's notice. This vintage favorite, made with brown sugar and pecans, gets its name from the prized family recipes that were often preserved in memory books for safekeeping.

Makes 6 dozen   Hands-on 15 minutes   Total 5 hours 10 minutes

1 cup butter, softened
2 cups firmly packed brown sugar
2 large eggs
1 teaspoon vanilla extract
3½ cups all-purpose flour

1 teaspoon baking soda
½ teaspoon table salt
1 cup chopped pecans
Parchment paper

1. Beat the butter at medium speed with an electric mixer; gradually add the sugar, beating well. Add the eggs and vanilla; beat until well blended.

2. Combine the flour, baking soda, and salt; gradually add to the butter mixture, beating well. Stir in the pecans. Shape the dough into 2 (12-inch) logs; wrap in plastic wrap, and chill at least 4 hours.

3. Preheat the oven to 375°F. Unwrap the dough, and cut into ⅓-inch-thick slices; place on parchment paper-lined baking sheets.

4. Bake at 375°F for 10 to 12 minutes or until the edges are lightly browned. Cool on wire racks.

Note: Dough may be frozen up to three months. Slice the dough while frozen, and bake as directed.

1990s

# ICEBOX BUTTER COOKIES

One recipe, infinite possibilities. Fragrant and buttery, but more delicate than shortbread, these classic cookies are the perfect canvas for delectable stir-ins. And that's just for starters. Try dipping the lemon-basil twist in melted white chocolate or the praline pecan in dark chocolate. Or, better yet, sandwich together pairs of java chip and dulce de leche.

Makes 8 to 10 dozen   Hands-on 20 minutes
Total 1 hour 45 minutes, plus chill time

1 cup butter, softened
1½ cups granulated sugar
½ cup firmly packed light
   brown sugar
1 tablespoon vanilla extract

2 large eggs
3½ cups all-purpose flour
½ teaspoon baking soda
½ teaspoon table salt
Parchment paper

1. Beat the first 4 ingredients at medium speed with an electric mixer until fluffy. Add the eggs, 1 at a time, beating just until blended after each addition.

2. Stir together the flour and next 2 ingredients; gradually add to the butter mixture, beating just until blended after each addition.

3. Shape the dough into 4 logs (about 2 inches in diameter); wrap each log in plastic wrap. Chill 8 hours to 3 days.

4. Preheat the oven to 350°F. Cut each log into ¼-inch-thick slices; place on parchment paper-lined baking sheets. Bake at 350°F for 8 to 12 minutes or until lightly browned. Remove from the baking sheets to wire racks, and cool completely (about 20 minutes).

---

## FRESH TAKE

### Try These Sweet Stir-ins

**Spiced Sweet Tea:** Add 3 Tbsp. unsweetened instant tea mix, 2 Tbsp. orange zest, 1 Tbsp. lemon zest, and 2 tsp. pumpkin pie spice with the first 4 ingredients in Step 1. Roll the logs in Demerara sugar before chilling.

**Praline Pecan:** Stir in 1½ cups roasted glazed pecan pieces after adding the flour mixture in Step 2.

**Lemon-Basil:** Add ¼ cup finely chopped fresh basil, 2 Tbsp. lemon zest, and 2 Tbsp. poppy seeds with the first 4 ingredients in Step 1.

# ✦ ACKNOWLEDGMENTS ✦

## Author Bio

Mary Allen Perry is a freelance artist, writer, and recipe developer. A longtime food editor of *Southern Living* magazine, she was a finalist for a James Beard Journalism Award in 2012, and received the Time Inc. Brilliant Lifestyle Award in 2013.

## Acknowledgments

This extraordinary collection of recipes would not have been possible without the contributions of past and present members of the *Southern Living* food staff. For fifty years this diverse and enthusiastic group of Southern food lovers have collaborated with readers across the region to produce a monthly offering of seasonal recipes and feature stories that together comprise the ultimate community cookbook.

Kaye Mabry Adams
Margaret Chason Agnew
Ashley Arthur
Sara Jane Ball
Elle Barrett
Cynthia Briscoe
Natalie Kelly Brown
Lyda Jones Burnette
Leslie Byars
Jane Cairns
Marian Cooper Cairns
Dana Adkins Campbell
Karen Collier
Lynnmarie P. Cook
Phyllis Young Cordell
Justin B. Craft
Cathy Criss
Kristi Michele Crowe
Sandra Day
Susan Payne Dobbs
Margaret Monroe Dickey
Helen Anne Dorrough
Susan Dosier
Julia Dowling

Charla Draper
Jane Elliot
Betsy Fannin
Judy Feagin
Donna Florio
Anna C. Fowler
Denise Gee
Susan Nash Gilpin
Rebecca Cracke Gordon
Holley Johnson Grainger
Julie Grimes
Shirley Harrington
Hannah Hayes
Monique Hicks
Martha Hinrichs
Diane Hogan
Andria Scott Hurst
Vanessa Taylor Johnson
Scott Jones
Carole King
Norman King
Gena Knox
Ashley Leath

Alison Lewis
Ann Lewis
Jean Wickstrom Liles
Lynne Lloyd
Jodie Jackson Loe
Pam Lolley
Deborah G. Lowery
Cindy Manning
Laura Martin
Marion McGahey
Susan M. McIntosh
Nola McKey
John McMillan
Robby Melvin
Erin Merhar
Jackie Mills, R.D.
Beverly Nesbit, R.D.
Laura Nestelroad
Nancy Nevins
Kate Nicholson
Karen Parker
Beverly Morrow Perrine
Vicki A. Poellnitz
Alyssa Porubcan

Jan Jacks Potter
Susan J. Reynolds
Vanessa McNeil Rocchio
Shannon Sliter Satterwhite
James Schend
Angela Sellers
Carroll Sessions
Connie Shedd
Peggy Smith
Lena Sturges
Kim Sunèe
Cybil Brown Talley
Donna Taylor
B. Ellen Templeton
Fran Tyler
Patty M. Vann
Vie Warshaw
Joann Weatherly
Linda Welch
Whitney Wright
Marilyn Wyrick
Pat York
Joy E. Zacharia

*A very special note of thanks to Oxmoor House Senior Editor and Brand Leader, Katherine Cobbs, whose creative vision, guidance, and keen editorial skills were invaluable in the writing of this book.*

# METRIC EQUIVALENTS

The recipes that appear in this cookbook use the standard U.S. method for measuring liquid and dry or solid ingredients (teaspoons, tablespoons, and cups). The information on this chart is provided to help cooks outside the United States successfully use these recipes. All equivalents are approximate.

## Metric Equivalents for Different Types of Ingredients

A standard cup measure of a dry or solid ingredient will vary in weight depending on the type of ingredient. A standard cup of liquid is the same volume for any type of liquid. Use the following chart when converting standard cup measures to grams (weight) or milliliters (volume).

| Standard Cup | Fine Powder (ex. flour) | Grain (ex. rice) | Granular (ex. sugar) | Liquid Solids (ex. butter) | Liquid (ex. milk) |
|---|---|---|---|---|---|
| 1 | 140 g | 150 g | 190 g | 200 g | 240 ml |
| ³/₄ | 105 g | 113 g | 143 g | 150 g | 180 ml |
| ²/₃ | 93 g | 100 g | 125 g | 133 g | 160 ml |
| ¹/₂ | 70 g | 75 g | 95 g | 100 g | 120 ml |
| ¹/₃ | 47 g | 50 g | 63 g | 67 g | 80 ml |
| ¹/₄ | 35 g | 38 g | 48 g | 50 g | 60 ml |
| ¹/₈ | 18 g | 19 g | 24 g | 25 g | 30 ml |

## Useful Equivalents for Liquid Ingredients by Volume

| | | | | | |
|---|---|---|---|---|---|
| ¹/₄ tsp | | | = | 1 ml | |
| ¹/₂ tsp | | | = | 2 ml | |
| 1 tsp | | | = | 5 ml | |
| 3 tsp | = 1 Tbsp | | = ¹/₂ fl oz | 15 ml | |
| | 2 Tbsp | = ¹/₈ cup | = 1 fl oz | 30 ml | |
| | 4 Tbsp | = ¹/₄ cup | = 2 fl oz | 60 ml | |
| | 5 ¹/₃ Tbsp | = ¹/₃ cup | = 3 fl oz | 80 ml | |
| | 8 Tbsp | = ¹/₂ cup | = 4 fl oz | 120 ml | |
| | 10 ²/₃ Tbsp | = ²/₃ cup | = 5 fl oz | 160 ml | |
| | 12 Tbsp | = ³/₄ cup | = 6 fl oz | 180 ml | |
| | 16 Tbsp | = 1 cup | = 8 fl oz | 240 ml | |
| | 1 pt | = 2 cups | = 16 fl oz | 480 ml | |
| | 1 qt | = 4 cups | = 32 fl oz | 960 ml | |
| | | | 33 fl oz | = 1000 ml | = 1 l |

## Useful Equivalents for Dry Ingredients by Weight

(To convert ounces to grams, multiply the number of ounces by 30.)

| | | | | |
|---|---|---|---|---|
| 1 oz | = | ¹/₁₆ lb | = | 30 g |
| 4 oz | = | ¹/₄ lb | = | 120 g |
| 8 oz | = | ¹/₂ lb | = | 240 g |
| 12 oz | = | ³/₄ lb | = | 360 g |
| 16 oz | = | 1 lb | = | 480 g |

## Useful Equivalents for Length

(To convert inches to centimeters, multiply the number of inches by 2.5.)

| | | | | |
|---|---|---|---|---|
| 1 in | | = | 2.5 cm | |
| 6 in | = ¹/₂ ft | = | 15 cm | |
| 12 in | = 1 ft | = | 30 cm | |
| 36 in | = 3 ft = 1 yd | = | 90 cm | |
| 40 in | | = | 100 cm | = 1 m |

## Useful Equivalents for Cooking/ Oven Temperatures

| | Fahrenheit | Celsius | Gas Mark |
|---|---|---|---|
| Freeze water | 32° F | 0° C | |
| Room temperature | 68° F | 20° C | |
| Boil water | 212° F | 100° C | |
| Bake | 325° F | 160° C | 3 |
| | 350° F | 180° C | 4 |
| | 375° F | 190° C | 5 |
| | 400° F | 200° C | 6 |
| | 425° F | 220° C | 7 |
| | 450° F | 230° C | 8 |
| Broil | | | Grill |

# ✦ VINTAGE RECIPE INDEX ✦

# ✦ RECIPE INDEX ✦

SWEET
BONUS!

# THE SOUTH'S MOST STORIED CAKES

By Mary Allen Perry
Photography by Hector Sanchez

# SOUTHERNERS HAVE HAD A LONG-STANDING LOVE AFFAIR WITH LAYER CAKES.

We bake them for birthdays and christenings, mount them on heirloom cake stands in honor of anniversaries and holiday homecomings, and immortalize them in great works of fiction. Few desserts are more impressive on a buffet. Vying with a dazzling parade of pies and meringue-topped banana puddings, a decadent layer cake will always be the star of the show at a church dinner. Tattered and scribbled with marginalia, the best-loved recipes are passed down from one generation to the next. Stories of their origin, both real and apocryphal, are as multilayered as the cakes themselves. Over the years, hundreds of readers, and SL staffers, have shared their favorite cake recipes in the pages of *Southern Living*.

# THE LANE CAKE

Serves 12 to 16   Hands-on 1 hour 30 minutes   Total 15 hours 35 minutes

## CAKE LAYERS:

2¼ cups sugar

1¼ cups butter, softened

8 large egg whites, at room temperature

3 cups all-purpose soft-wheat flour (such as White Lily)

4 teaspoons baking powder

1 cup water

1 tablespoon vanilla extract

Shortening

## PEACH FILLING:

Boiling water

8 ounces dried peach halves

½ cup butter, melted

1 cup sugar

8 large egg yolks

¾ cup sweetened flaked coconut

¾ cup chopped toasted pecans

½ cup bourbon

2 teaspoons vanilla extract

## PEACH SCHNAPPS FROSTING:

2 large egg whites

1½ cups sugar

½ cup peach schnapps

2 teaspoons light corn syrup

⅛ teaspoon table salt

1. Prepare the Cake Layers: Preheat the oven to 350°F. Beat the first 2 ingredients at medium speed with an electric mixer until fluffy. Gradually add the 8 egg whites, 2 at a time, beating well after each addition.

2. Sift together the flour and baking powder; gradually add to the butter mixture alternately with 1 cup water, beginning and ending with the flour mixture. Stir in 1 tablespoon vanilla. Spoon the batter into 4 greased (with shortening) and floured 9-inch round shiny cake pans (about 1¾ cups batter in each pan).

3. Bake at 350°F for 14 to 16 minutes or until a wooden pick inserted in the center comes out clean. Cool in pans on wire racks 10 minutes; remove from pans to wire racks, and cool completely (about 30 minutes).

4. Prepare the Filling: Pour boiling water to cover over dried peach halves in a medium bowl; let stand 30 minutes. Drain well, and cut into ¼-inch pieces. (After plumping and dicing, you should have about 2 cups peaches.)

5. Whisk together the melted butter and next 2 ingredients in a heavy saucepan. Cook over medium-low, whisking constantly, 10 to 12 minutes or until thickened. Remove from the heat, and stir in the diced peaches, coconut, and next 3 ingredients. Cool completely (about 30 minutes).

6. Spread the filling between cake layers (a little over 1 cup per layer). Cover cake with plastic wrap, and chill 12 hours.

7. Prepare the Frosting: Pour water to a depth of 1½ inches into a small saucepan; bring to a boil over medium. Whisk together 2 egg whites, 1½ cups sugar, and next 3 ingredients in a heatproof bowl; place the bowl over boiling water. Beat the egg white mixture at medium-high speed with a handheld electric mixer 12 to 15 minutes or until stiff glossy peaks form and the frosting is spreading consistency. Remove from the heat, and spread immediately over the top and the sides of the cake.

Note: Find dried peaches at Sprouts Farmers Market and Whole Foods Market.

## THE LANE CAKE

**More than 100 years ago,** Emma Rylander Lane of Clayton, Alabama, entered the annual baking competition at the county fair in Columbus, Georgia. She took first prize. No doubt the judges were swayed by her cake's filling: a richly yolked custard heavily spiked with bourbon. The recipe, entitled Prize Cake, can be found in *Some Good Things to Eat*, a collection of personal favorites she published in 1898. Though later versions add shredded coconut and pecans to the filling, the original recipe calls for raisins only. Like Lady Baltimore Cake, it's one of many spirited fruit-filled cakes of the era that became a holiday tradition. In July 1960, Lane Cake gained literary fame in *To Kill a Mockingbird*. And in March 1966, *Southern Living* featured a recipe for Lane Cake in its second issue. Our latest twist? Dried peaches (finely diced and ridiculously delicious) stand in for raisins, and the traditional meringue frosting gets a spirited makeover with a triple shot of peach schnapps.

## THE LEMON CHEESE LAYER CAKE

**Expecting a twist on cheesecake?** You're in for an even sweeter surprise. These layers are filled with a buttery rich lemon curd instead. Recipes dating back to the early 1800s called for acidulating cream with lemon juice, then separating the curds and whey. Over the years, the original recipe for lemon cheese evolved into one using butter and eggs. By the 1940s, almost every good cook south of the Mason-Dixon Line had a recipe for lemon cheese layer cake in her repertoire. And if you've ever lived anywhere near Hartford in southeast Alabama you know of the local ladies still famous for their 14-layer lemon cheese cakes. Numerous versions of this nostalgic classic pay homage to Robert E. Lee, who allegedly fancied sponge cakes filled with a sugary mix of finely grated lemons and oranges. Until now, a lemon cheese riff on Robert E. Lee Cake from the *Southern Living* 1990 Five-Star Recipe Collection used to be our favorite. But this one trumps them all.

# THE LEMON CHEESE LAYER CAKE

Serves 12 to 16   Hands-on 1 hour 30 minutes   Total 22 hours 45 minutes

LEMON CURD:

1 3/4 cups granulated sugar

3/4 cup butter, softened

4 large eggs

3 large egg yolks

1 tablespoon lemon zest

3/4 cup fresh lemon juice

CAKE LAYERS:

1 3/4 cups granulated sugar

1 cup butter, softened

4 large eggs, separated, at room temperature

1 tablespoon orange zest

3 cups cake flour

2 1/2 teaspoons baking powder

1/4 teaspoon table salt

1 cup fresh orange juice

Shortening

3 (4-inch) wooden skewers

LEMON-ORANGE BUTTERCREAM FROSTING:

3 cups powdered sugar, sifted

1/2 cup butter, softened

1 tablespoon orange zest

1. Prepare the Lemon Curd: Beat first 2 ingredients at medium speed with an electric mixer until blended. Add the 4 eggs and 3 egg yolks, 1 at a time, to the butter mixture, beating just until blended after each addition. Stir in the lemon zest. Gradually add the lemon juice to the butter mixture, beating at low speed just until blended after each addition. (The mixture will look curdled.) Transfer to a large heavy saucepan.

2. Cook the mixture over medium-low, whisking constantly, 14 to 16 minutes or until it thickens, coats the back of a spoon, and starts to mound slightly when stirred. Transfer the mixture to a bowl.

3. Place heavy-duty plastic wrap directly on the surface of the warm curd (to prevent a film from forming), and cool 1 hour. Chill 8 hours.

4. Prepare the Cake Layers: Preheat the oven to 350°F. Beat 1 3/4 cups granulated sugar and 1 cup softened butter at medium speed with an electric mixer until fluffy. Add 4 egg yolks, 1 at a time, beating just until blended after each addition. Stir in the orange zest.

5. Sift together the flour and next 2 ingredients; gradually add to butter mixture alternately with 1 cup orange juice, beginning and ending with flour mixture, beating just until blended after each addition.

6. Beat 4 egg whites at medium-high speed with mixer until stiff peaks form. Fold one-third of egg whites into batter; fold remaining egg whites into batter. Pour batter into 4 greased (with shortening) and floured 8-inch round shiny cake pans (about 1 3/4 cups batter in each pan).

7. Bake at 350°F for 17 to 20 minutes or until a wooden pick inserted in center comes out clean. Cool in pans on wire racks 10 minutes; remove to wire racks, and cool completely (about 30 minutes).

8. Reserve and refrigerate 1 cup Lemon Curd. Spread the remaining Lemon Curd between the cake layers and on top of the cake (about 1/2 cup per layer). Insert skewers 2 to 3 inches apart into the cake to prevent layers from sliding. Immediately wrap cake tightly in plastic wrap, and chill 12 to 24 hours. (The layers of the cake and the Lemon Curd will set and firm up overnight, ripening the flavor and making the cake more secure and easier to frost.)

9. Prepare the Frosting: Beat 1 cup of the powdered sugar, 1/2 cup softened butter, and 1 tablespoon orange zest at low speed with electric mixer until blended. Add 1/2 cup reserved Lemon Curd alternately with remaining 2 cups powdered sugar, beating until blended after each addition. Increase speed to high, and beat 1 to 2 minutes or until fluffy.

10. Remove skewers from the cake; discard skewers. Spread the frosting on the sides of the cake. Spread remaining 1/2 cup reserved Lemon Curd over top of cake. (Adding a bit of extra Lemon Curd to the top of the cake creates a luxe decorative finish.)

# THE RED VELVET CAKE

Serves 12 to 16   Hands-on 1 hour 10 minutes   Total 2 hours 10 minutes

## CAKE LAYERS:

1 1/2 cups granulated sugar
1 cup butter, softened
1/2 cup firmly packed light brown sugar
4 large eggs, at room temperature
2 tablespoons red liquid food coloring
1 tablespoon vanilla extract
1 (8-ounce) container sour cream
1/2 cup water
2 1/2 cups all-purpose soft-wheat flour
   (such as White Lily)
1/2 cup unsweetened cocoa
1 teaspoon baking soda
1/2 teaspoon table salt
Shortening

## STRAWBERRY GLAZE:

3/4 cup strawberry preserves
1/4 cup almond liqueur

## STRAWBERRY FROSTING:

3/4 cup butter, softened
5 cups powdered sugar, sifted
1 3/4 cups diced fresh strawberries

1. Prepare the Cake Layers: Preheat the oven to 350°F. Beat the first 3 ingredients at medium speed with an electric mixer until fluffy. Add the eggs, 1 at a time, beating just until blended after each addition. Add the red food coloring and vanilla, beating at low speed just until blended.

2. Stir together the sour cream and 1/2 cup water until blended. Sift together the flour and next 3 ingredients; gradually add to butter mixture alternately with sour cream mixture, beginning and ending with flour mixture. Spoon the batter into 3 greased (with shortening) and floured 9-inch round shiny cake pans (about 2 1/2 cups batter in each pan).

3. Bake at 350°F for 20 to 24 minutes or until a wooden pick inserted in the center comes out clean. Cool in pans 10 minutes; remove from pans to wire racks, and cool completely (about 30 minutes).

4. Prepare the Glaze: Pulse the strawberry preserves in a food processor until smooth; transfer to a microwave-safe bowl. Microwave the strawberry preserves at HIGH 30 to 45 seconds or until melted; stir in the almond liqueur. Brush 1/4 cup warm glaze over the top of each cooled cake layer. Reserve remaining 1/4 cup glaze.

5. Prepare the Frosting: Beat 3/4 cup softened butter at medium speed 20 seconds or until fluffy. Gradually add 5 cups powdered sugar and 1/2 cup of the diced strawberries, beating at low speed until creamy. Add 1/4 cup of the diced strawberries, 1 tablespoon at a time, beating until frosting reaches desired consistency. Reserve remaining 1 cup diced strawberries.

6. Place 1 cake layer, glazed side up, on a serving platter. Spread one-third of the frosting over the cake layer; sprinkle with 1/2 cup reserved diced strawberries. Repeat the procedure with the second cake layer. Top with remaining cake layer; spread with remaining frosting. Drizzle remaining 1/4 cup strawberry glaze over cake.

Note: If your berries are juicy, you may not need the entire amount in the frosting.

## THE RED VELVET CAKE

**Velvet cakes (minus the jolt of red)** were popular in Victorian times when savvy cooks blended flour and cornstarch to create fine-crumbed cake layers with a velvety texture. The subtle hue of Mahogany Velvet Cake, and later Red Devil's Food Cake, was the result of baking soda interacting with natural cocoa and other acids in the batter. Legend has it that chefs at the Waldorf Astoria dreamed up a hybrid "Red Velvet" cake during the 1930s and served a slice to the owner of the Texas-based Adams Extract Company while he was a hotel guest. By the 40s, Mr. Adams was marketing red food coloring to the masses with recipe cards for a Red Velvet Cake his wife, Betty, developed. In 1989, an armadillo-shaped groom's cake in *Steel Magnolias* kicked off a cult following for red velvet. The craze has continued, fueled in part by the red velvet cakes that have graced the *Southern Living* Christmas cover three times.

## THE JAM CAKE

**The origins of jam cake** lie deep in Appalachia where store-bought sugar was once scarce. Cakes were often sweetened with homemade jams, filled with wild berries and mountain fruits. The payoff for the genius swap? Rich, dense cake layers with a depth of flavor sugar alone can't deliver. Vintage cookbooks offer century-old favorites, from Alice May Cresswell's Blackberry Jam Cake to Zella McDowell's extravaganza made with strawberry jam and fig preserves. Most recipes start with a tangy buttermilk batter ramped up with one or more flavors of jam and a flurry of ground spices. Foraged hickories and black walnuts, or wind-fallen pecans were added along with raisins and dates. Optional flourishes ranged from cocoa and freshly grated apple to pickled watermelon rind. This latest addition to our archives is finished with a quick caramel cream cheese frosting instead of the traditional burnt sugar icing. And yes, it's every bit as luscious as it looks.

# THE JAM CAKE

Serves 12 to 16   Hands-on 1 hour   Total 2 hours

CAKE LAYERS:
1 ½ cups sugar
1 cup butter, softened
4 large eggs, at room temperature
3 cups all-purpose flour
2 tablespoons unsweetened cocoa
2 teaspoons pumpkin pie spice
1 cup buttermilk
1 teaspoon baking soda
1 ½ cups seedless blackberry jam
1 tablespoon vanilla extract

1 ½ cups finely chopped toasted pecans
1 cup peeled and grated Granny Smith apple
   (about 1 large)
Shortening

CARAMEL-CREAM CHEESE FROSTING:
2 (8-ounce) packages cream cheese, softened
¼ cup butter, softened
2 (13.4-ounce) cans dulce de leche
2 to 4 tablespoons whipping cream

1. Prepare the Cake Layers: Preheat the oven to 350°F. Beat first 2 ingredients at medium speed with an electric mixer until light and fluffy. Add the eggs, 1 at a time, beating just until blended after each addition.

2. Stir together the flour and next 2 ingredients. Stir together the buttermilk and baking soda in a 2-cup glass measuring cup. Add the flour mixture to butter mixture alternately with buttermilk mixture, beginning and ending with flour mixture. Beat at low speed just until blended after each addition.

3. Stir the jam until smooth. Add the jam and vanilla to butter mixture, and beat at low speed just until blended. Stir in the toasted pecans and grated apple. Spoon the batter into 4 greased (with shortening) and floured 9-inch round shiny cake pans (about 2 ½ cups batter in each pan).

4. Bake at 350°F for 20 to 22 minutes or until a wooden pick inserted in center comes out clean. Cool in pans 10 minutes; remove from pans to wire racks, and cool completely (about 30 minutes).

5. Prepare the Frosting: Beat the cream cheese and ¼ cup softened butter at medium speed with an electric mixer until creamy. Add the dulce de leche, 1 can at a time, beating until blended after each addition. Gradually add 2 tablespoons whipping cream, 1 tablespoon at a time, and beat at medium speed. Add up to 2 tablespoons additional cream, 1 tablespoon at a time, and beat until the frosting is desired spreading consistency. Spread the frosting between each layer and on the top and the sides of the cake.

Note: We tested with Nestlé La Lechera Dulce de Leche.

# THE COCONUT CHIFFON CAKE

Serves 12 to 16   Hands-on 1 hour 15 minutes   Total 14 hours 25 minutes

CAKE LAYERS:

2 1/2 cups sifted cake flour
1 1/3 cups granulated sugar
1 tablespoon baking powder
1/2 teaspoon table salt
1/2 cup canola oil
5 large eggs, separated, at room temperature
1 tablespoon vanilla extract
3/4 cup water
1/2 teaspoon cream of tartar
Shortening

COCONUT-MASCARPONE FILLING:

1 (8-ounce) container mascarpone cheese
1/2 cup powdered sugar

1 tablespoon vanilla extract
3/4 cup whipping cream
1 (6-ounce) package frozen grated coconut, thawed

WHITE CHOCOLATE BUTTERCREAM FROSTING:

1 1/2 (4-ounce) white chocolate baking bars, chopped
2 tablespoons whipping cream
1 cup butter, softened
3 cups sifted powdered sugar
2 teaspoons vanilla extract
3 cups sweetened flaked coconut

1. Prepare the Cake Layers: Preheat the oven to 350°F. Stir together the sifted cake flour and next 3 ingredients in bowl of a heavy-duty electric stand mixer. Make a well in the center of the flour mixture; add the oil, egg yolks, vanilla, and 3/4 cup water. Beat at medium speed 1 to 2 minutes or until smooth.

2. Beat the egg whites and cream of tartar at medium-high speed until stiff peaks form. Fold one-third of egg whites into batter; fold remaining whites into the batter. Spoon the batter into 4 greased (with shortening) and floured 8-inch round shiny cake pans (about 2 cups batter in each pan).

3. Bake at 350°F for 12 to 14 minutes or until a wooden pick inserted in center comes out clean. (Do not overbake—cakes will be a very pale golden color.) Cool in pans on wire racks 10 minutes; remove from pans to wire racks, and cool completely (about 30 minutes).

4. Prepare the Filling: Stir together the mascarpone cheese, 1/2 cup powdered sugar, and 1 tablespoon vanilla in a large bowl just until blended.

5. Beat 3/4 cup cream at low speed with an electric mixer until foamy; increase speed to medium-high, and beat until soft peaks form. Fold the whipped cream into the mascarpone mixture until well blended. Add the thawed grated coconut, and stir just until blended. Spread the mixture between the cake layers (about 1 1/3 cups per layer). Cover with plastic wrap, and chill 12 hours.

6. Prepare the White Chocolate Buttercream Frosting: Microwave the chopped white chocolate and 2 tablespoons whipping cream in a microwave-safe bowl at MEDIUM (50% power) 1 to 1 1/2 minutes or until melted and smooth, stirring at 30-second intervals. Cool completely (about 20 minutes).

7. Beat 1 cup softened butter and 2 cups of the powdered sugar at low speed with an electric mixer until blended. Add the white chocolate mixture, 2 teaspoons vanilla, and remaining 1 cup powdered sugar, and beat at high speed 2 to 3 minutes or until fluffy. Spread the frosting on the top and the sides of the cake. Cover the top and the sides of the cake with 3 cups flaked coconut, gently pressing the coconut into the frosting.

Test Kitchen Tip: Be sure to measure the flour after sifting. (If you measure before sifting, you'll end up with too much flour and a dry cake.) Check for doneness at the minimum bake time—even 1 or 2 minutes of extra baking can also create a dry cake.

Note: We tested with Birds Eye Tropic Isle Fresh Frozen Flake Grated Coconut and Mounds Sweetened Coconut Flakes.

## THE COCONUT CHIFFON CAKE

**White as a Sunday glove,** coconut is the doyenne of Southern layer cakes, a masterpiece of home cookery that has crowned dining room sideboards for more than a hundred years. Purists sing the praises of simple but divine, opting for coconut water-doused cake layers and dreamy swirls of meringue. No argument there. In fact, it's one of our favorites too. But flip through back issues of *Southern Living* and you'll find more than 40 top-rated twists too good to pass up. Often requested: Nanny's Famous Coconut-Pineapple Cake leavened with 7-Up, sent in by a reader in 1997. Fifty-one years earlier Eudora Welty chose a coconut cake as the culinary centerpiece of *Delta Wedding*. Faulkner gives it a shout-out in *The Unvanquished*. One of the earliest published recipes appears in *Mrs. Hill's New Cook Book*. Writing from her rural Georgia kitchen in 1867, Mrs. Annabella P. Hill advises to make the filling "as thick and rich as desired," which is exactly what we did with our latest creation.

# Layer Cake Wisdom

◆

Layer cakes have a reputation for being both wickedly delicious and troublesome to make, which is exactly why they're so prized. Follow our Test Kitchen's tips, learned from 50 years of baking and building cover-worthy cakes, and you'll have a perfect layer cake on your buffet in no time.

## FILL YOUR FREEZER
If you want to get a jump on things, bake and freeze cake layers up to three months ahead. Allow layers to cool completely before wrapping individually in plastic wrap and placing in zip-top plastic freezer bags. Bonus: Partially frozen layers are easy to frost and rarely require a crumb coat.

## ASSEMBLE EARLY
Filled layer cakes can be assembled ahead of time; in fact, many taste better if you give the cake layers and filling time to ripen and meld. Assemble the cake, and let it rest in the refrigerator overnight; then, frost it the next day before serving. The Lane Cake (page 374), Lemon Cheese Layer Cake (page 377), and Coconut Chiffon Cake (page 382) are the perfect recipes for this do-ahead technique.

## BE PRECISE
Follow the recipe and measurements exactly. Prep cake pans and any special ingredients, such as chopped fruits or toasted nuts, before starting to mix the batter. Use a scale or dry measuring cup to distribute batter evenly between pans.

## MAXIMIZE VOLUME
Room temperature ingredients incorporate more evenly than cold, trapping air and giving rise to tender cake layers. Soften butter at room temperature for about 30 minutes, then test by gently pressing the top of the stick with your index finger. If an indentation remains but the stick of butter still holds its shape, it's perfectly softened.

## KNOW YOUR OVEN
Get an inexpensive oven thermometer to see if your oven is calibrated correctly. (Some ovens can be off by as much as 50°F.) Bake layer cakes on the middle rack in the center of the oven, leaving plenty of room for hot air to circulate.

## DITCH DARK CAKE PANS
Dark cake pans absorb heat, so they turn out cakes with overcooked edges. Instead, opt for shiny, light-colored pans that will reflect heat away from the cake, creating a tender, golden crust.